THE PUNISHER

IN THE BEGINNING

WRITER:
Garth Ennis
PENCILER:
Lewis Larosa
INKER:
Tom Palmer
COLORS:
Dean White
LETTERS:
VC's Randy Gentile, Dave Sharpe & Cory Petit
COVER ART:
Tim Bradstreet
ASSISTANT EDITOR: **John Miesegaes**
EDITOR: **Axel Alonso**

COLLECTION EDITOR: **Jennifer Grünwald**
ASSISTANT EDITORS: **Alex Starbuck & Nelson Ribeiro**
EDITOR, SPECIAL PROJECTS: **Mark D. Beazley**
SENIOR EDITOR, SPECIAL PROJECTS: **Jeff Youngquist**
SENIOR VICE PRESIDENT OF SALES: **David Gabriel**
SVP OF BRAND PLANNING & COMMUNICATIONS: **Michael Pasciullo**
BOOK DESIGNER: **Patrick McGrath**

EDITOR IN CHIEF: **Axel Alonso**
CHIEF CREATIVE OFFICER: **Joe Quesada**
PUBLISHER: **Dan Buckley**
EXECUTIVE PRODUCER: **Alan Fine**

PUNISHER MAX VOL. 1: IN THE BEGINNING. Contains material originally published in magazine form as PUNISHER #1-6.
Sixth printing 2011. ISBN# 978-0-7851-1391-1. Published by MARVEL WORLDWIDE, INC., a subsidiary of MARVEL ENTER-
TAINMENT, LLC. OFFICE OF PUBLICATION: 135 West 50th Street, New York, NY 10020. Copyright © 2004 Marvel Characters,
Inc. All rights reserved. $14.99 per copy in the U.S. and $16.50 in Canada (GST #R127032852); Canadian Agreement
#40668537. All characters featured in this issue and the distinctive names and likenesses thereof, and all related indicia are
trademarks of Marvel Characters, Inc. No similarity between any of the names, characters, persons, and/or institutions in
this magazine with those of any living or dead person or institution is intended, and any such similarity which may exist is
purely coincidental. **Printed in the U.S.A. ALAN** FINE, EVP - Office of the President, Marvel Worldwide, Inc. and EVP & CMO
Marvel Characters B.V.; DAN BUCKLEY, Publisher & President - Print, Animation & Digital Divisions; JOE QUESADA, Chief
Creative Officer; JIM SOKOLOWSKI, Chief Operating Officer; DAVID BOGART, SVP of Business Affairs & Talent Management;
TOM BREVOORT, SVP of Publishing; C.B. CEBULSKI, SVP of Creator & Content Development; DAVID GABRIEL, SVP of Publish-
ing Sales & Circulation; MICHAEL PASCIULLO, SVP of Brand Planning & Communications; JIM O'KEEFE, VP of Operations
& Logistics; DAN CARR, Executive Director of Publishing Technology; JUSTIN F. GABRIE, Director of Publishing & Editorial
Operations; SUSAN CRESPI, Editorial Operations Manager; ALEX MORALES, Publishing Operations Manager; STAN LEE,
Chairman Emeritus. For information regarding advertising in Marvel Comics or on Marvel.com, please contact John Dokes,
SVP Integrated Sales and Marketing, at jdokes@marvel.com. For Marvel subscription inquiries, please call 800-217-9158.
Manufactured between 6/6/11 and 6/21/11 by QUAD/GRAPHICS, DUBUQUE, IA, USA.
10 9 8 7 6

#1

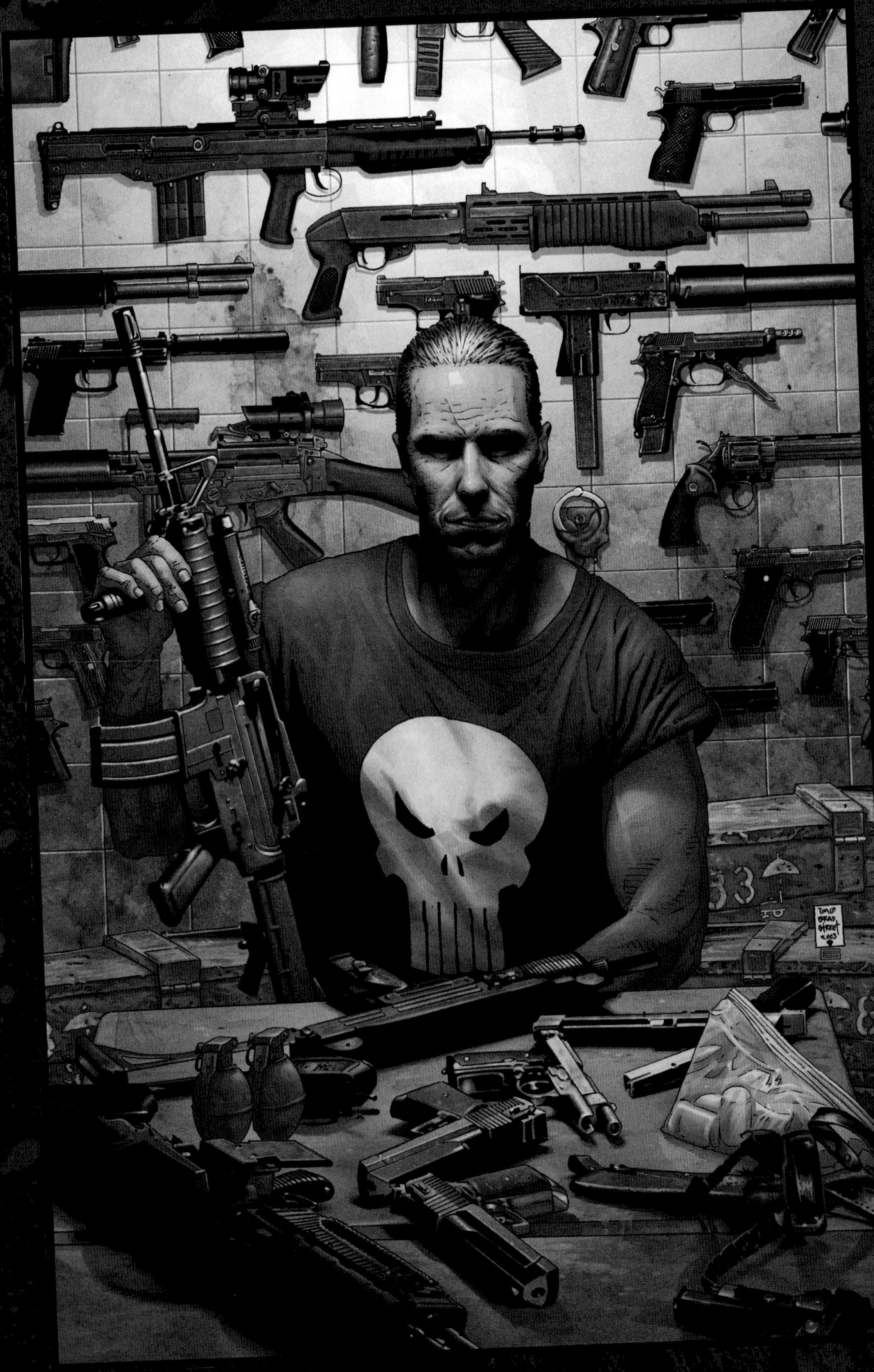

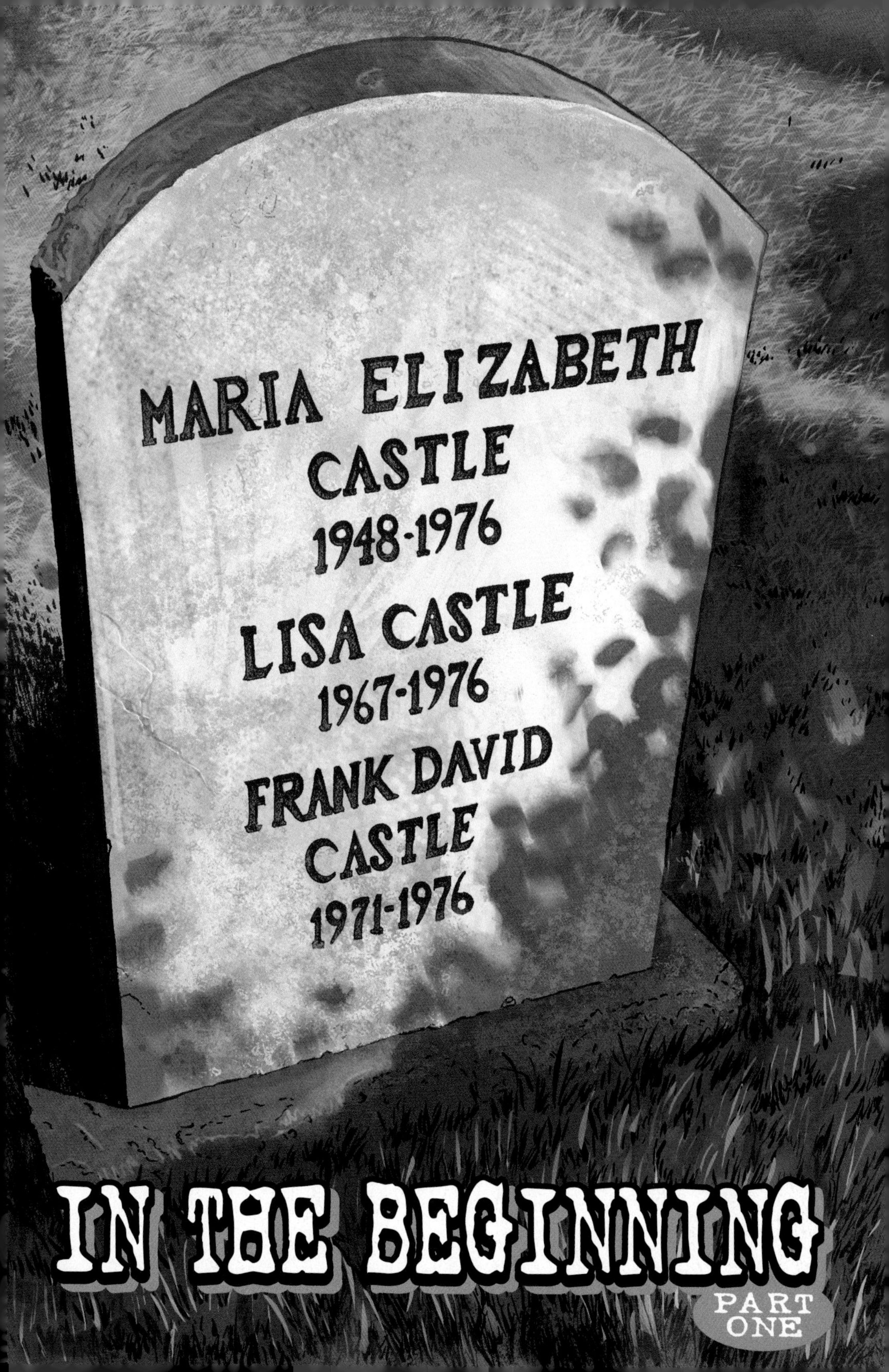
MARIA ELIZABETH
CASTLE
1948-1976
LISA CASTLE
1967-1976
FRANK DAVID
CASTLE
1971-1976
IN THE BEGINNING
PART ONE

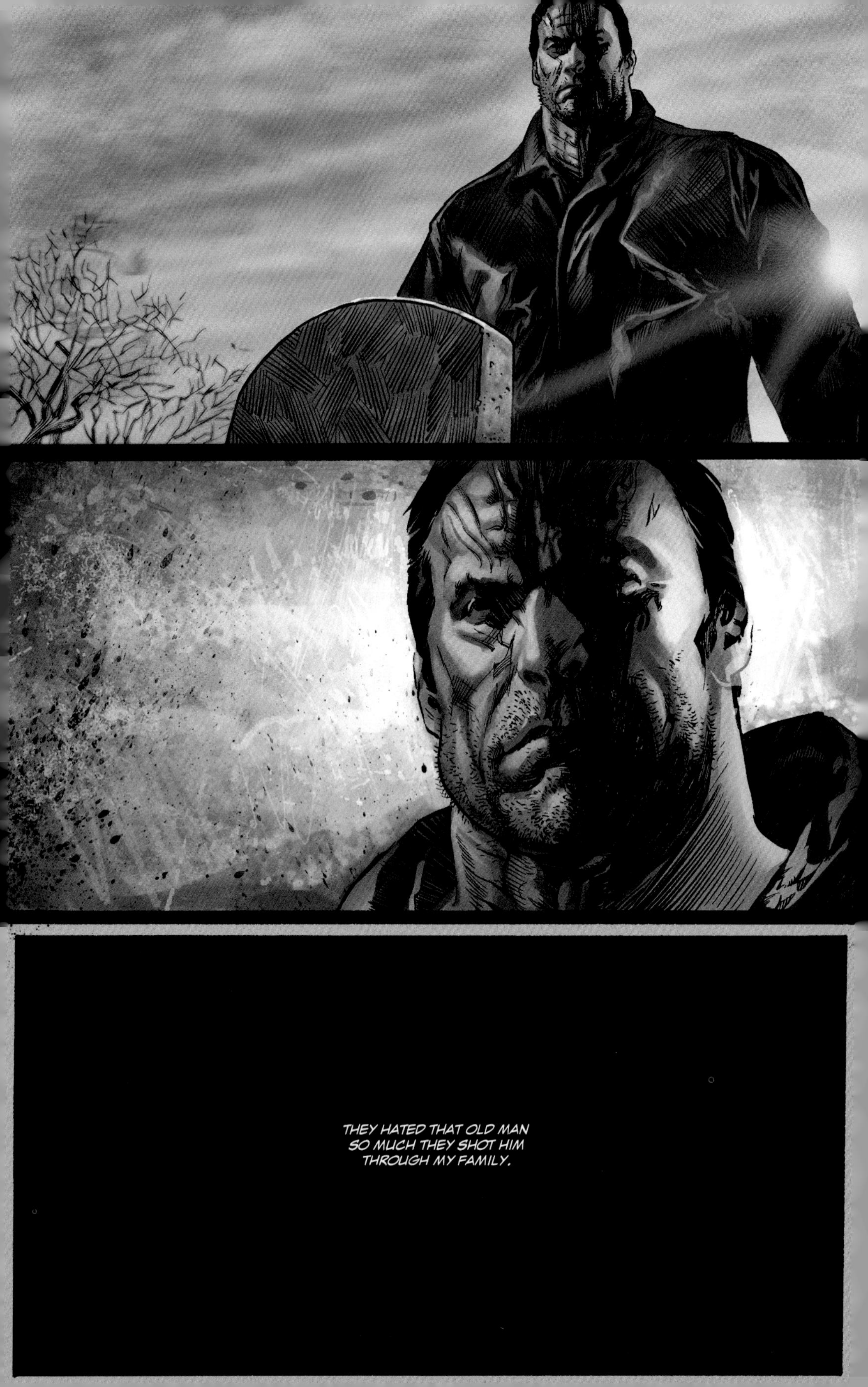
THEY HATED THAT OLD MAN SO MUCH THEY SHOT HIM THROUGH MY FAMILY.

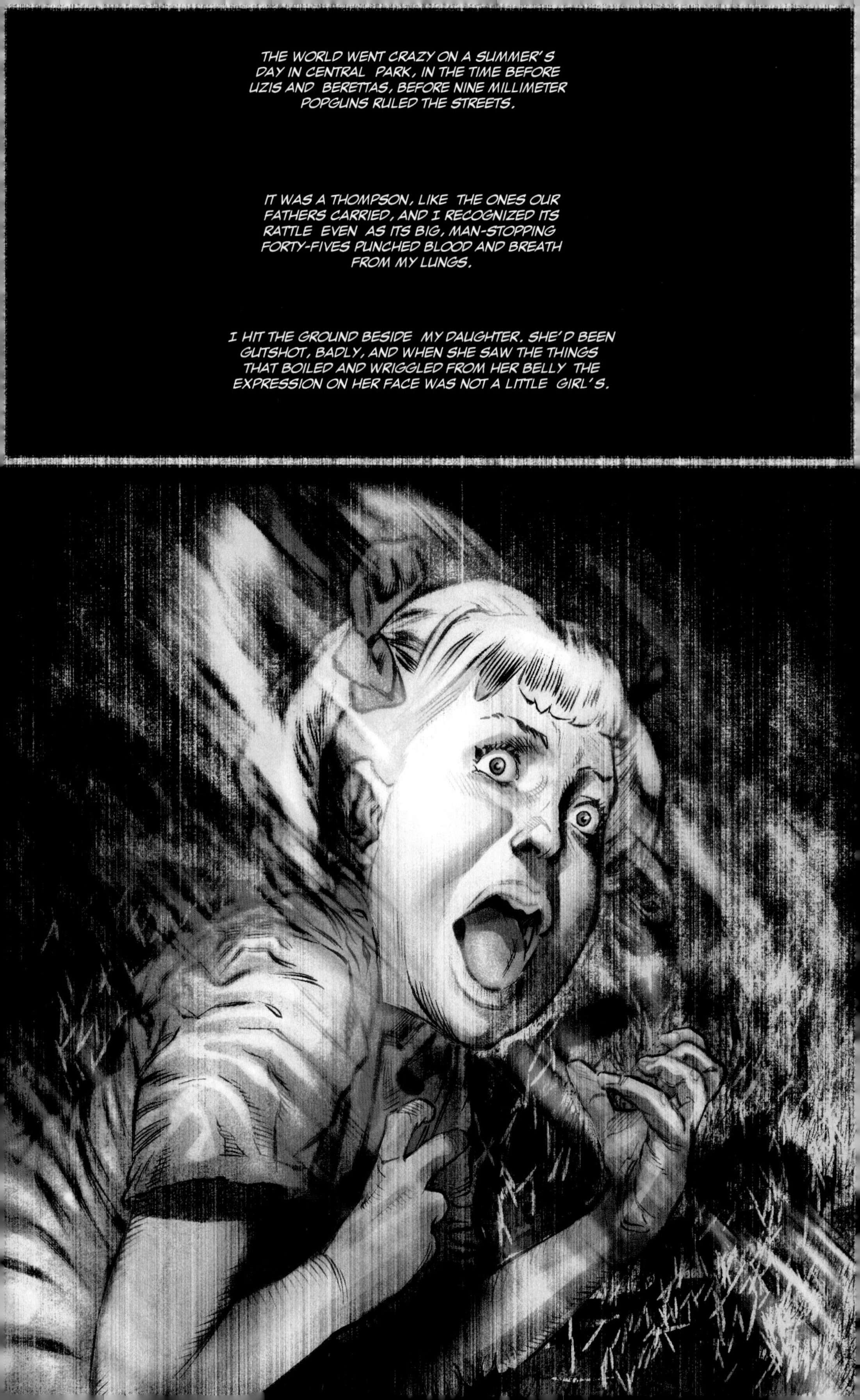
THE WORLD WENT CRAZY ON A SUMMER'S DAY IN CENTRAL PARK, IN THE TIME BEFORE UZIS AND BERETTAS, BEFORE NINE MILLIMETER POPGUNS RULED THE STREETS.
IT WAS A THOMPSON, LIKE THE ONES OUR FATHERS CARRIED, AND I RECOGNIZED ITS RATTLE EVEN AS ITS BIG, MAN-STOPPING FORTY-FIVES PUNCHED BLOOD AND BREATH FROM MY LUNGS.
I HIT THE GROUND BESIDE MY DAUGHTER. SHE'D BEEN GUTSHOT, BADLY, AND WHEN SHE SAW THE THINGS THAT BOILED AND WRIGGLED FROM HER BELLY THE EXPRESSION ON HER FACE WAS NOT A LITTLE GIRL'S.

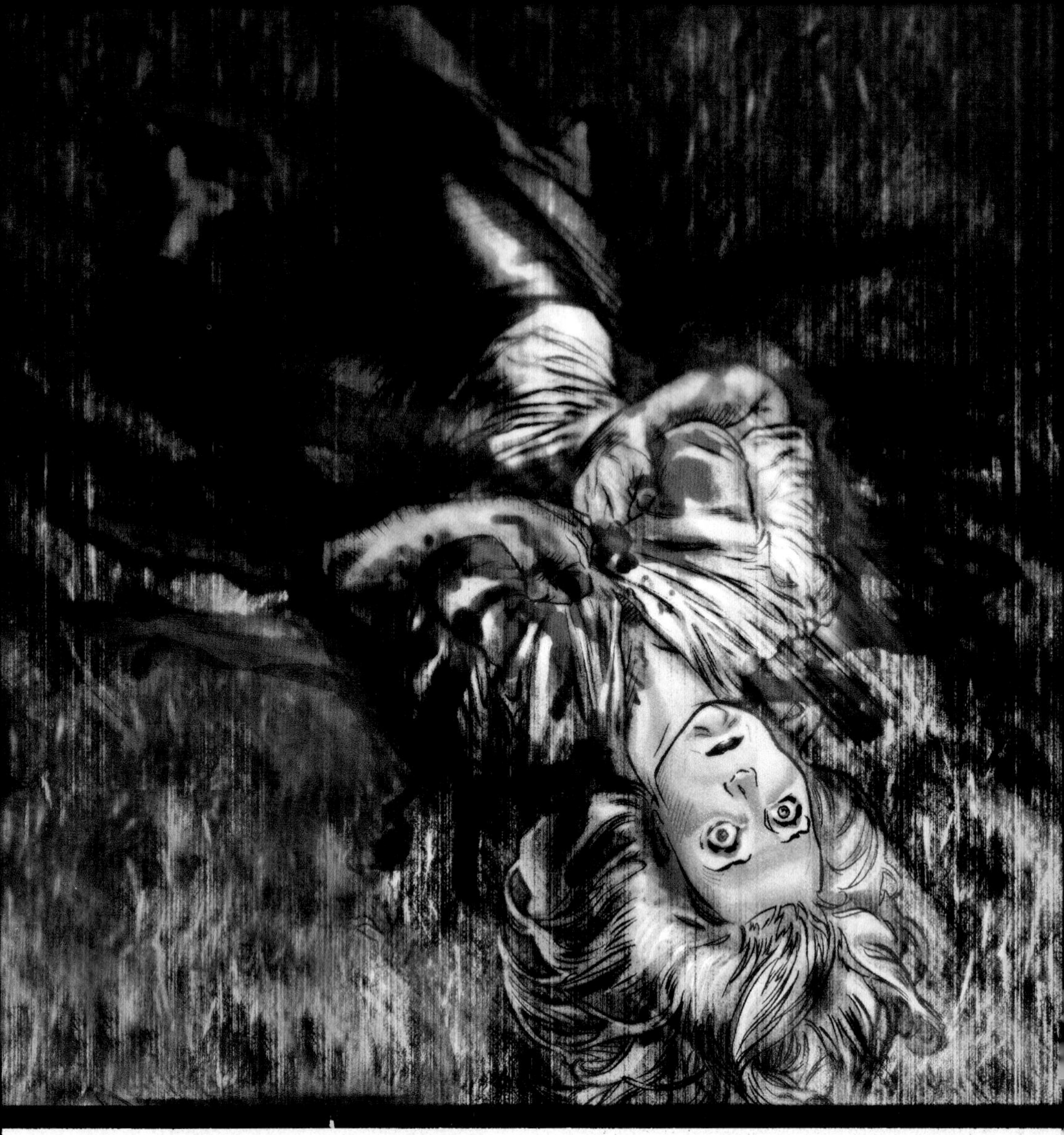

MY WIFE BLED OUT LATER ON THE OPERATING TABLE, HER HEART A GAPING HOLE HER LIFE DRAINED THROUGH. WHENEVER I GET CARELESS, THAT YEARNING IN HER EYES CREEPS UP AND BRINGS ME TO MY KNEES.

RIGHT THEN THE OLD MAN'S SOLDIERS STARTED SHOOTING BACK. MY SON DROPPED WORDLESSLY, WITHOUT A MARK ON HIM.

I TOOK A BREATH THAT CUT LIKE GLASS, SPAT BLOOD, ROSE TO MY KNEES, PICKED UP THE BOY AND SEARCHED IN VAIN FOR ENTRY WOUNDS.

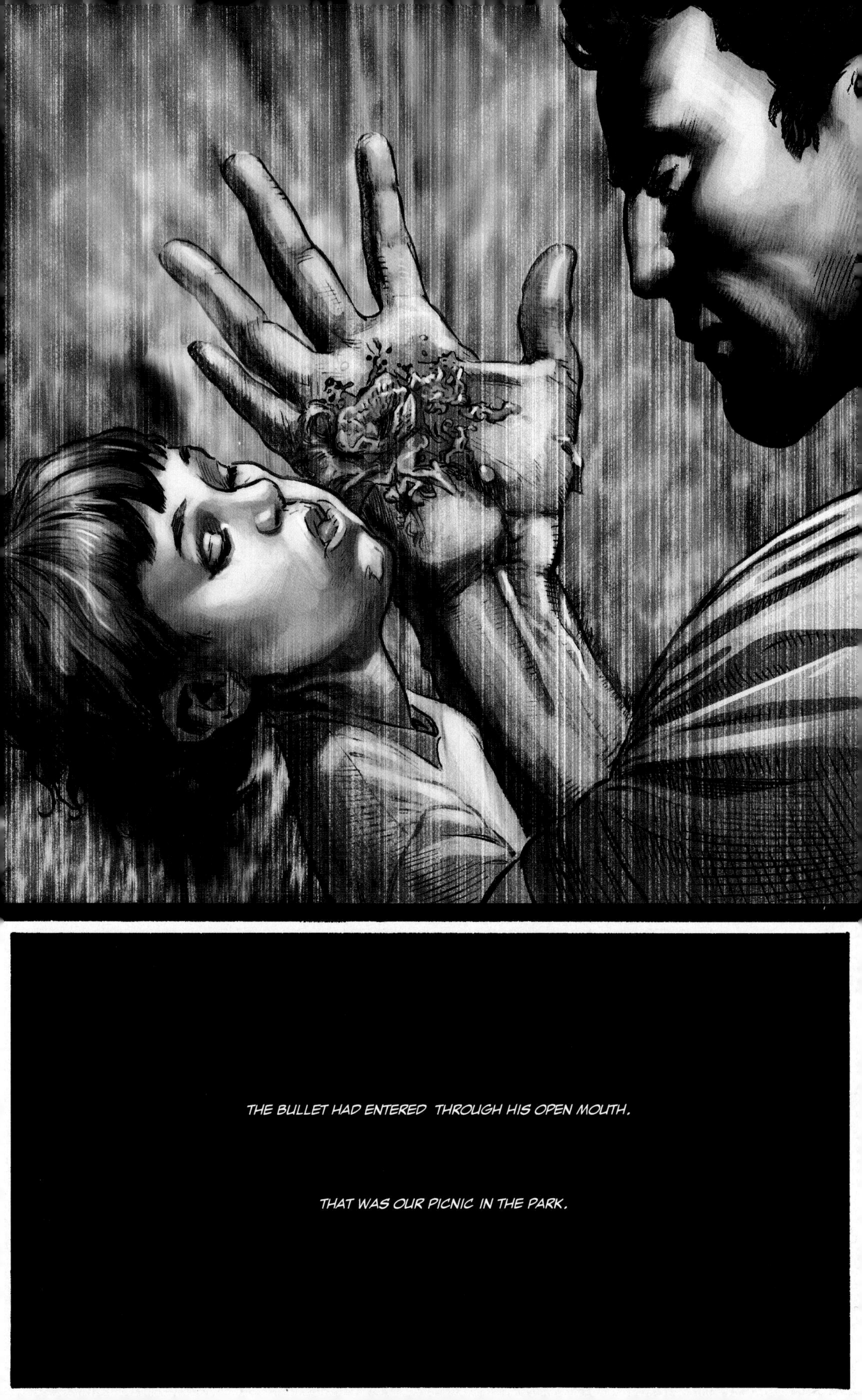
THE BULLET HAD ENTERED THROUGH HIS OPEN MOUTH.
THAT WAS OUR PICNIC IN THE PARK.

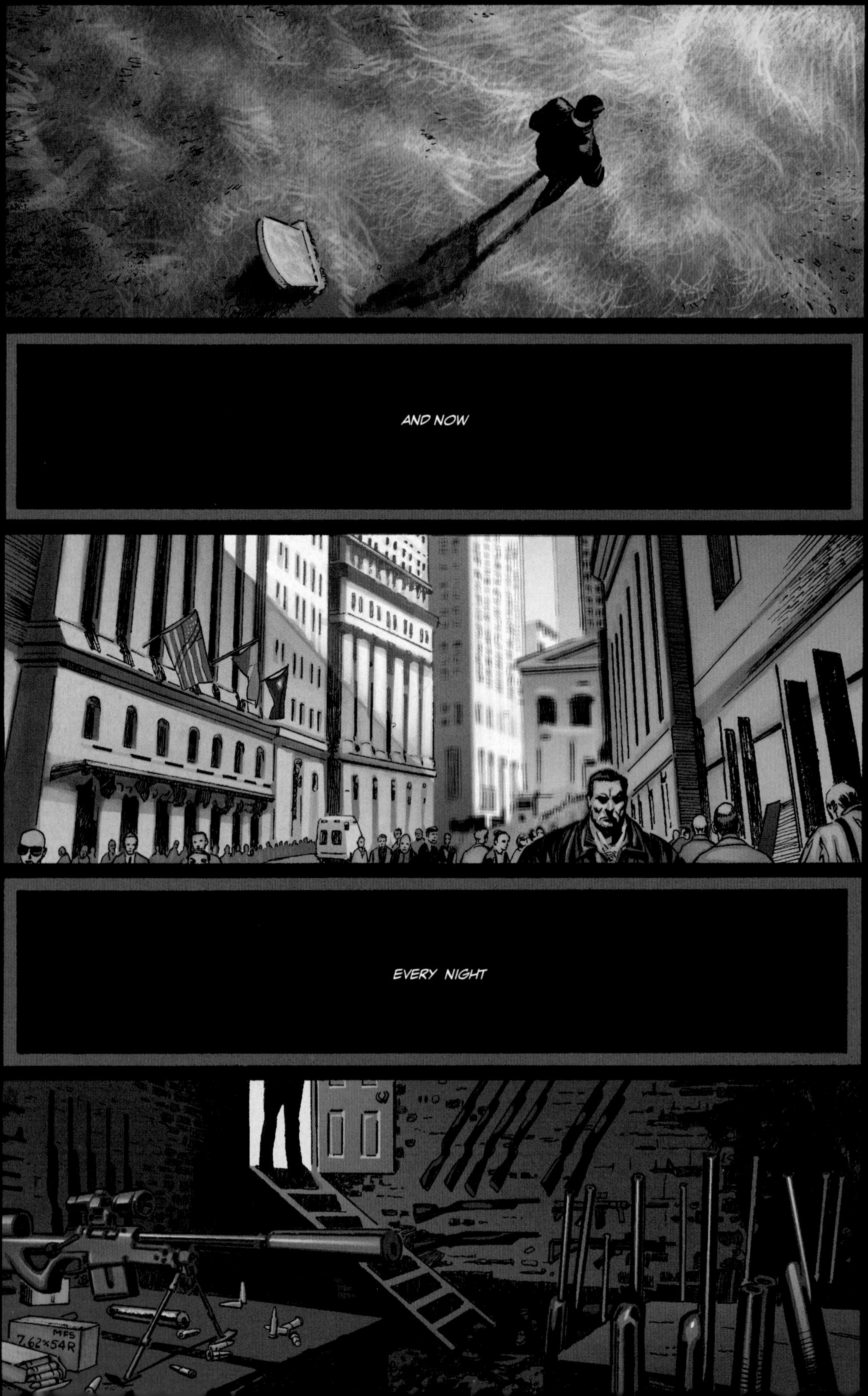
AND NOW
EVERY NIGHT
MFS
7.62x54R

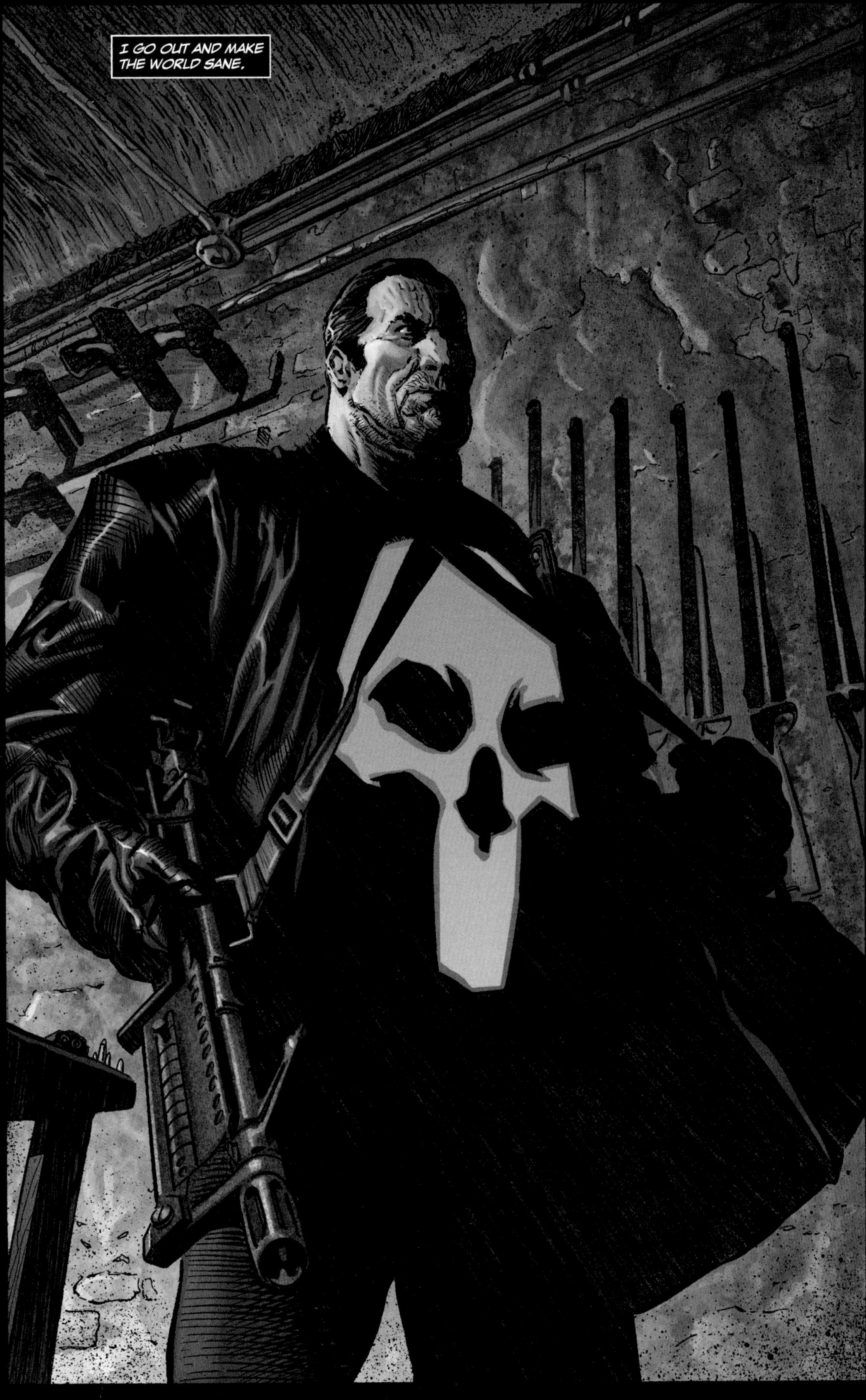
I GO OUT AND MAKE THE WORLD SANE.

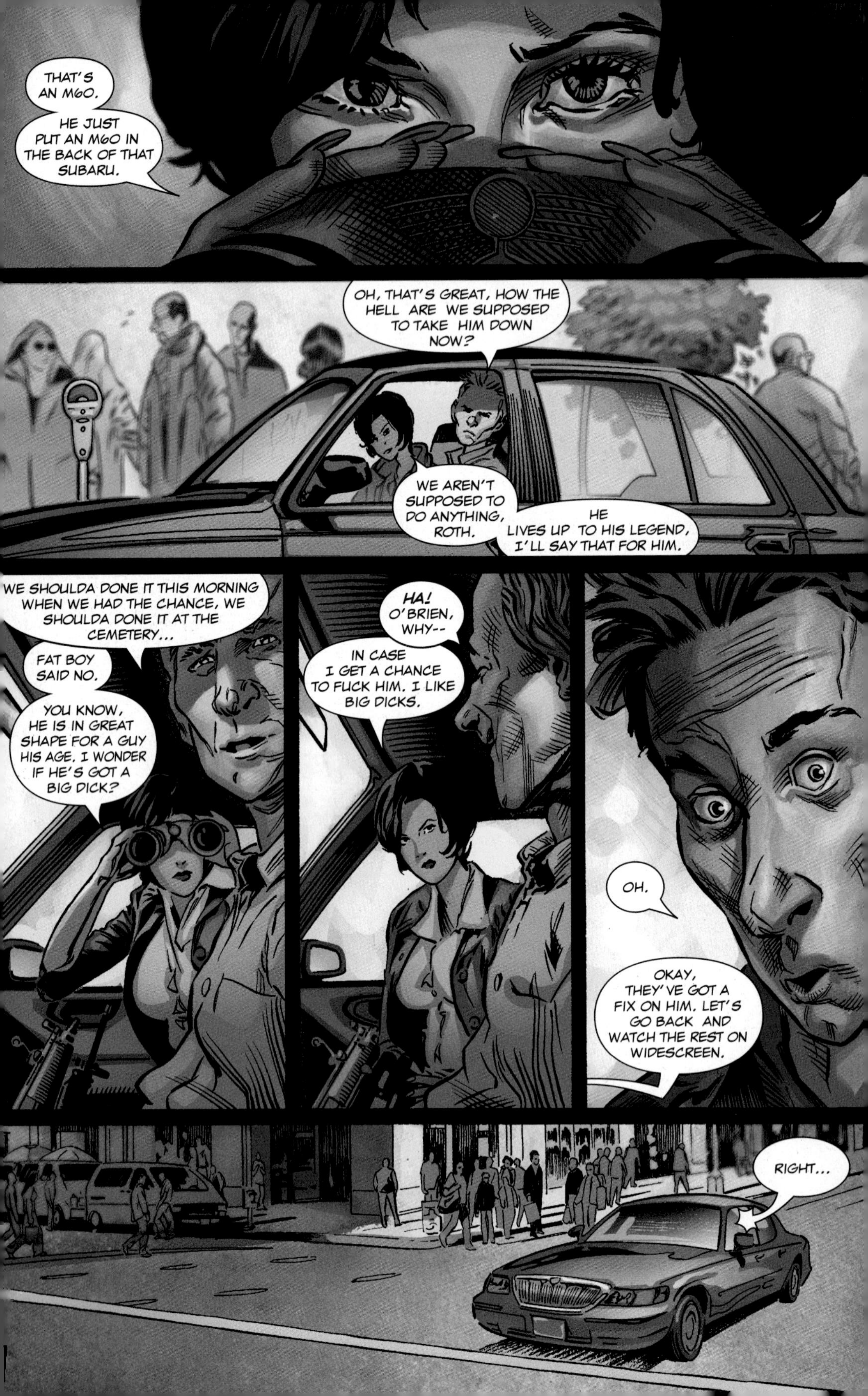
THAT'S AN M60.
HE JUST PUT AN M60 IN THE BACK OF THAT SUBARU.
OH, THAT'S GREAT, HOW THE HELL ARE WE SUPPOSED TO TAKE HIM DOWN NOW?
WE AREN'T SUPPOSED TO DO ANYTHING, ROTH.
HE LIVES UP TO HIS LEGEND, I'LL SAY THAT FOR HIM.
WE SHOULDA DONE IT THIS MORNING WHEN WE HAD THE CHANCE, WE SHOULDA DONE IT AT THE CEMETERY...
FAT BOY SAID NO.
YOU KNOW, HE IS IN GREAT SHAPE FOR A GUY HIS AGE. I WONDER IF HE'S GOT A BIG DICK?
HA! O'BRIEN, WHY--
IN CASE I GET A CHANCE TO FUCK HIM. I LIKE BIG DICKS.
OH.
OKAY, THEY'VE GOT A FIX ON HIM. LET'S GO BACK AND WATCH THE REST ON WIDESCREEN.
RIGHT...

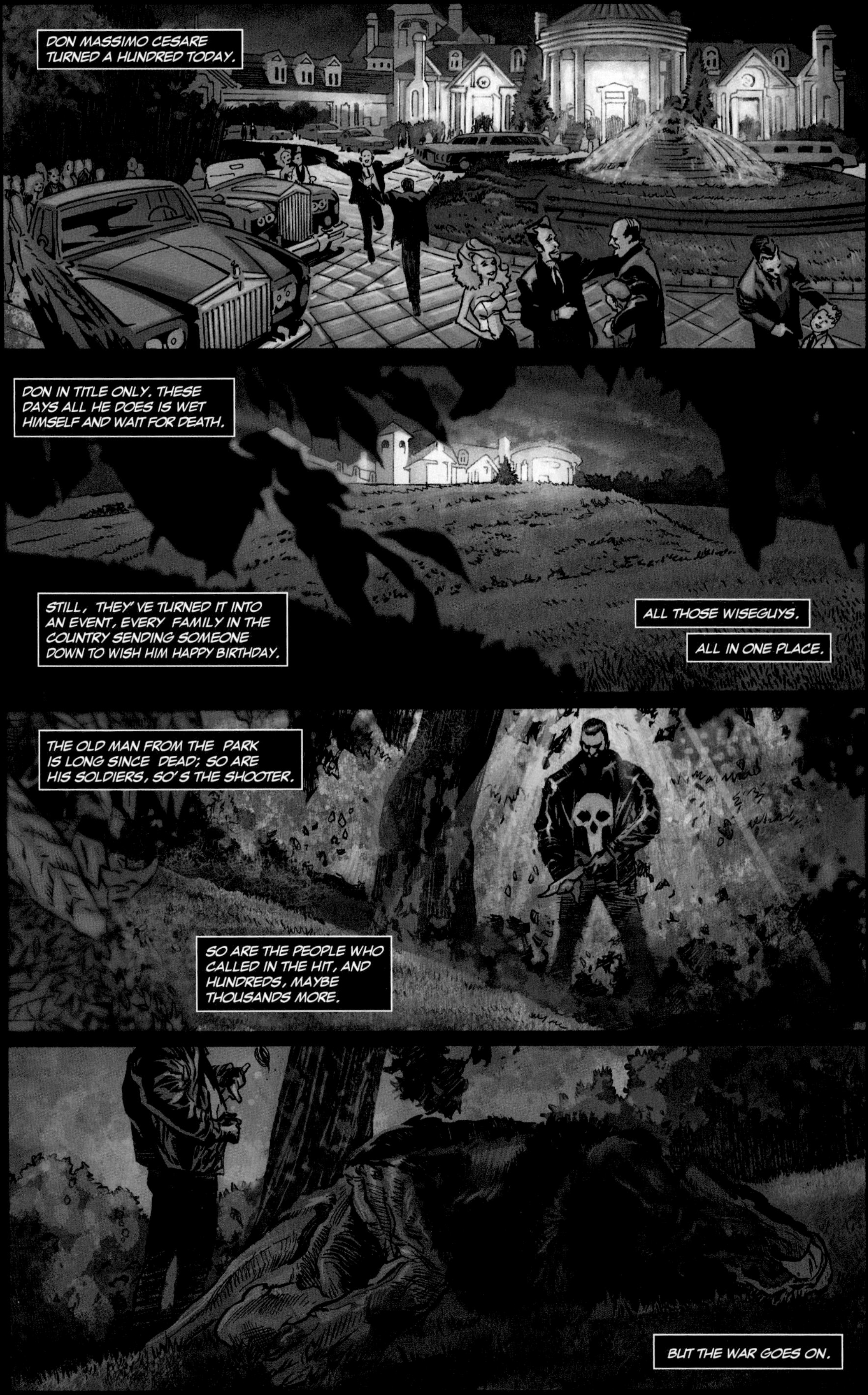
DON MASSIMO CESARE TURNED A HUNDRED TODAY.
DON IN TITLE ONLY. THESE DAYS ALL HE DOES IS WET HIMSELF AND WAIT FOR DEATH.
STILL, THEY'VE TURNED IT INTO AN EVENT, EVERY FAMILY IN THE COUNTRY SENDING SOMEONE DOWN TO WISH HIM HAPPY BIRTHDAY.
ALL THOSE WISEGUYS.
ALL IN ONE PLACE.
THE OLD MAN FROM THE PARK IS LONG SINCE DEAD; SO ARE HIS SOLDIERS, SO'S THE SHOOTER.
SO ARE THE PEOPLE WHO CALLED IN THE HIT, AND HUNDREDS, MAYBE THOUSANDS MORE.
BUT THE WAR GOES ON.

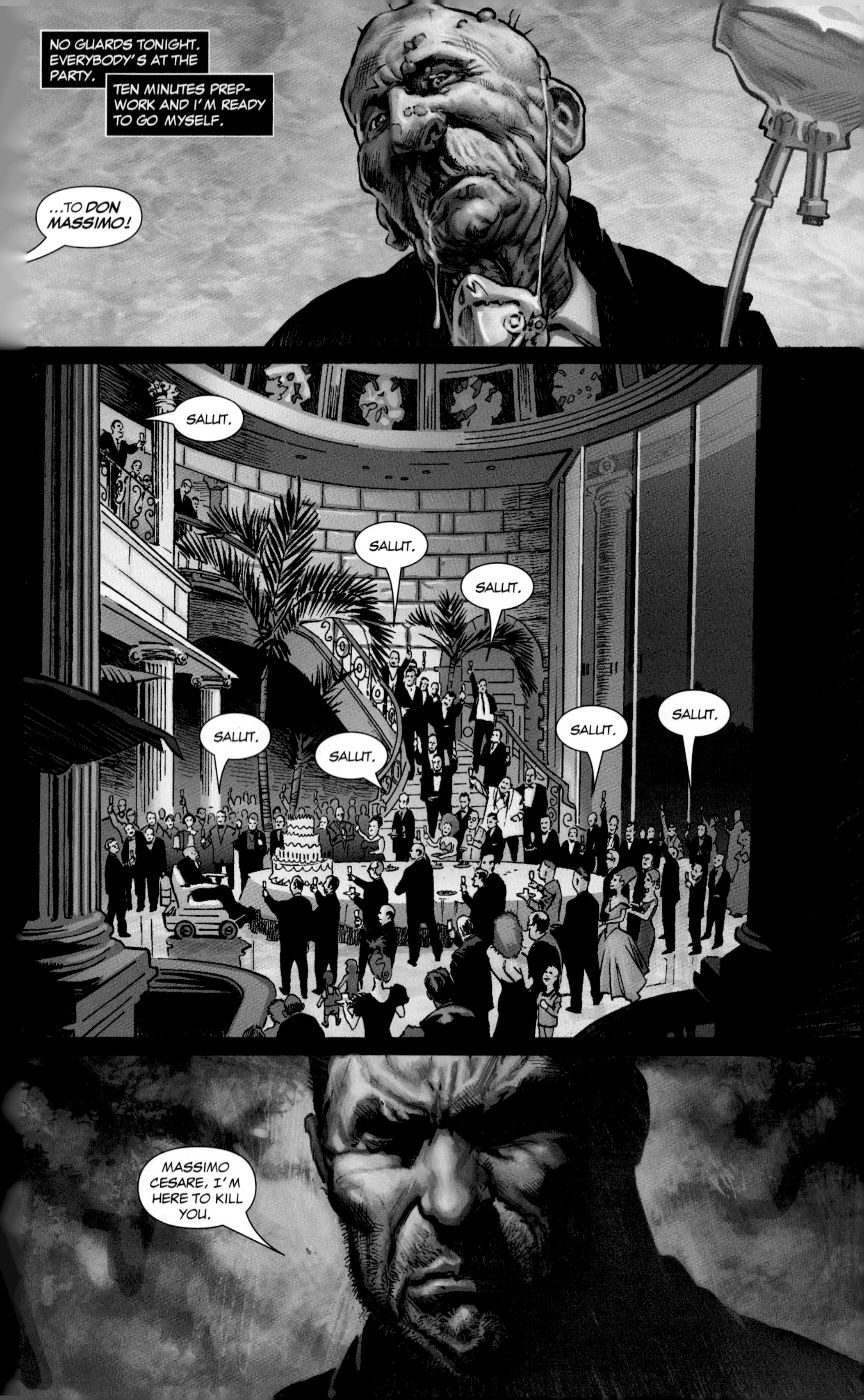
NO GUARDS TONIGHT. EVERYBODY'S AT THE PARTY.
TEN MINUTES PREP-WORK AND I'M READY TO GO MYSELF.
...TO DON MASSIMO!
SALUT.
SALUT.
SALUT.
SALUT.
SALUT.
SALUT.
SALUT.
MASSIMO CESARE, I'M HERE TO KILL YOU.

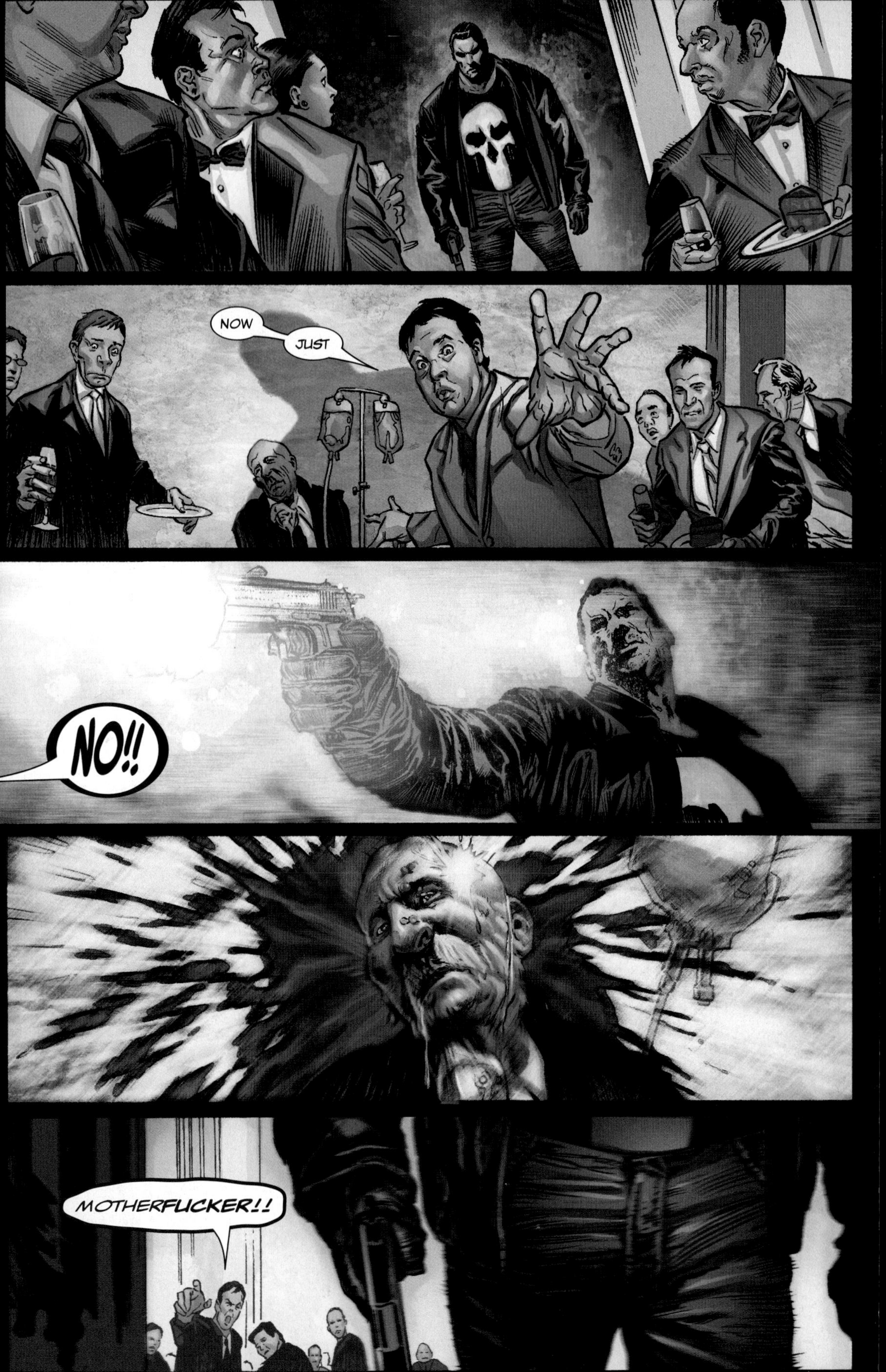
NOW
JUST
NO!!
MOTHERFUCKER!!

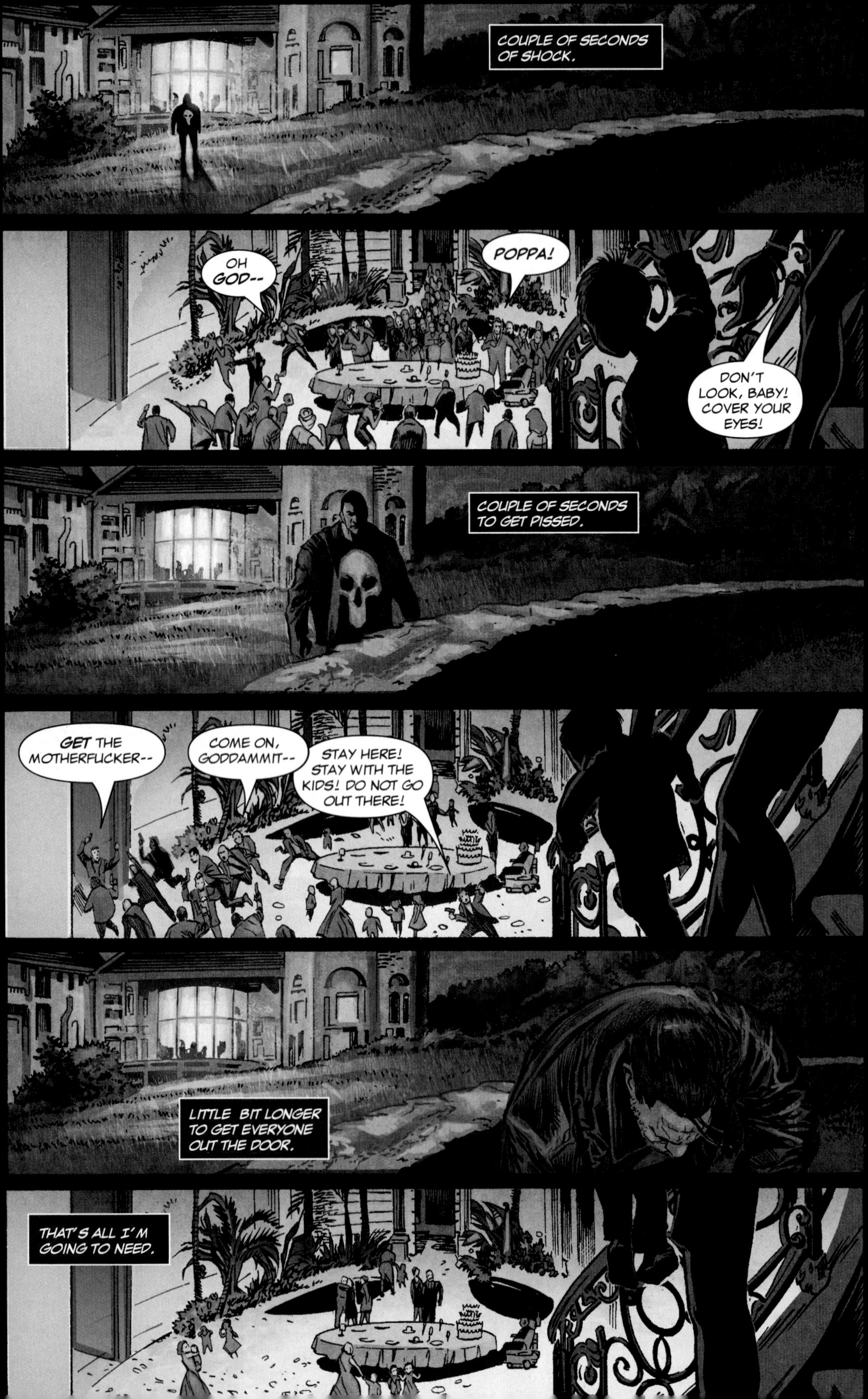
COUPLE OF SECONDS OF SHOCK.
OH GOD--
POPPA!
DON'T LOOK, BABY! COVER YOUR EYES!
COUPLE OF SECONDS TO GET PISSED.
GET THE MOTHERFUCKER--
COME ON, GODDAMMIT--
STAY HERE! STAY WITH THE KIDS! DO NOT GO OUT THERE!
LITTLE BIT LONGER TO GET EVERYONE OUT THE DOOR.
THAT'S ALL I'M GOING TO NEED.

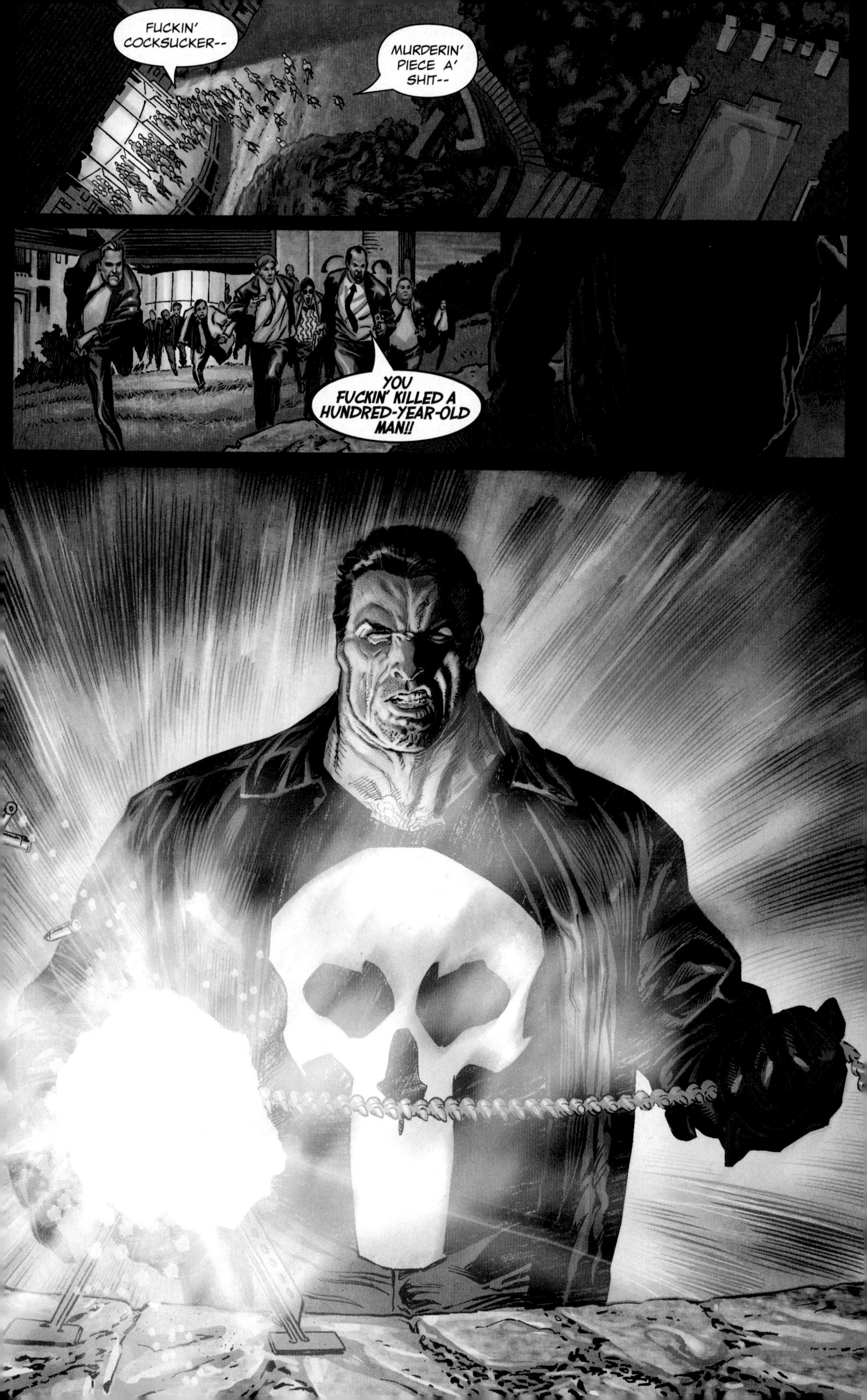
FUCKIN' COCKSUCKER--
MURDERIN' PIECE A' SHIT--
YOU FUCKIN' KILLED A HUNDRED-YEAR-OLD MAN!!

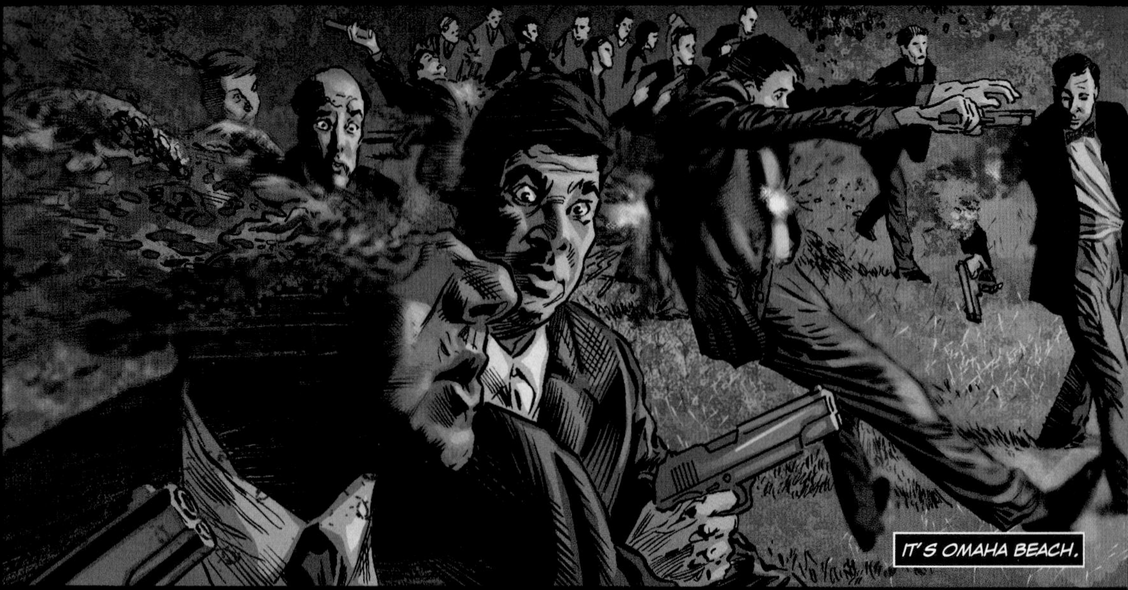
IT'S OMAHA BEACH.

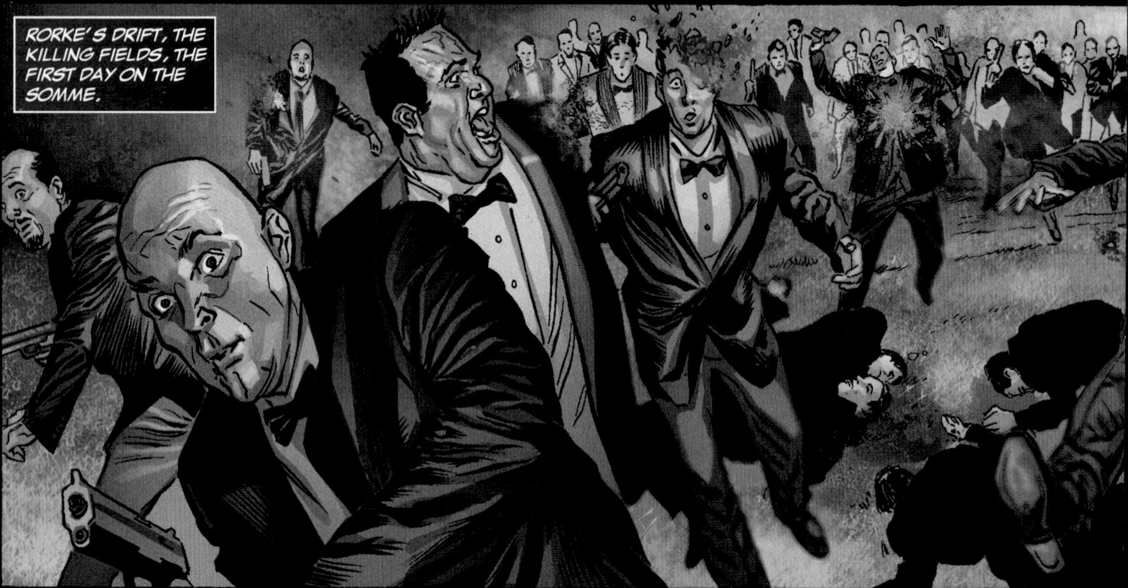
RORKE'S DRIFT, THE KILLING FIELDS, THE FIRST DAY ON THE SOMME.

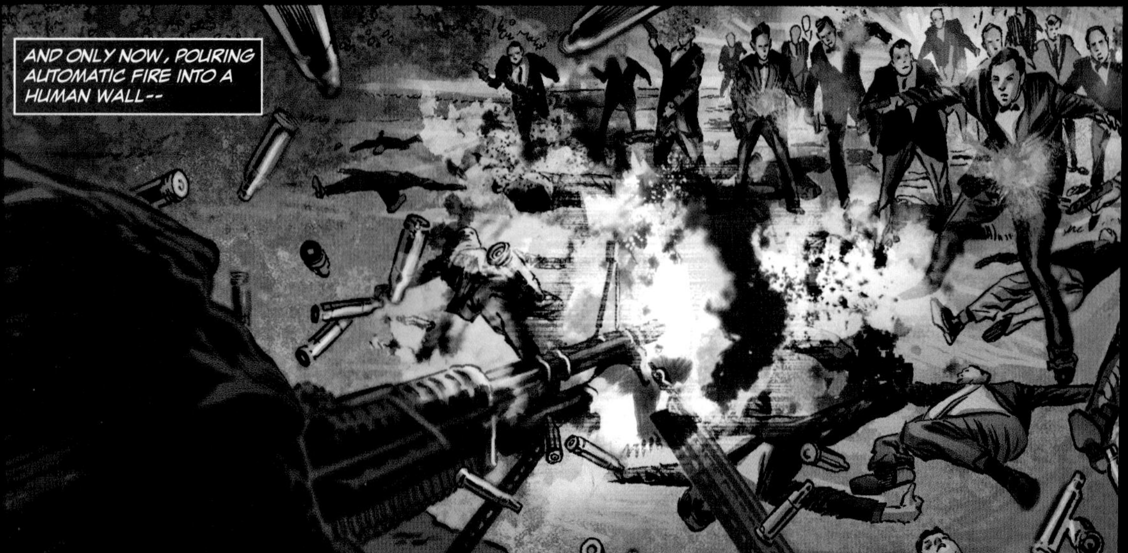
AND ONLY NOW, POURING AUTOMATIC FIRE INTO A HUMAN WALL--

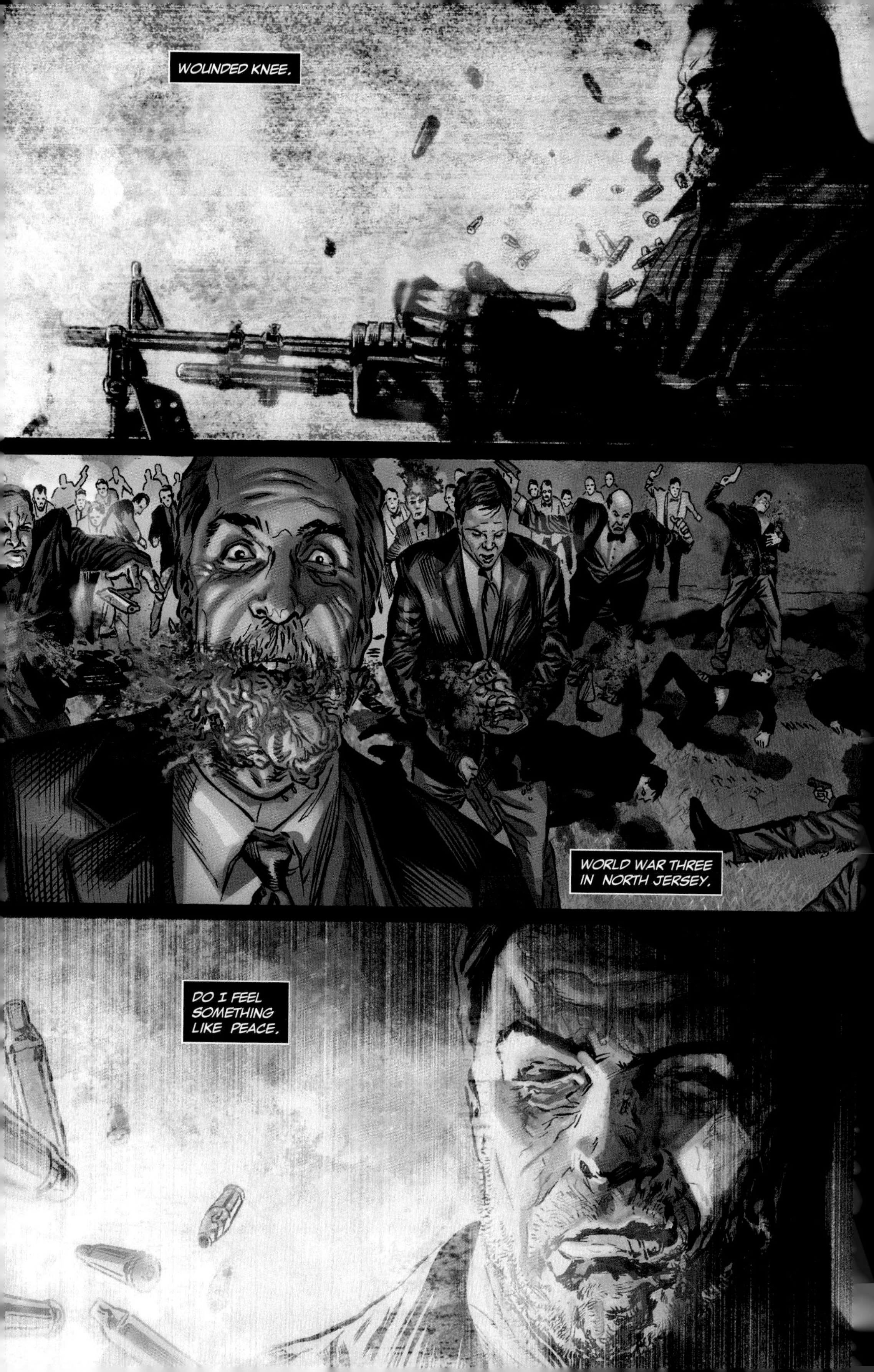
WOUNDED KNEE.
WORLD WAR THREE IN NORTH JERSEY.
DO I FEEL SOMETHING LIKE PEACE.

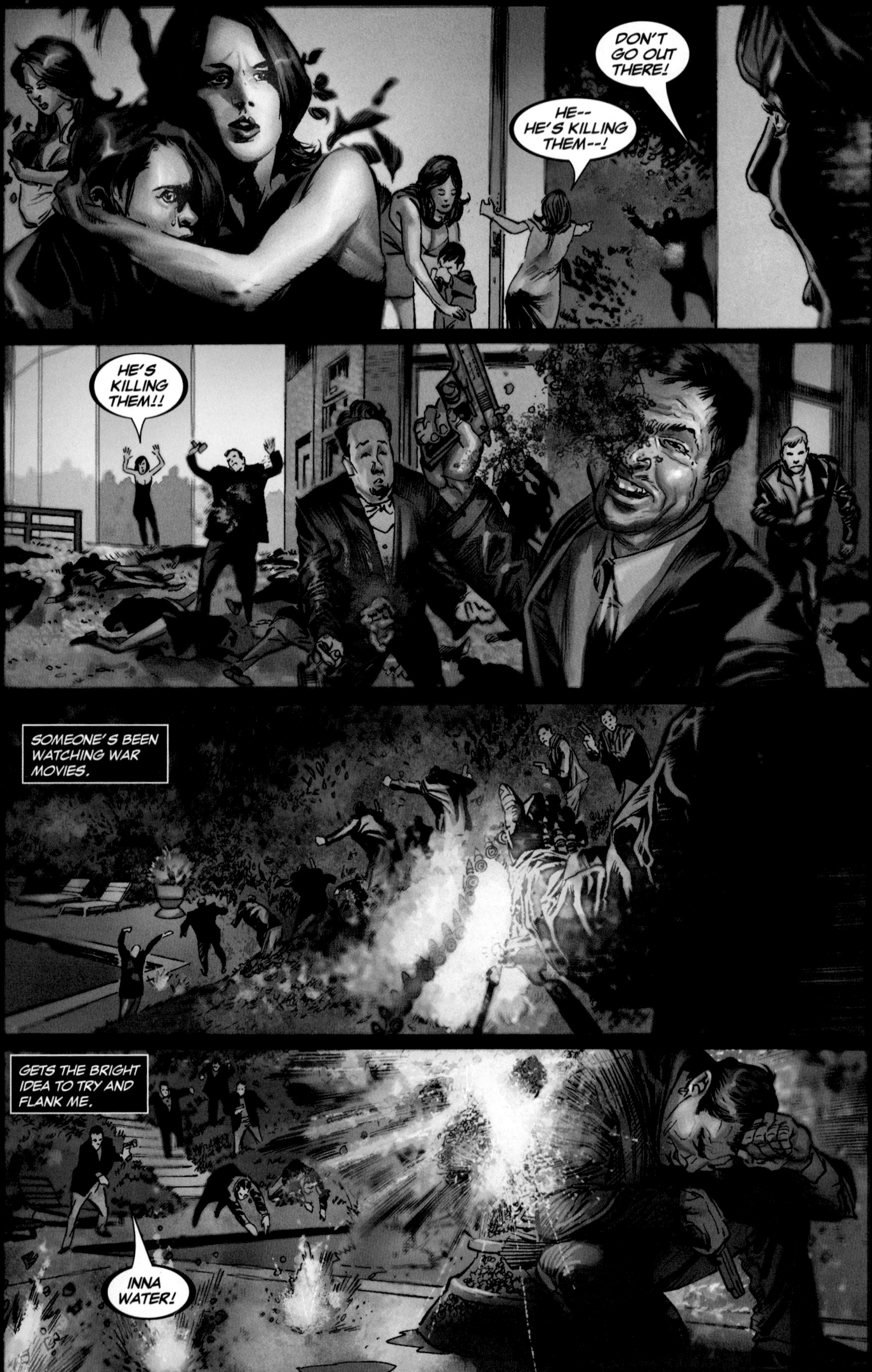
DON'T GO OUT THERE!
HE-- HE'S KILLING THEM--!
HE'S KILLING THEM!!
SOMEONE'S BEEN WATCHING WAR MOVIES.
GETS THE BRIGHT IDEA TO TRY AND FLANK ME.
INNA WATER!

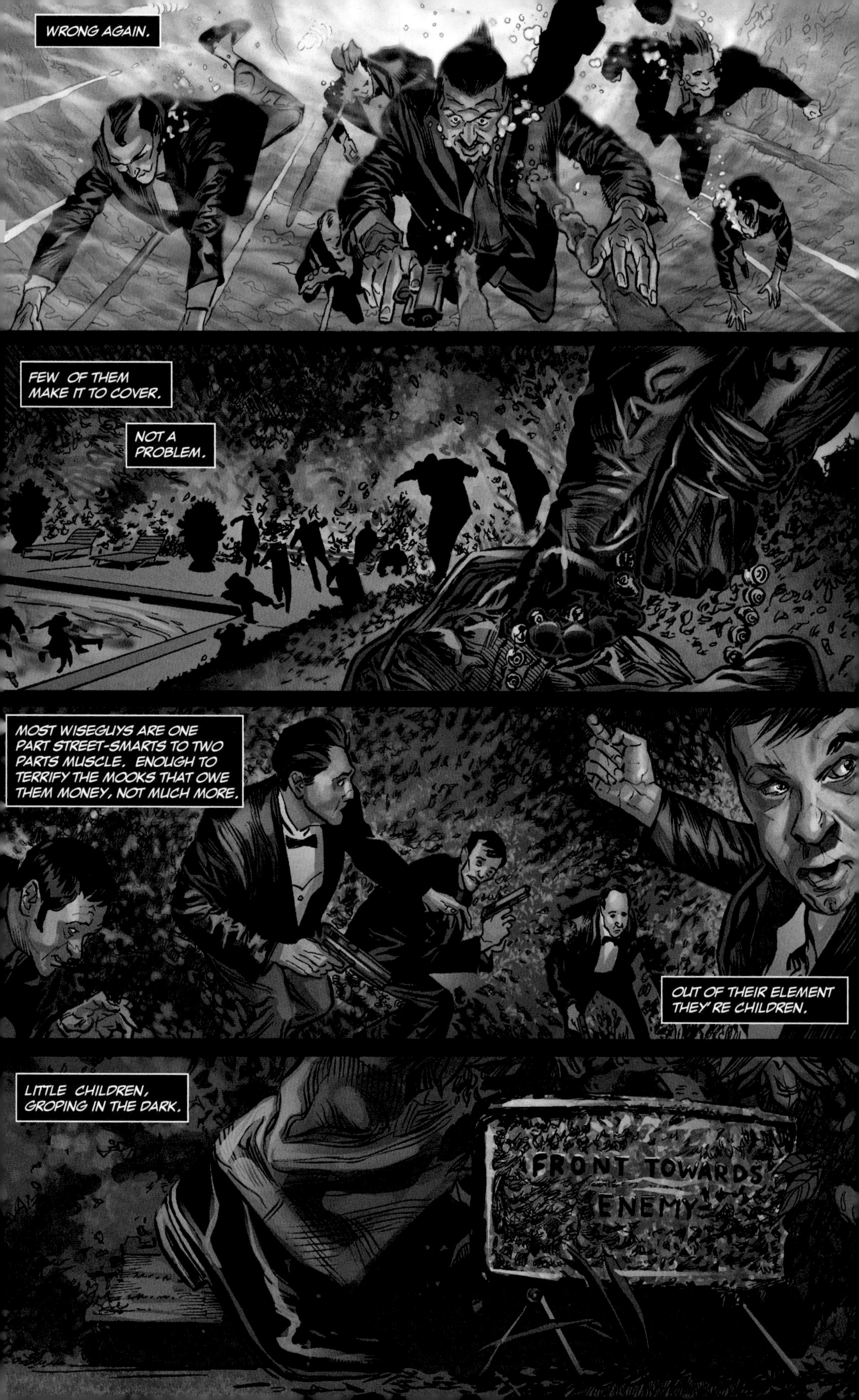

WRONG AGAIN.
FEW OF THEM MAKE IT TO COVER.
NOT A PROBLEM.
MOST WISEGUYS ARE ONE PART STREET-SMARTS TO TWO PARTS MUSCLE. ENOUGH TO TERRIFY THE MOOKS THAT OWE THEM MONEY, NOT MUCH MORE.
OUT OF THEIR ELEMENT THEY'RE CHILDREN.
LITTLE CHILDREN, GROPING IN THE DARK.
FRONT TOWARDS ENEMY

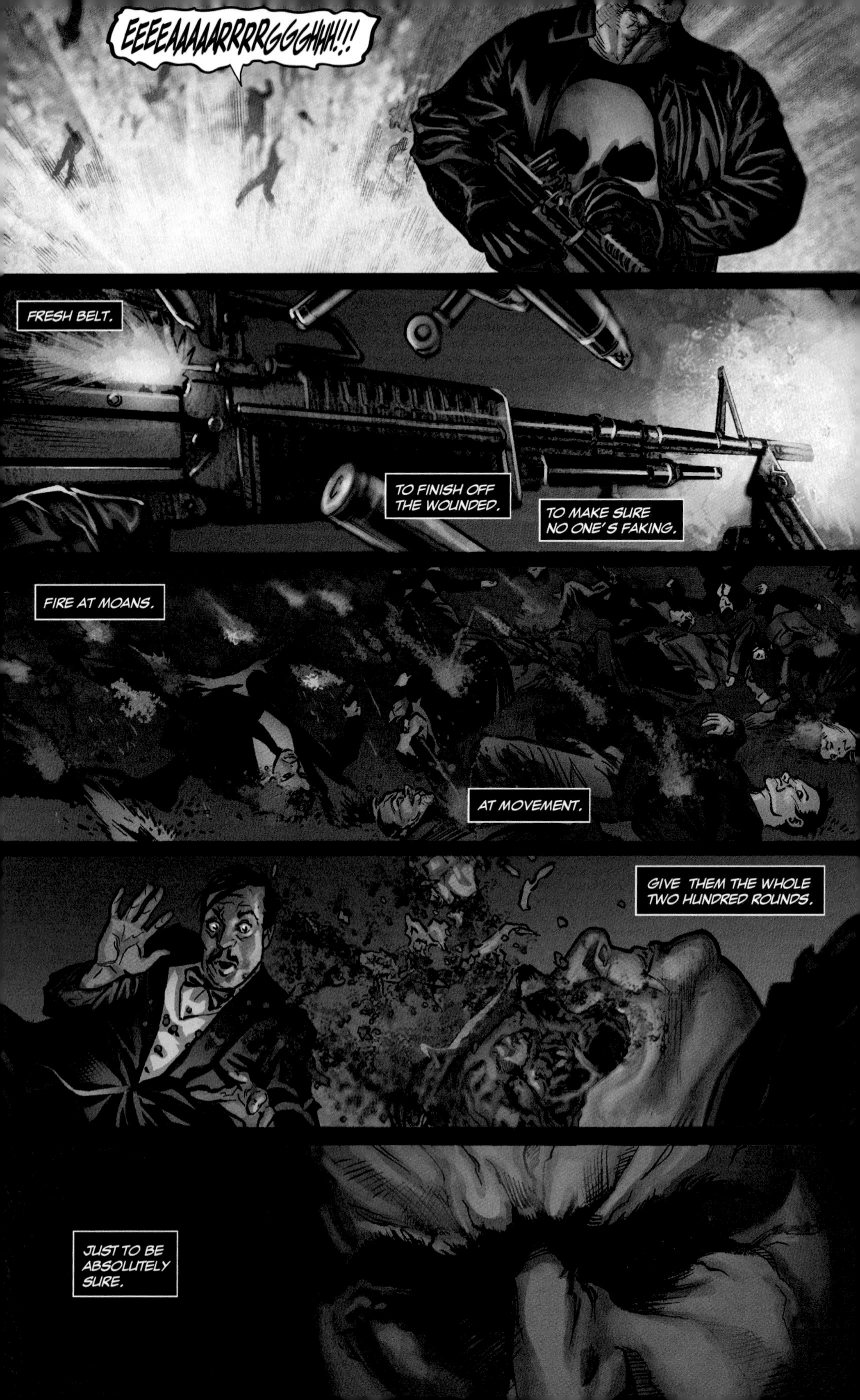
EEEEAAAAARRRRGGGHH!!!
FRESH BELT.
TO FINISH OFF THE WOUNDED.
TO MAKE SURE NO ONE'S FAKING.
FIRE AT MOANS.
AT MOVEMENT.
GIVE THEM THE WHOLE TWO HUNDRED ROUNDS.
JUST TO BE ABSOLUTELY SURE.

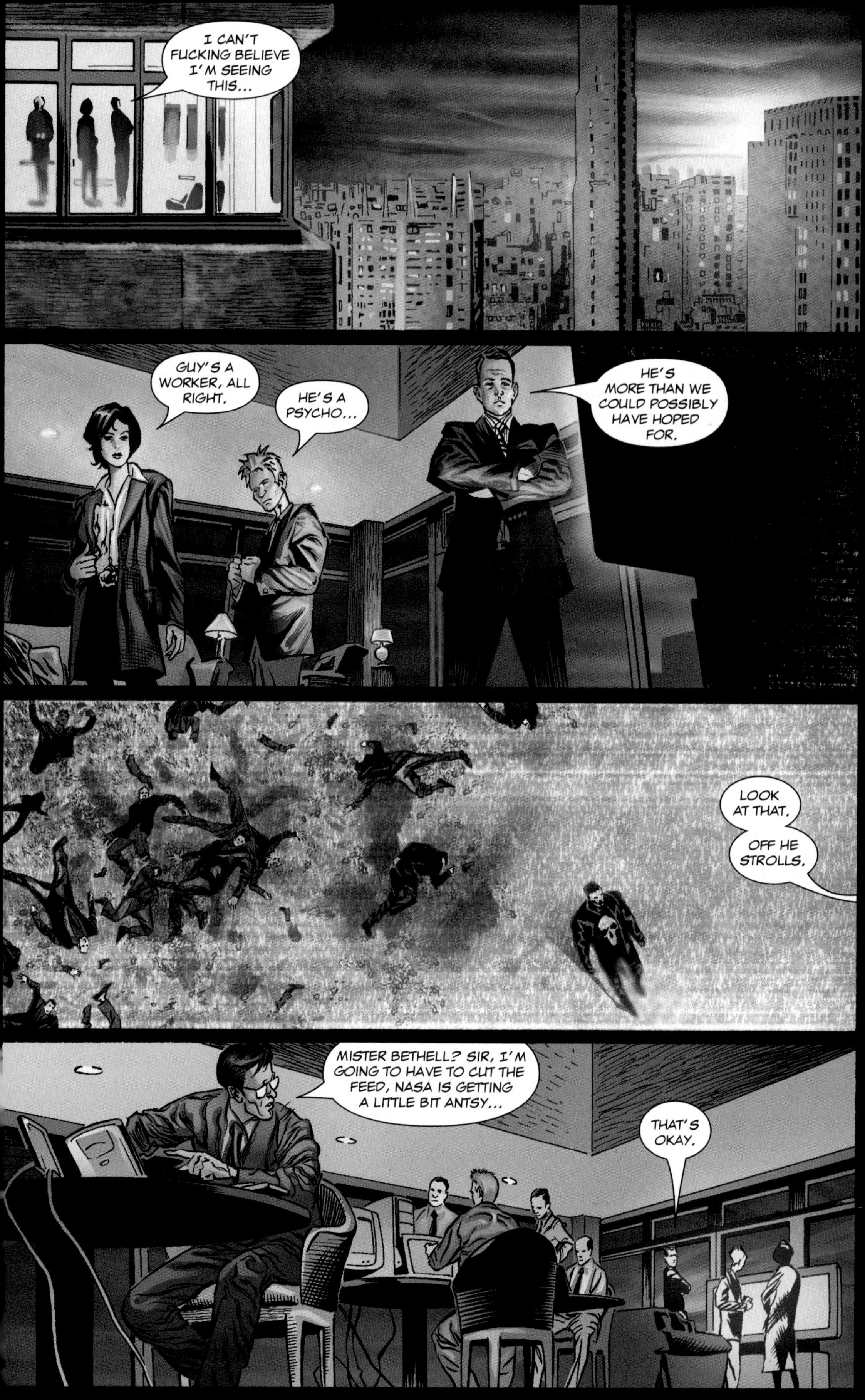
I CAN'T FUCKING BELIEVE I'M SEEING THIS...
GUY'S A WORKER, ALL RIGHT.
HE'S A PSYCHO...
HE'S MORE THAN WE COULD POSSIBLY HAVE HOPED FOR.
LOOK AT THAT.
OFF HE STROLLS.
MISTER BETHELL? SIR, I'M GOING TO HAVE TO CUT THE FEED, NASA IS GETTING A LITTLE BIT ANTSY...
THAT'S OKAY.

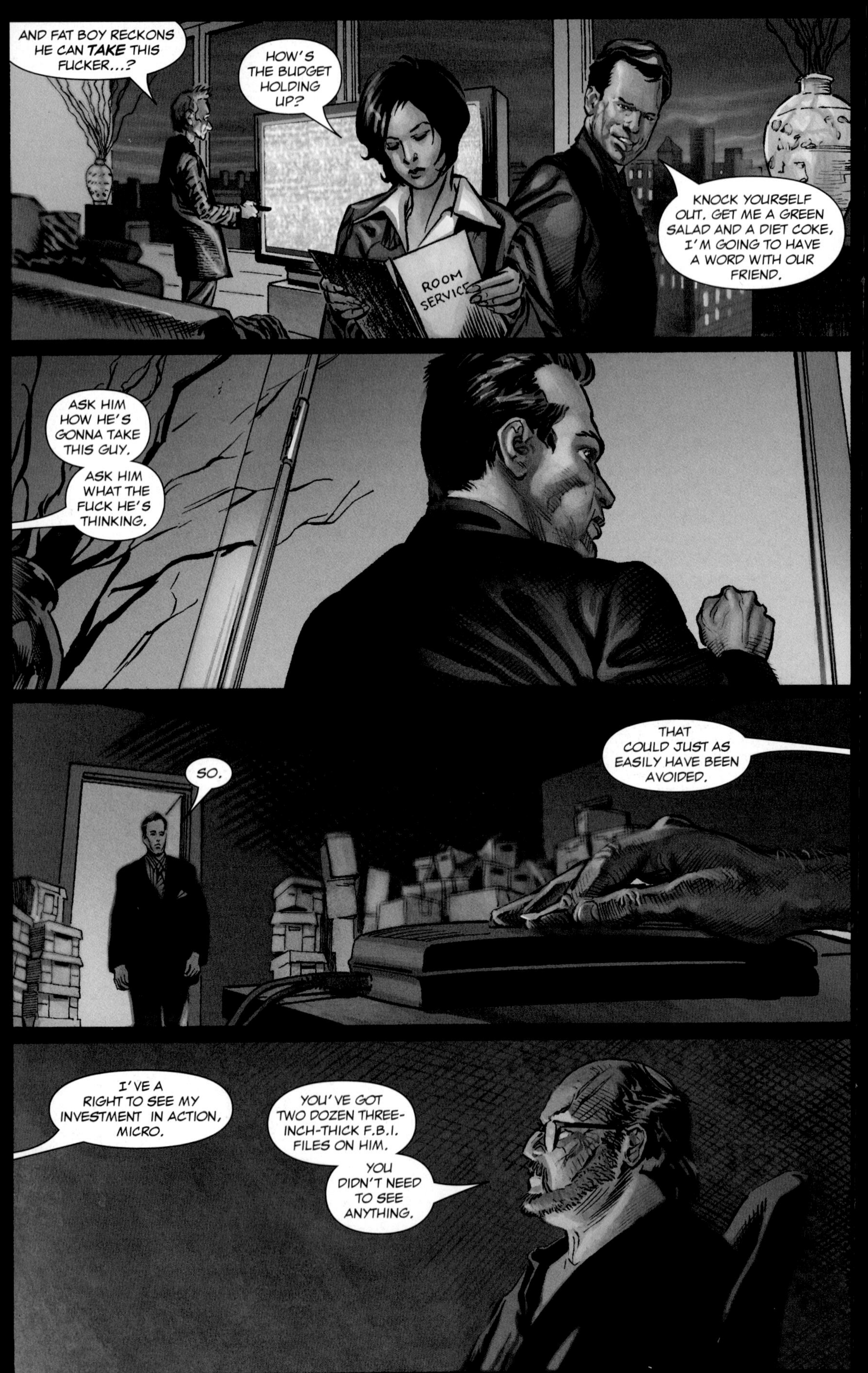
AND FAT BOY RECKONS HE CAN TAKE THIS FUCKER...?
HOW'S THE BUDGET HOLDING UP?
KNOCK YOURSELF OUT. GET ME A GREEN SALAD AND A DIET COKE, I'M GOING TO HAVE A WORD WITH OUR FRIEND.
ROOM SERVICE
ASK HIM HOW HE'S GONNA TAKE THIS GUY.
ASK HIM WHAT THE FUCK HE'S THINKING.
SO.
THAT COULD JUST AS EASILY HAVE BEEN AVOIDED.
I'VE A RIGHT TO SEE MY INVESTMENT IN ACTION, MICRO.
YOU'VE GOT TWO DOZEN THREE-INCH-THICK F.B.I. FILES ON HIM.
YOU DIDN'T NEED TO SEE ANYTHING.

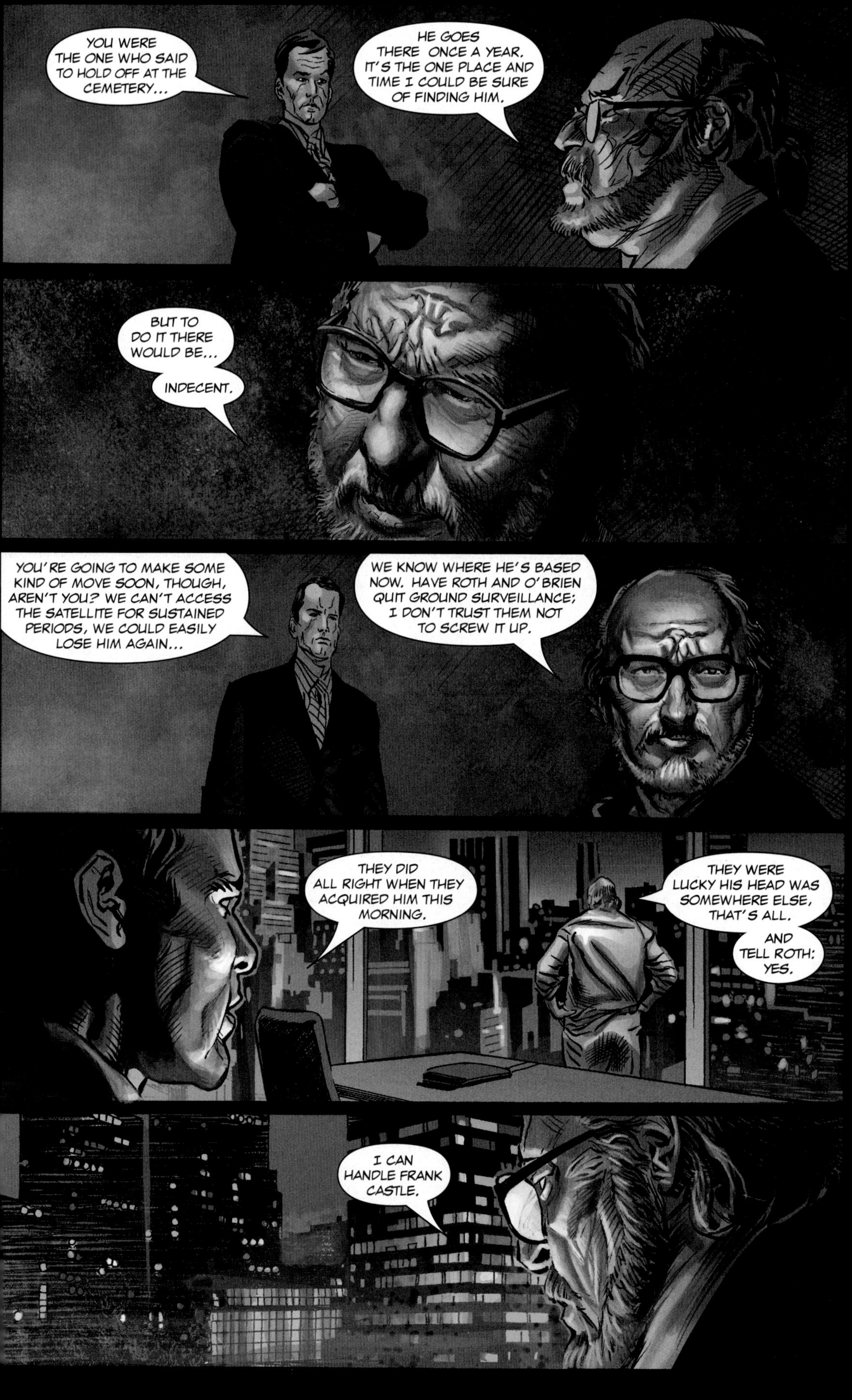
YOU WERE THE ONE WHO SAID TO HOLD OFF AT THE CEMETERY...
HE GOES THERE ONCE A YEAR. IT'S THE ONE PLACE AND TIME I COULD BE SURE OF FINDING HIM.
BUT TO DO IT THERE WOULD BE...
INDECENT.
YOU'RE GOING TO MAKE SOME KIND OF MOVE SOON, THOUGH, AREN'T YOU? WE CAN'T ACCESS THE SATELLITE FOR SUSTAINED PERIODS, WE COULD EASILY LOSE HIM AGAIN...
WE KNOW WHERE HE'S BASED NOW. HAVE ROTH AND O'BRIEN QUIT GROUND SURVEILLANCE; I DON'T TRUST THEM NOT TO SCREW IT UP.
THEY DID ALL RIGHT WHEN THEY ACQUIRED HIM THIS MORNING.
THEY WERE LUCKY HIS HEAD WAS SOMEWHERE ELSE, THAT'S ALL.
AND TELL ROTH: YES.
I CAN HANDLE FRANK CASTLE.

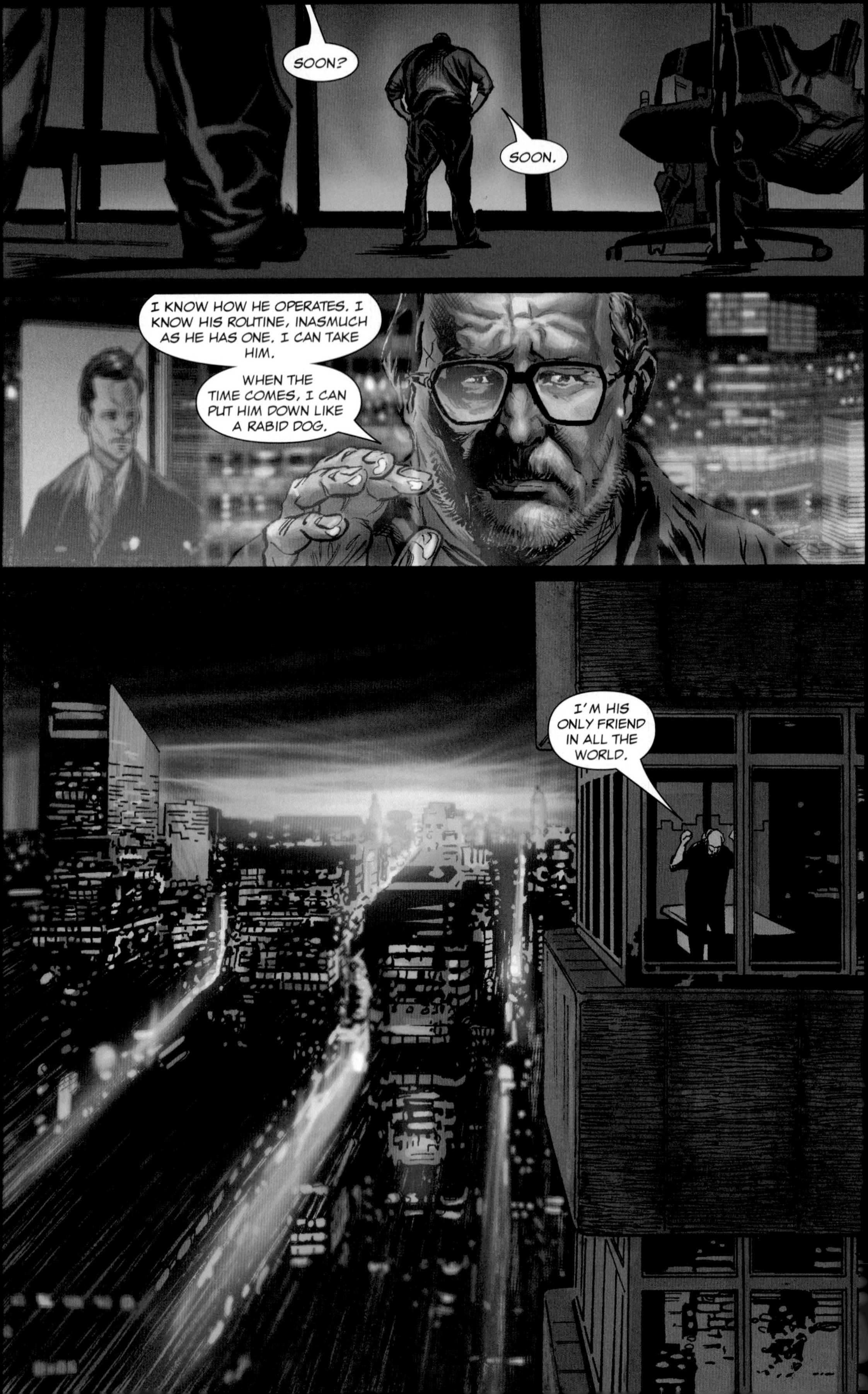
SOON?
SOON.
I KNOW HOW HE OPERATES. I KNOW HIS ROUTINE, INASMUCH AS HE HAS ONE. I CAN TAKE HIM.
WHEN THE TIME COMES, I CAN PUT HIM DOWN LIKE A RABID DOG.
I'M HIS ONLY FRIEND IN ALL THE WORLD.

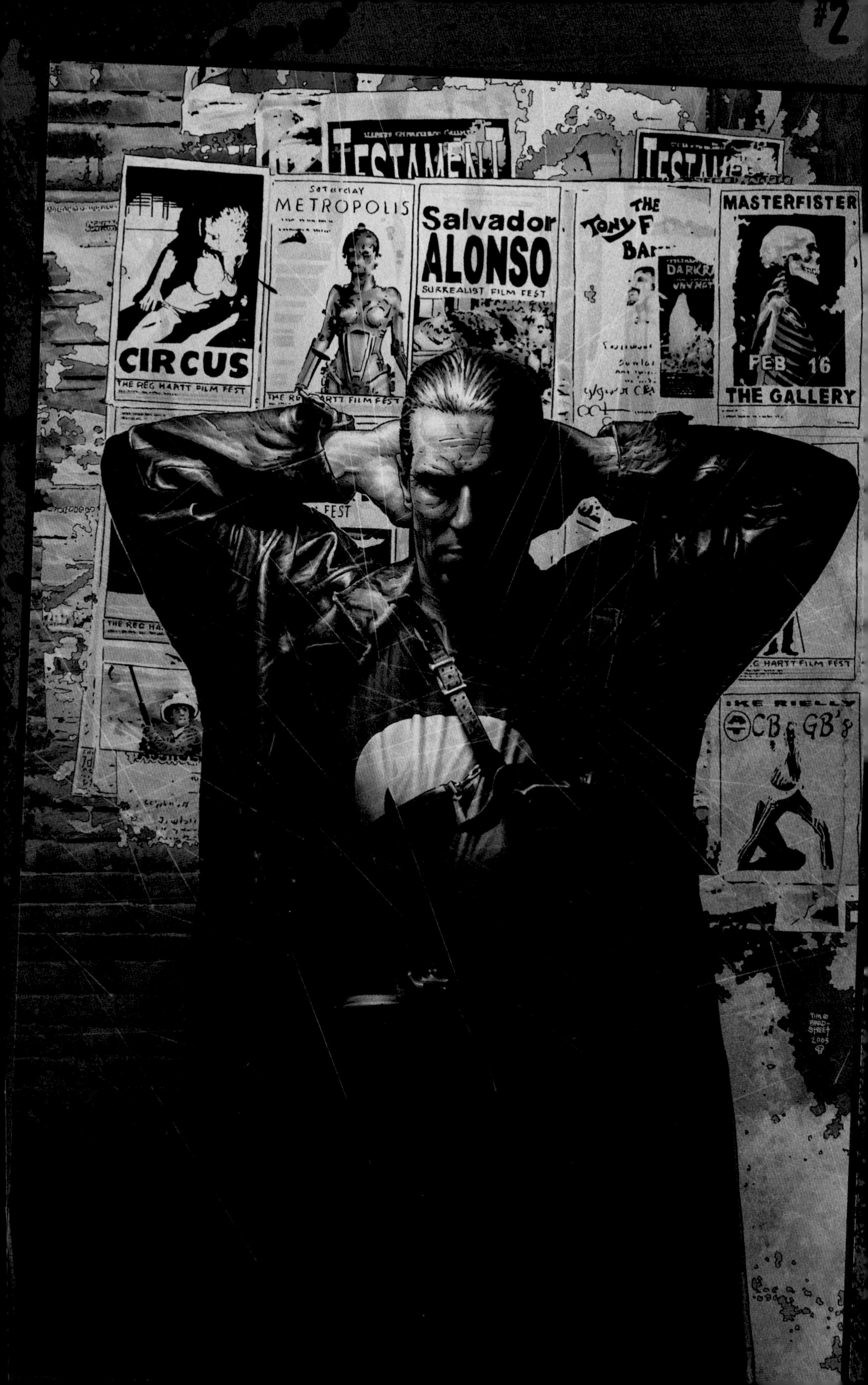

#2
saturday
METROPOLIS
Salvador
ALONSO
SURREALIST FILM FEST
CIRCUS
THE REG HARTT FILM FEST
MASTERFISTER
FEB 16
THE GALLERY
TIM BRADSTREET 2003

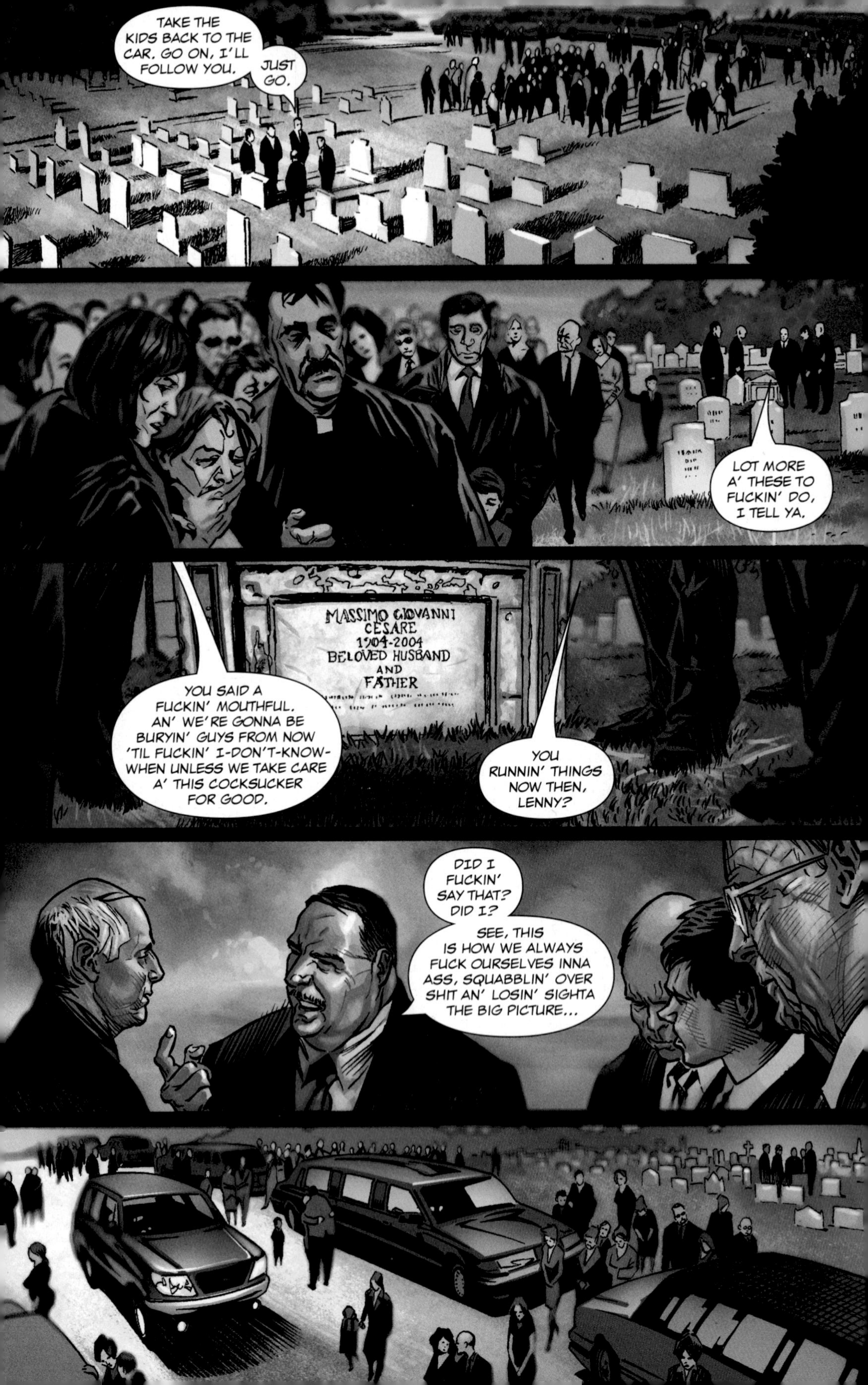
TAKE THE KIDS BACK TO THE CAR. GO ON, I'LL FOLLOW YOU.
JUST GO.
LOT MORE A' THESE TO FUCKIN' DO, I TELL YA.
MASSIMO GIOVANNI CESARE 1904-2004 BELOVED HUSBAND AND FATHER
YOU SAID A FUCKIN' MOUTHFUL. AN' WE'RE GONNA BE BURYIN' GUYS FROM NOW 'TIL FUCKIN' I-DON'T-KNOW-WHEN UNLESS WE TAKE CARE A' THIS COCKSUCKER FOR GOOD.
YOU RUNNIN' THINGS NOW THEN, LENNY?
DID I FUCKIN' SAY THAT? DID I?
SEE, THIS IS HOW WE ALWAYS FUCK OURSELVES INNA ASS, SQUABBLIN' OVER SHIT AN' LOSIN' SIGHTA THE BIG PICTURE...

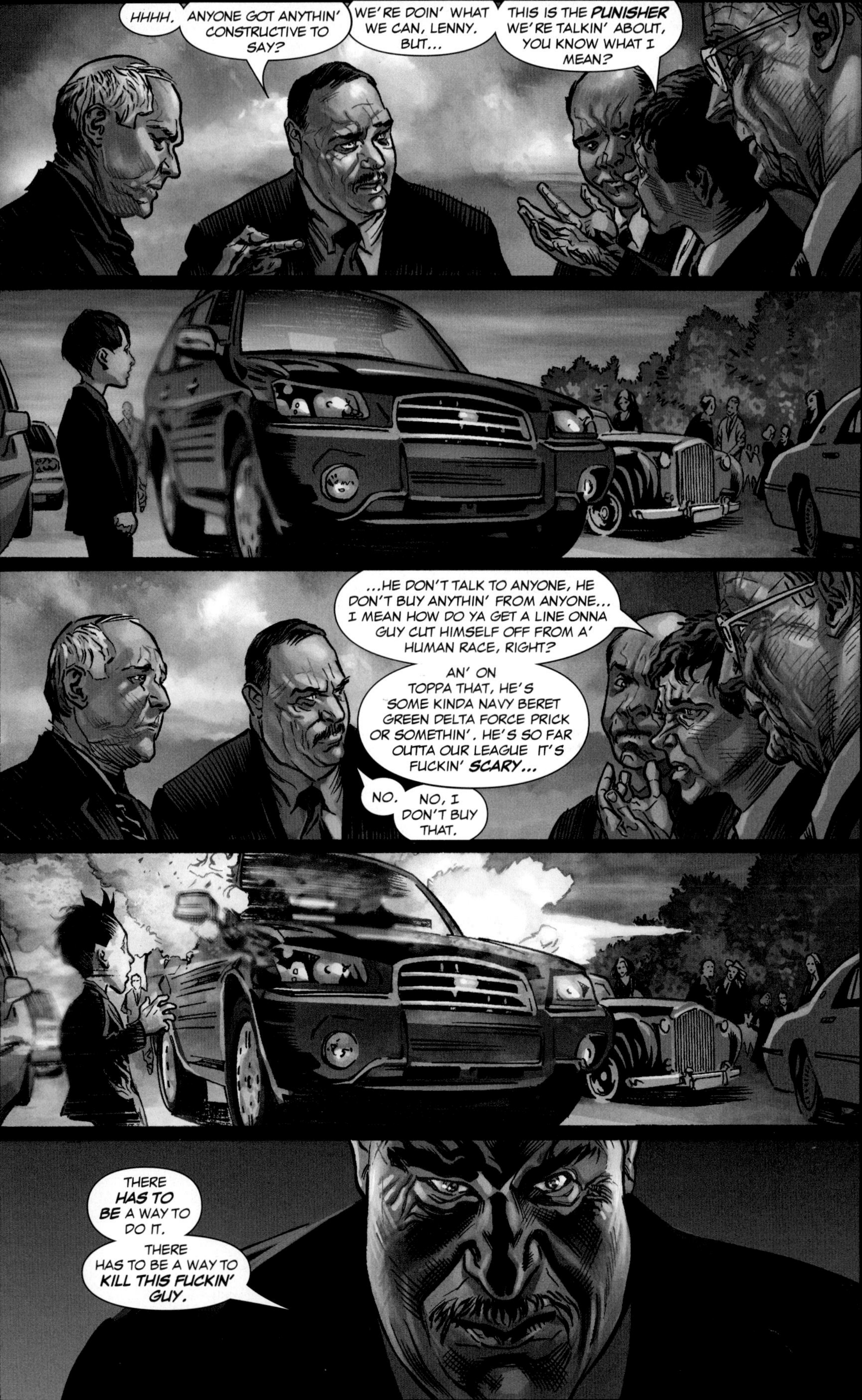
HHHH.
ANYONE GOT ANYTHIN' CONSTRUCTIVE TO SAY?
WE'RE DOIN' WHAT WE CAN, LENNY. BUT...
THIS IS THE PUNISHER WE'RE TALKIN' ABOUT, YOU KNOW WHAT I MEAN?
...HE DON'T TALK TO ANYONE, HE DON'T BUY ANYTHIN' FROM ANYONE... I MEAN HOW DO YA GET A LINE ONNA GUY CUT HIMSELF OFF FROM A' HUMAN RACE, RIGHT?
AN' ON TOPPA THAT, HE'S SOME KINDA NAVY BERET GREEN DELTA FORCE PRICK OR SOMETHIN'. HE'S SO FAR OUTTA OUR LEAGUE IT'S FUCKIN' SCARY...
NO.
NO, I DON'T BUY THAT.
THERE HAS TO BE A WAY TO DO IT.
THERE HAS TO BE A WAY TO KILL THIS FUCKIN' GUY.

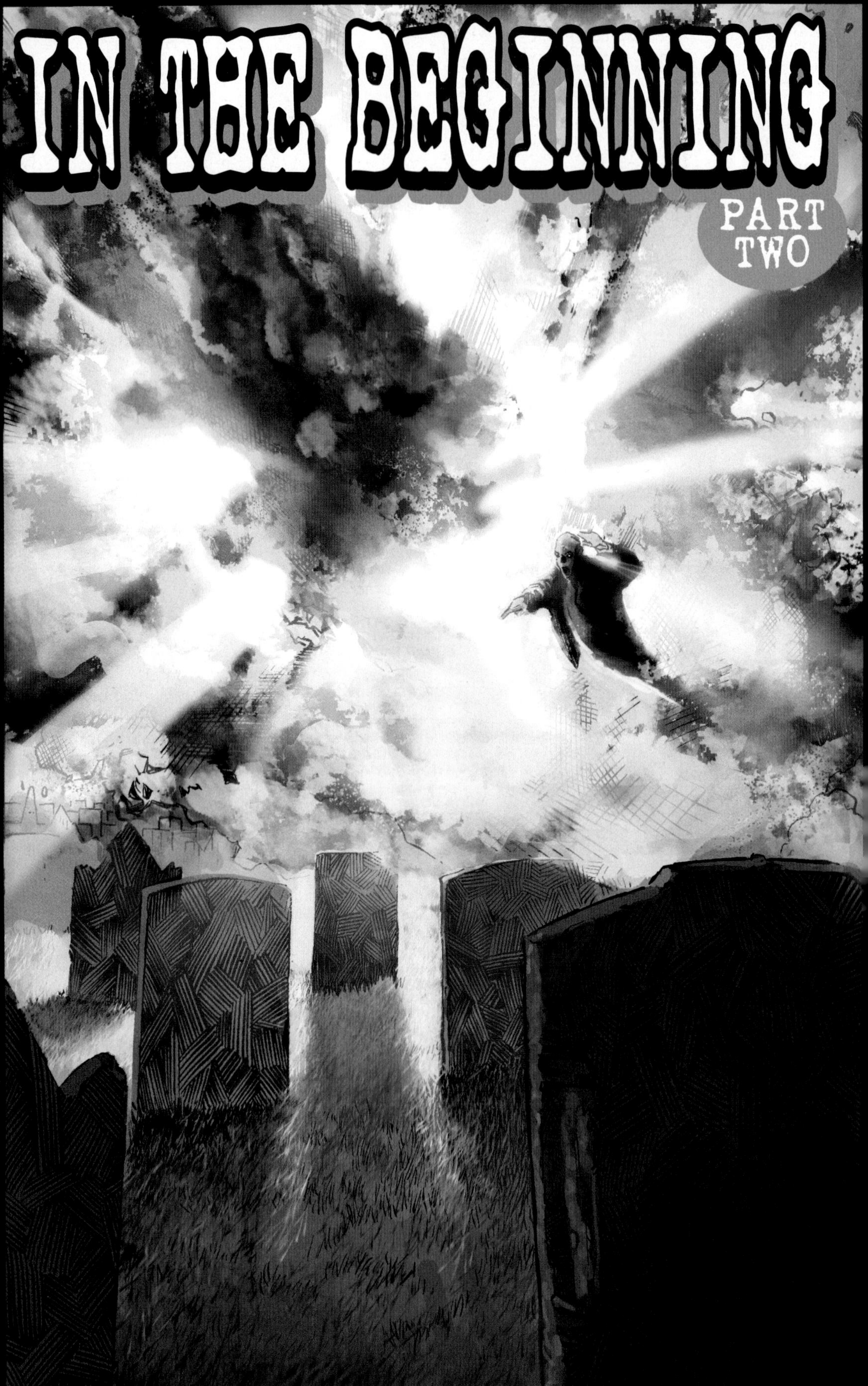
IN THE BEGINNING
PART TWO

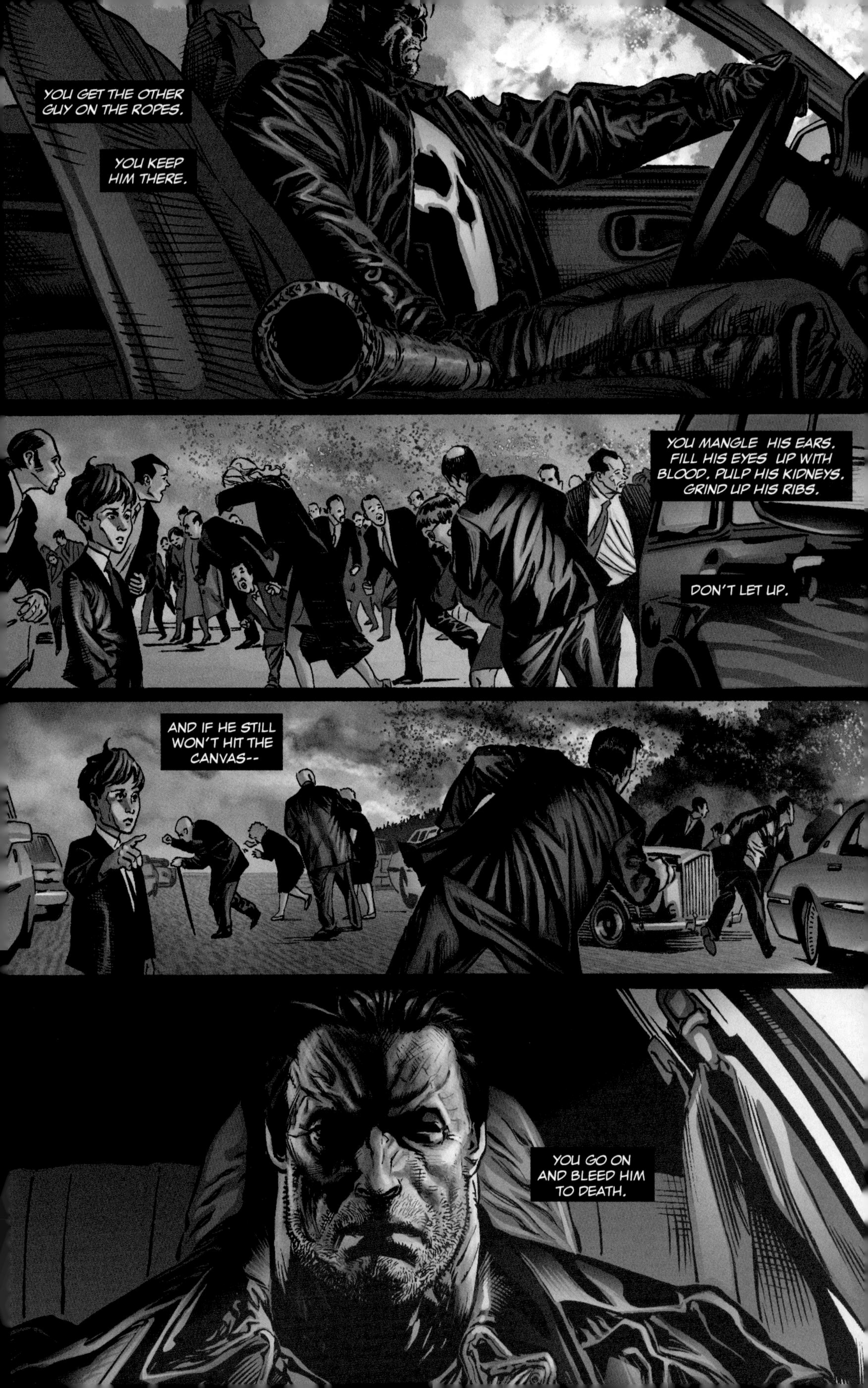
YOU GET THE OTHER GUY ON THE ROPES.
YOU KEEP HIM THERE.
YOU MANGLE HIS EARS. FILL HIS EYES UP WITH BLOOD. PULP HIS KIDNEYS. GRIND UP HIS RIBS.
DON'T LET UP.
AND IF HE STILL WON'T HIT THE CANVAS--
YOU GO ON AND BLEED HIM TO DEATH.

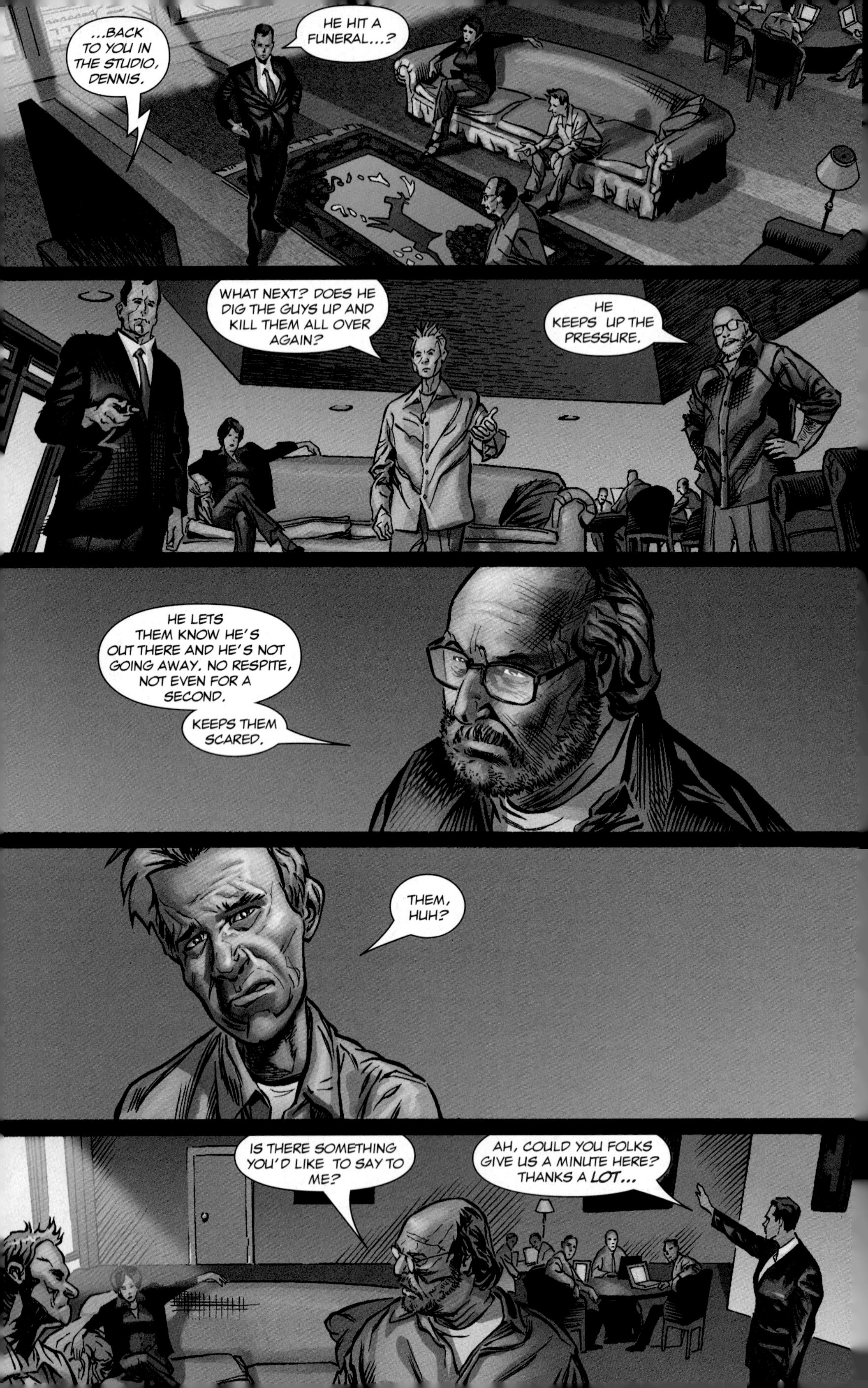
...BACK TO YOU IN THE STUDIO, DENNIS.
HE HIT A FUNERAL...?
WHAT NEXT? DOES HE DIG THE GUYS UP AND KILL THEM ALL OVER AGAIN?
HE KEEPS UP THE PRESSURE.
HE LETS THEM KNOW HE'S OUT THERE AND HE'S NOT GOING AWAY. NO RESPITE, NOT EVEN FOR A SECOND.
KEEPS THEM SCARED.
THEM, HUH?
IS THERE SOMETHING YOU'D LIKE TO SAY TO ME?
AH, COULD YOU FOLKS GIVE US A MINUTE HERE? THANKS A **LOT**...

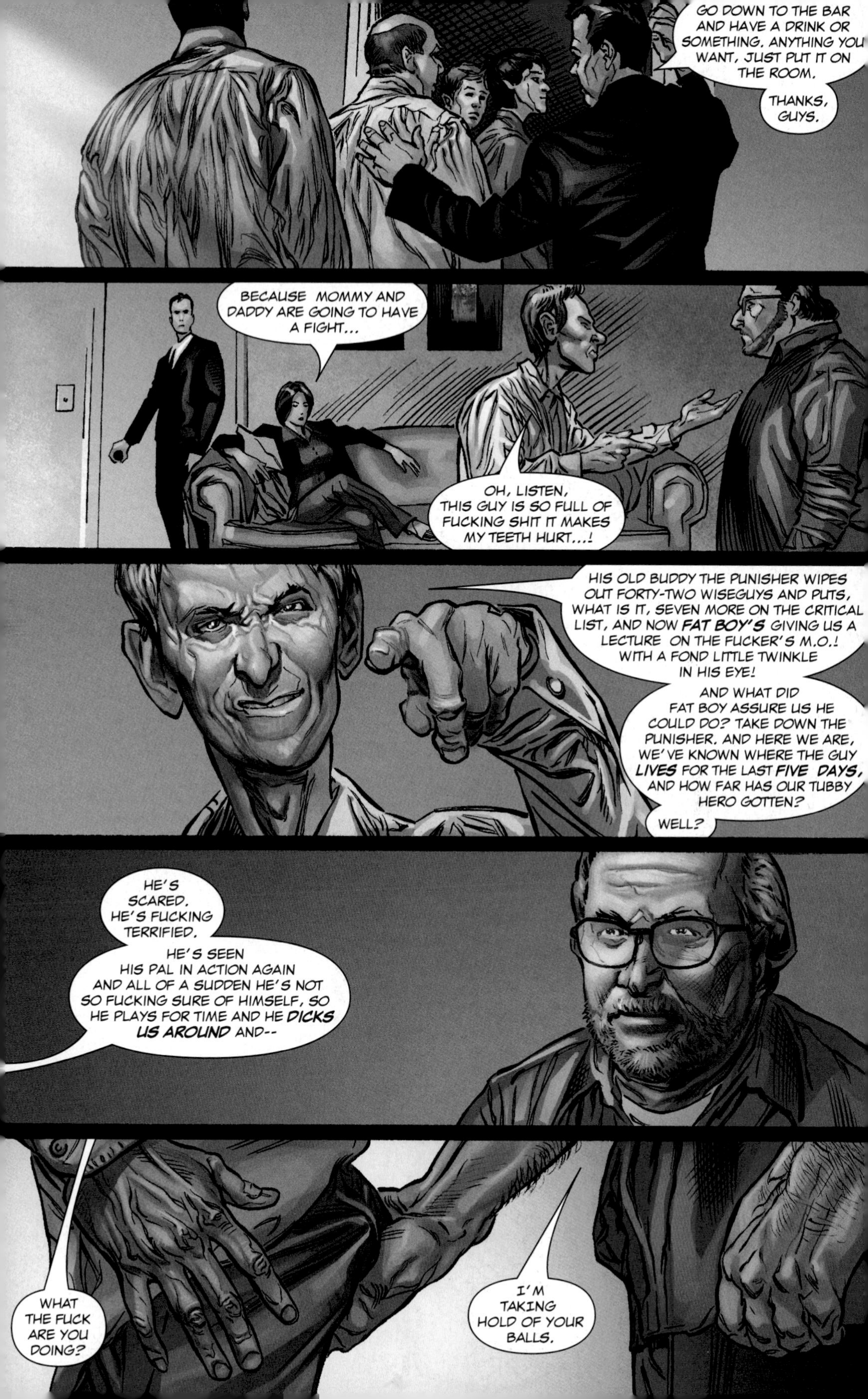
GO DOWN TO THE BAR AND HAVE A DRINK OR SOMETHING. ANYTHING YOU WANT, JUST PUT IT ON THE ROOM.
THANKS, GUYS.
BECAUSE MOMMY AND DADDY ARE GOING TO HAVE A FIGHT...
OH, LISTEN, THIS GUY IS SO FULL OF FUCKING SHIT IT MAKES MY TEETH HURT...!
HIS OLD BUDDY THE PUNISHER WIPES OUT FORTY-TWO WISEGUYS AND PUTS, WHAT IS IT, SEVEN MORE ON THE CRITICAL LIST, AND NOW FAT BOY'S GIVING US A LECTURE ON THE FUCKER'S M.O.! WITH A FOND LITTLE TWINKLE IN HIS EYE!
AND WHAT DID FAT BOY ASSURE US HE COULD DO? TAKE DOWN THE PUNISHER. AND HERE WE ARE, WE'VE KNOWN WHERE THE GUY LIVES FOR THE LAST FIVE DAYS, AND HOW FAR HAS OUR TUBBY HERO GOTTEN?
WELL?
HE'S SCARED. HE'S FUCKING TERRIFIED.
HE'S SEEN HIS PAL IN ACTION AGAIN AND ALL OF A SUDDEN HE'S NOT SO FUCKING SURE OF HIMSELF, SO HE PLAYS FOR TIME AND HE DICKS US AROUND AND--
WHAT THE FUCK ARE YOU DOING?
I'M TAKING HOLD OF YOUR BALLS.

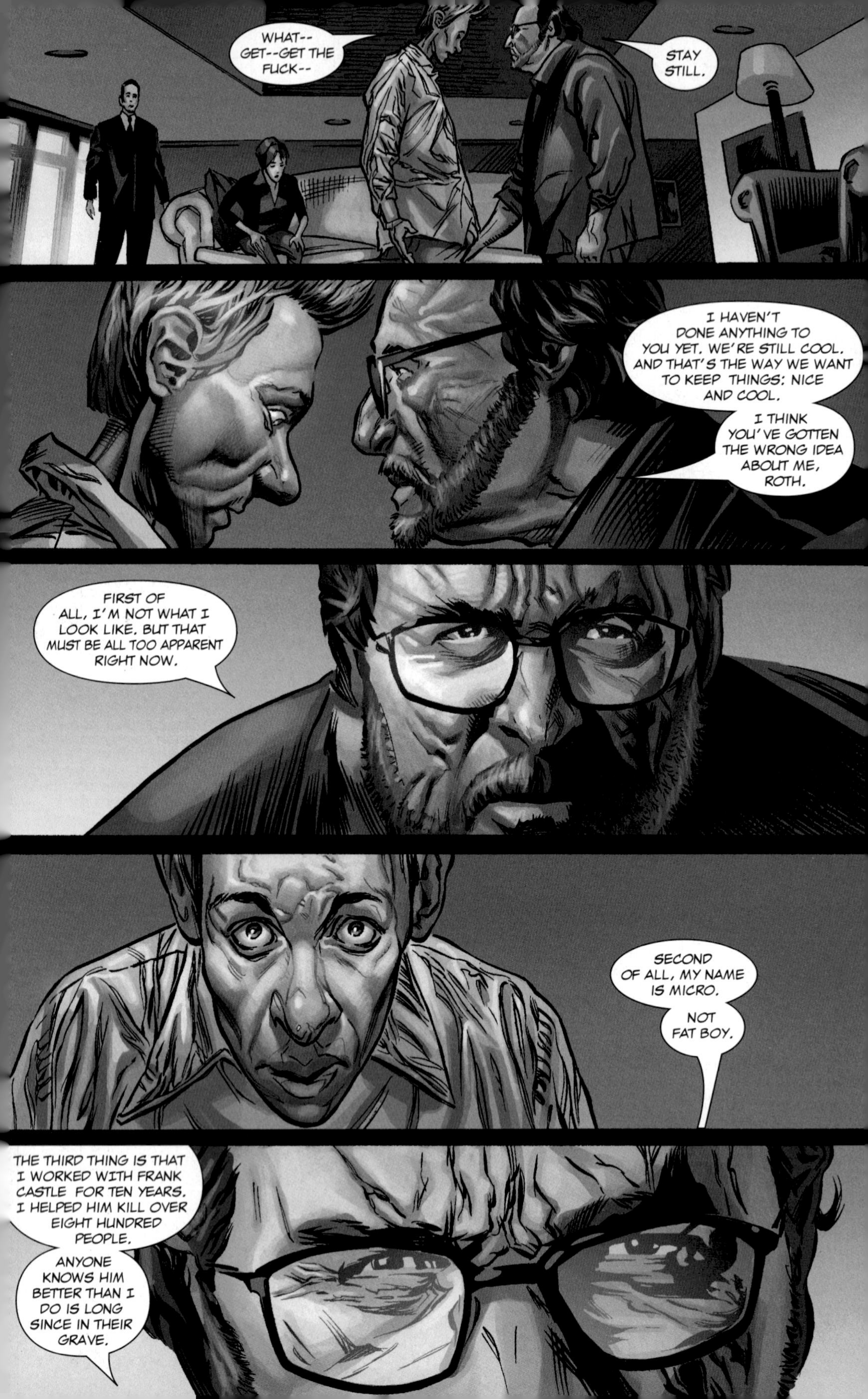
WHAT-- GET--GET THE FUCK--
STAY STILL.
I HAVEN'T DONE ANYTHING TO YOU YET. WE'RE STILL COOL. AND THAT'S THE WAY WE WANT TO KEEP THINGS: NICE AND COOL.
I THINK YOU'VE GOTTEN THE WRONG IDEA ABOUT ME, ROTH.
FIRST OF ALL, I'M NOT WHAT I LOOK LIKE. BUT THAT MUST BE ALL TOO APPARENT RIGHT NOW.
SECOND OF ALL, MY NAME IS MICRO.
NOT FAT BOY.
THE THIRD THING IS THAT I WORKED WITH FRANK CASTLE FOR TEN YEARS. I HELPED HIM KILL OVER EIGHT HUNDRED PEOPLE.
ANYONE KNOWS HIM BETTER THAN I DO IS LONG SINCE IN THEIR GRAVE.

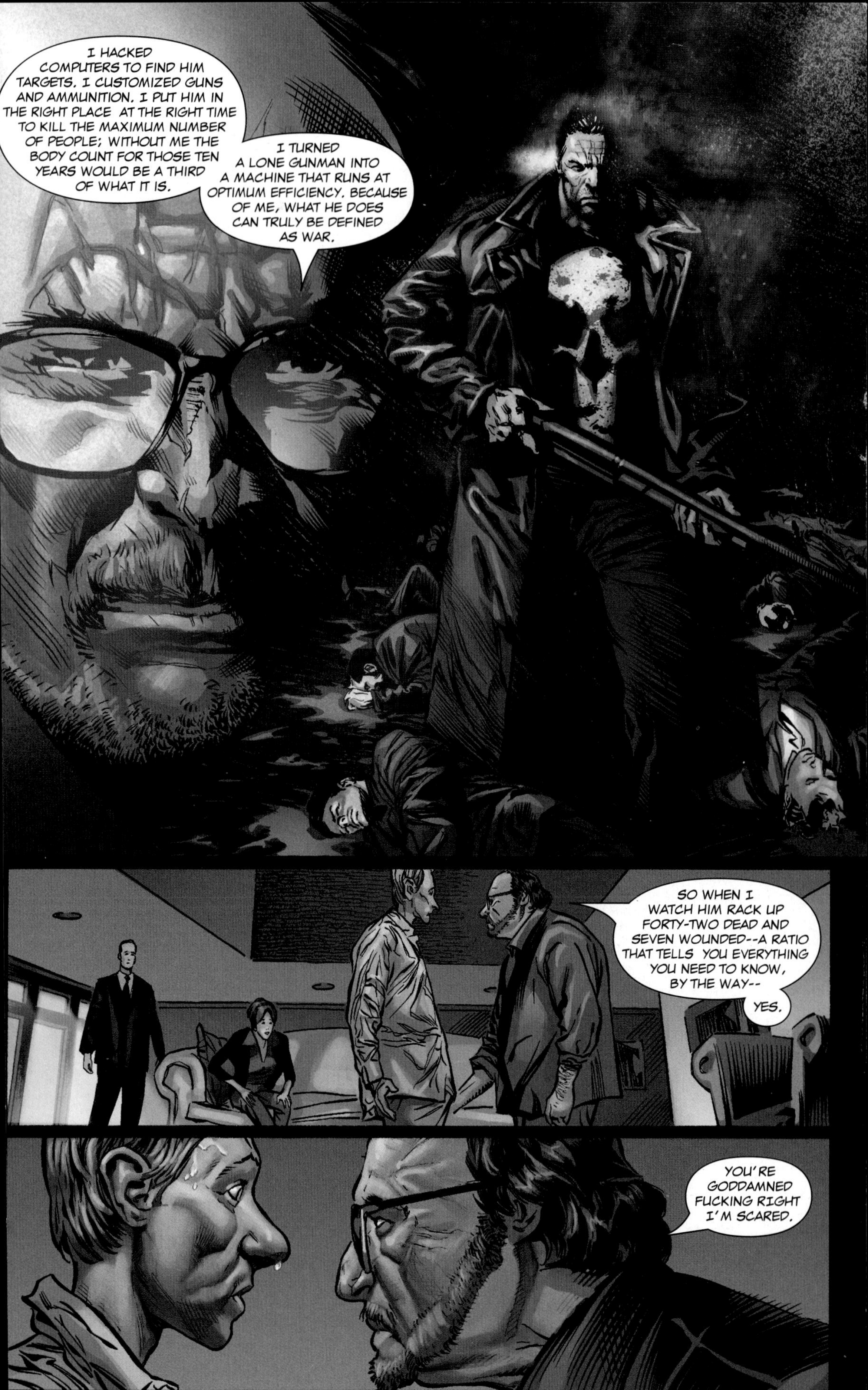
I HACKED COMPUTERS TO FIND HIM TARGETS. I CUSTOMIZED GUNS AND AMMUNITION. I PUT HIM IN THE RIGHT PLACE AT THE RIGHT TIME TO KILL THE MAXIMUM NUMBER OF PEOPLE; WITHOUT ME THE BODY COUNT FOR THOSE TEN YEARS WOULD BE A THIRD OF WHAT IT IS.
I TURNED A LONE GUNMAN INTO A MACHINE THAT RUNS AT OPTIMUM EFFICIENCY. BECAUSE OF ME, WHAT HE DOES CAN TRULY BE DEFINED AS WAR.
SO WHEN I WATCH HIM RACK UP FORTY-TWO DEAD AND SEVEN WOUNDED--A RATIO THAT TELLS YOU EVERYTHING YOU NEED TO KNOW, BY THE WAY--
YES.
YOU'RE GODDAMNED FUCKING RIGHT I'M SCARED.

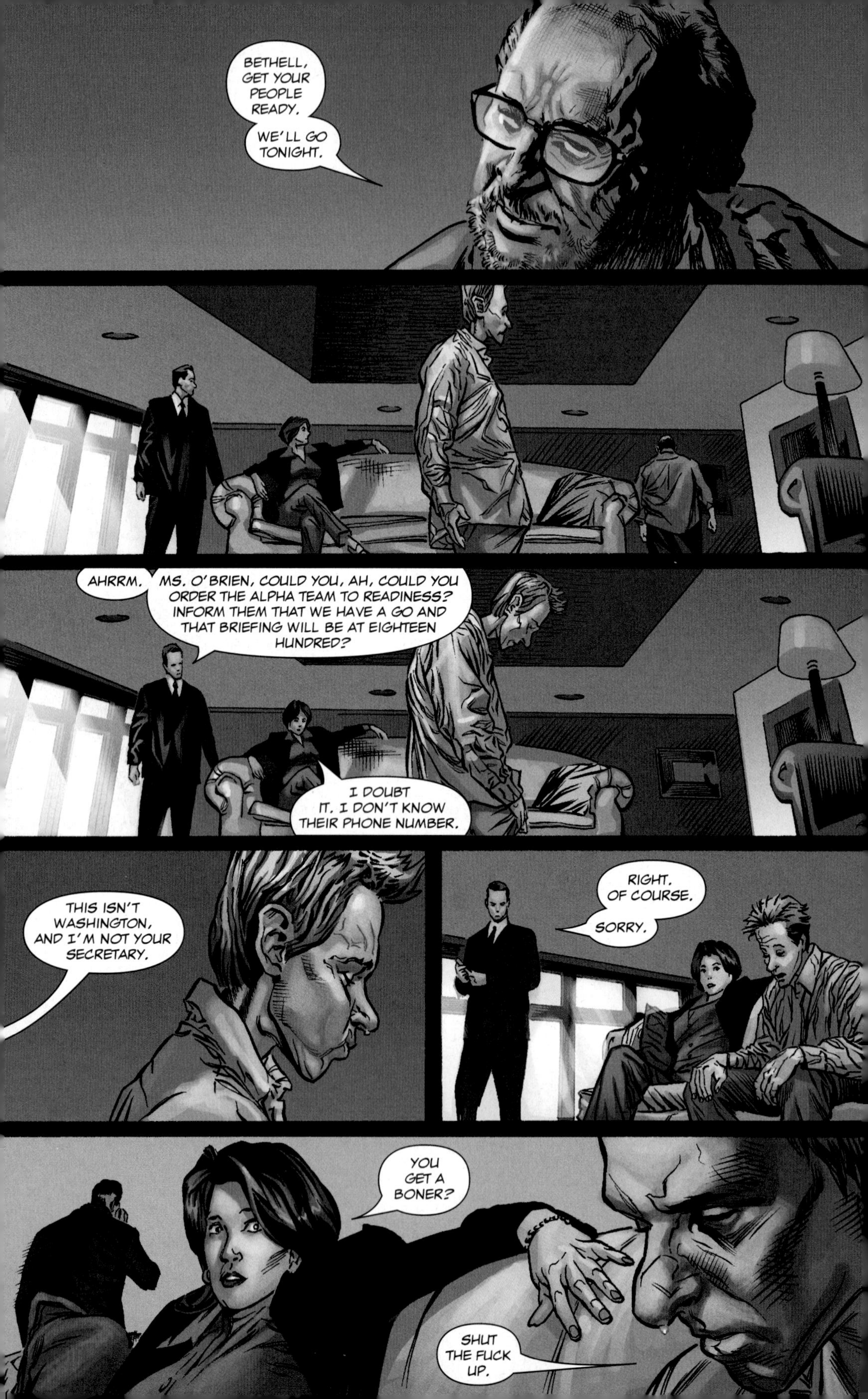
BETHELL, GET YOUR PEOPLE READY.
WE'LL GO TONIGHT.
AHRRM.
MS. O'BRIEN, COULD YOU, AH, COULD YOU ORDER THE ALPHA TEAM TO READINESS? INFORM THEM THAT WE HAVE A GO AND THAT BRIEFING WILL BE AT EIGHTEEN HUNDRED?
I DOUBT IT. I DON'T KNOW THEIR PHONE NUMBER.
THIS ISN'T WASHINGTON, AND I'M NOT YOUR SECRETARY.
RIGHT. OF COURSE.
SORRY.
YOU GET A BONER?
SHUT THE FUCK UP.

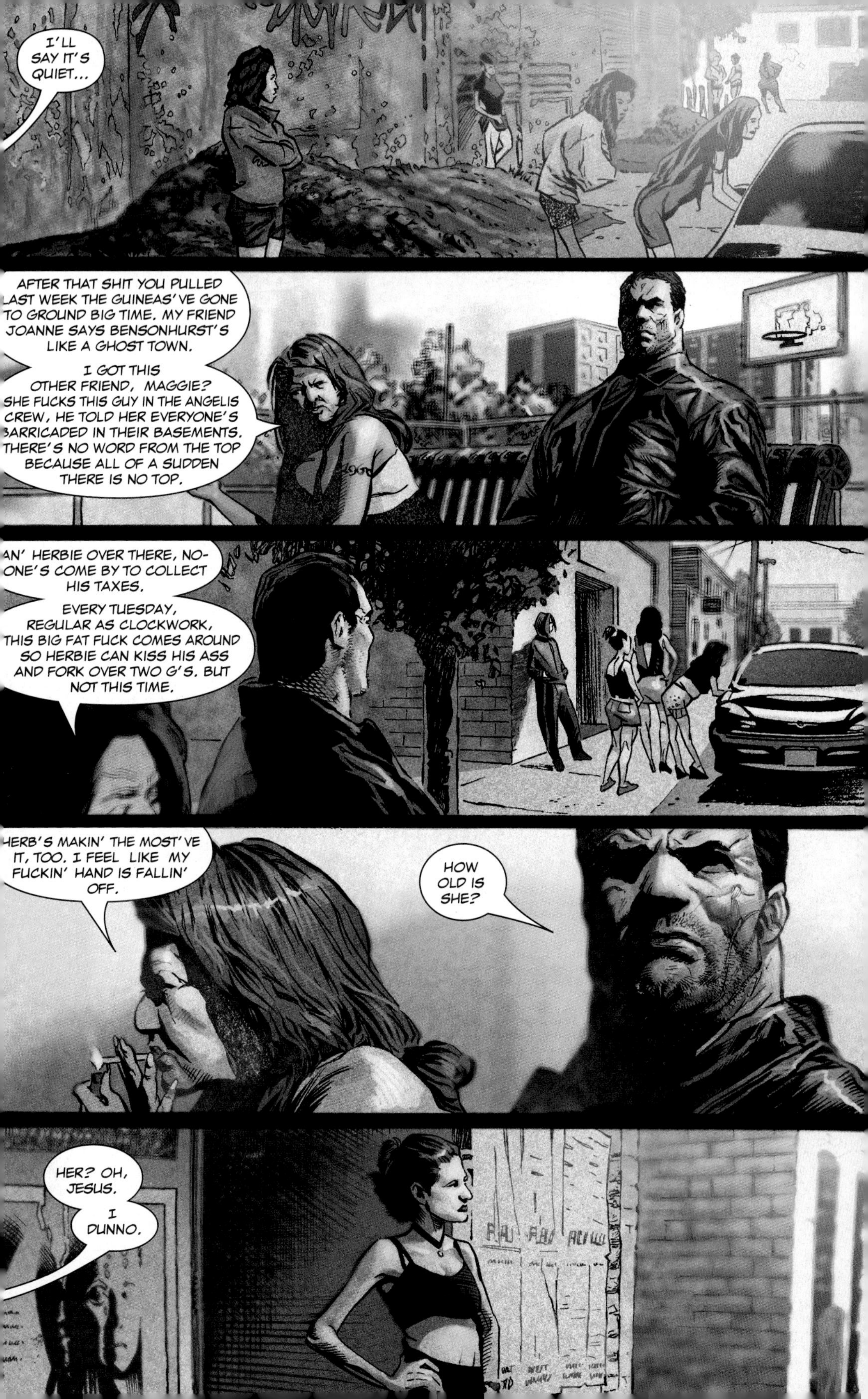
I'LL SAY IT'S QUIET...
AFTER THAT SHIT YOU PULLED LAST WEEK THE GUINEAS'VE GONE TO GROUND BIG TIME. MY FRIEND JOANNE SAYS BENSONHURST'S LIKE A GHOST TOWN.
I GOT THIS OTHER FRIEND, MAGGIE? SHE FUCKS THIS GUY IN THE ANGELIS CREW, HE TOLD HER EVERYONE'S BARRICADED IN THEIR BASEMENTS. THERE'S NO WORD FROM THE TOP BECAUSE ALL OF A SUDDEN THERE IS NO TOP.
AN' HERBIE OVER THERE, NO-ONE'S COME BY TO COLLECT HIS TAXES.
EVERY TUESDAY, REGULAR AS CLOCKWORK, THIS BIG FAT FUCK COMES AROUND SO HERBIE CAN KISS HIS ASS AND FORK OVER TWO G'S. BUT NOT THIS TIME.
HERB'S MAKIN' THE MOST'VE IT, TOO. I FEEL LIKE MY FUCKIN' HAND IS FALLIN' OFF.
HOW OLD IS SHE?
HER? OH, JESUS.
I DUNNO.

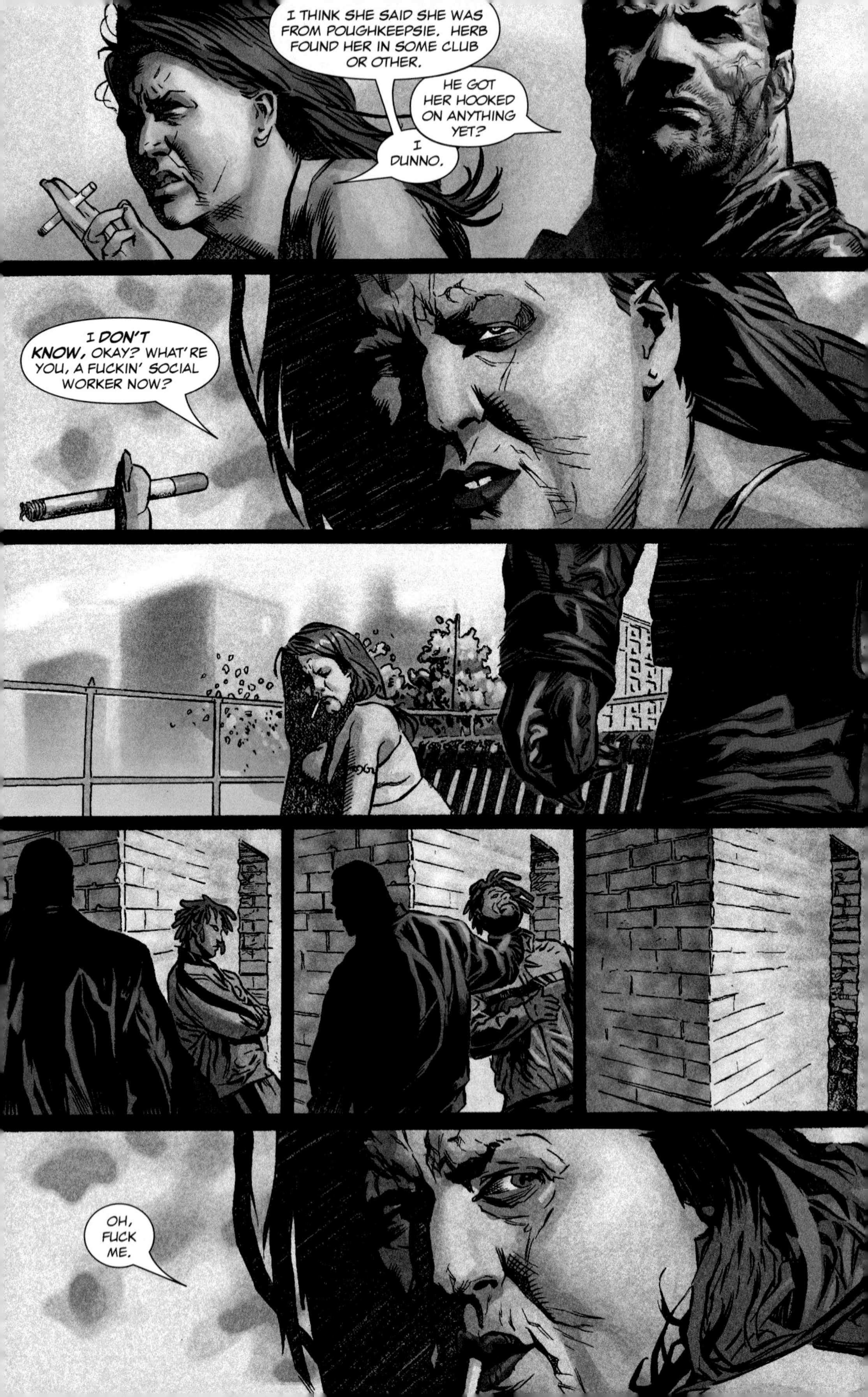
I THINK SHE SAID SHE WAS FROM POUGHKEEPSIE. HERB FOUND HER IN SOME CLUB OR OTHER.
HE GOT HER HOOKED ON ANYTHING YET?
I DUNNO.
I DON'T KNOW, OKAY? WHAT'RE YOU, A FUCKIN' SOCIAL WORKER NOW?
OH, FUCK ME.

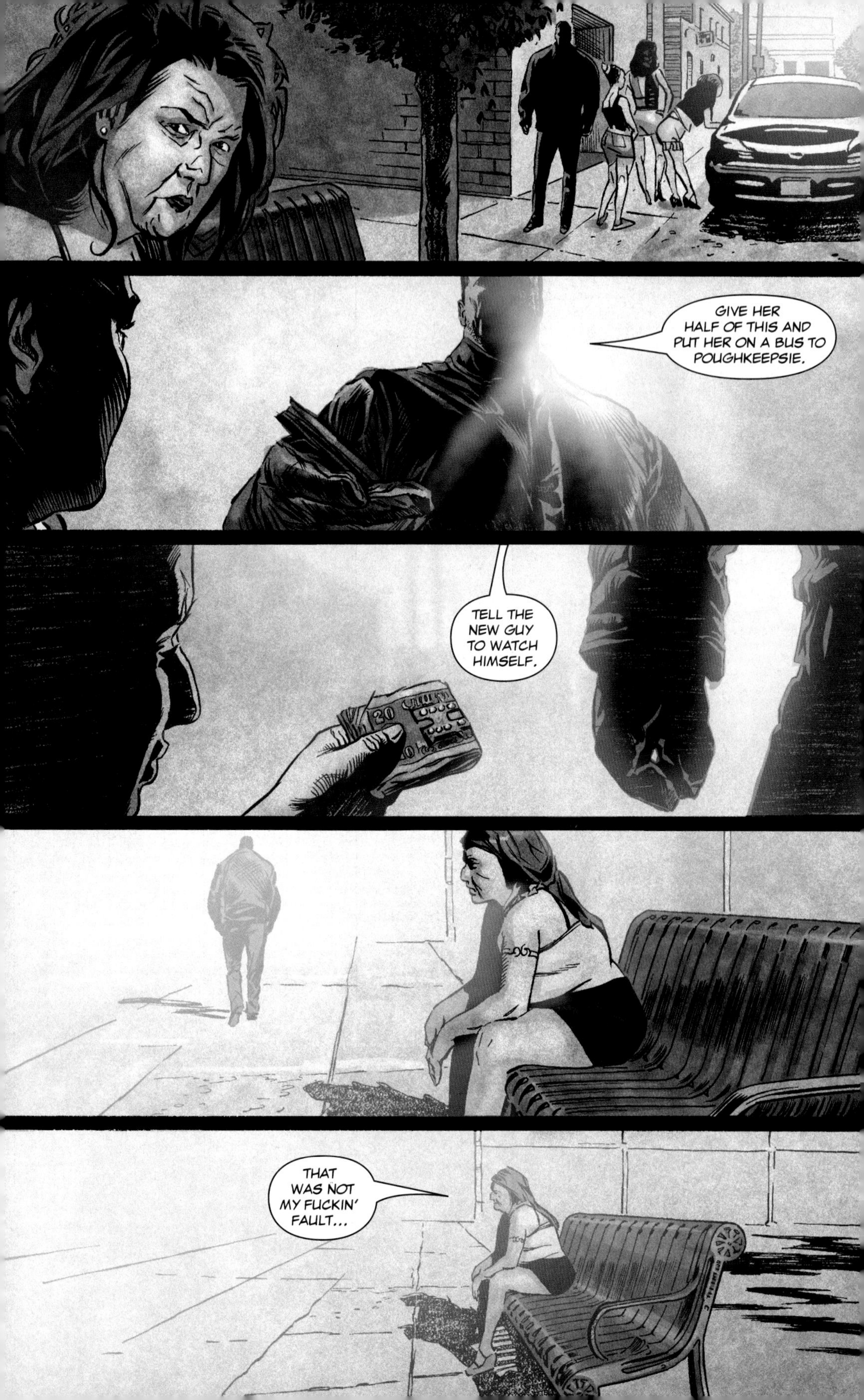
GIVE HER HALF OF THIS AND PUT HER ON A BUS TO POUGHKEEPSIE.
TELL THE NEW GUY TO WATCH HIMSELF.
THAT WAS NOT MY FUCKIN' FAULT...

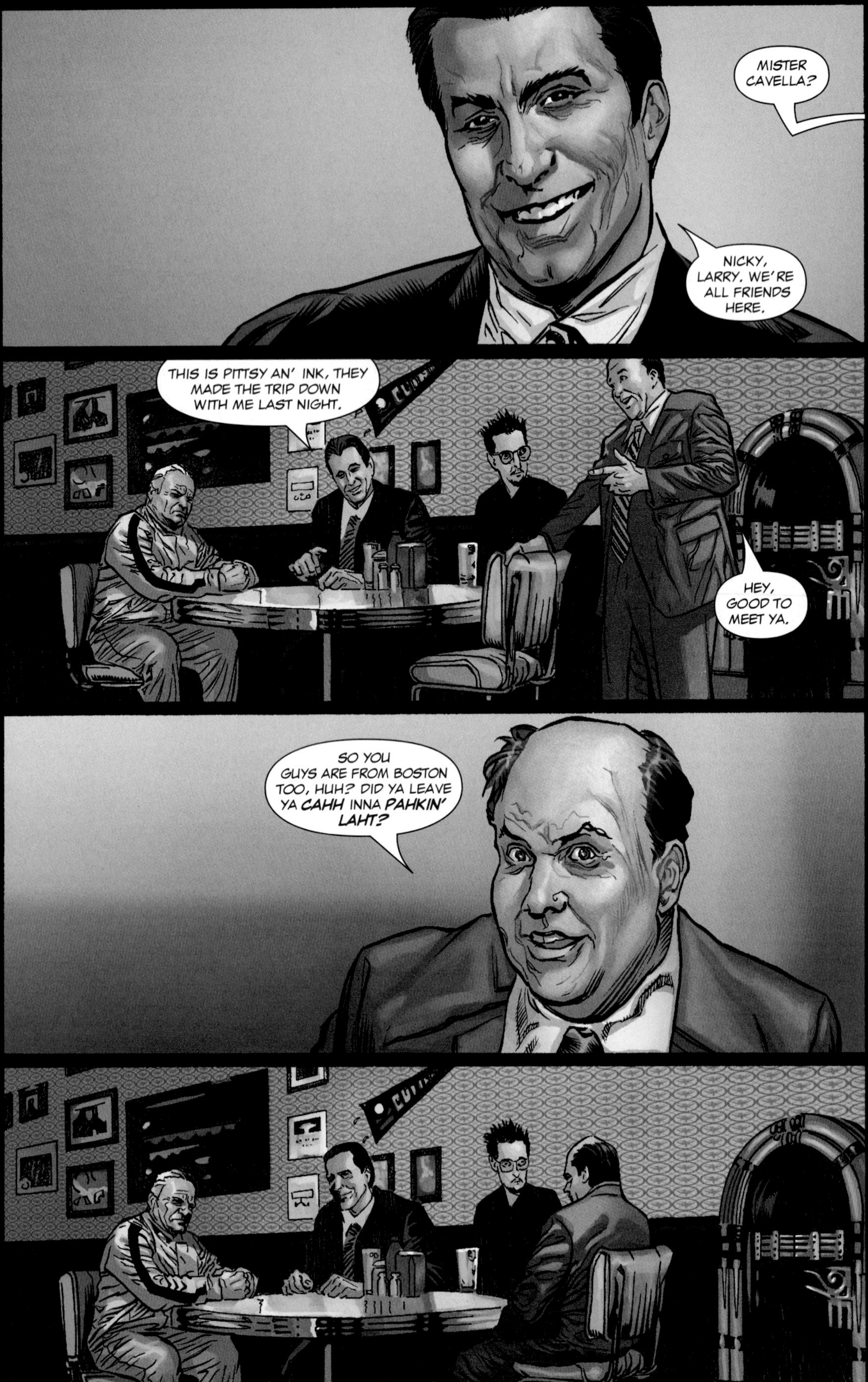
MISTER CAVELLA?
NICKY, LARRY. WE'RE ALL FRIENDS HERE.
THIS IS PITTSY AN' INK, THEY MADE THE TRIP DOWN WITH ME LAST NIGHT.
HEY, GOOD TO MEET YA.
SO YOU GUYS ARE FROM BOSTON TOO, HUH? DID YA LEAVE YA ***CAHH*** INNA ***PAHKIN' LAHT?***

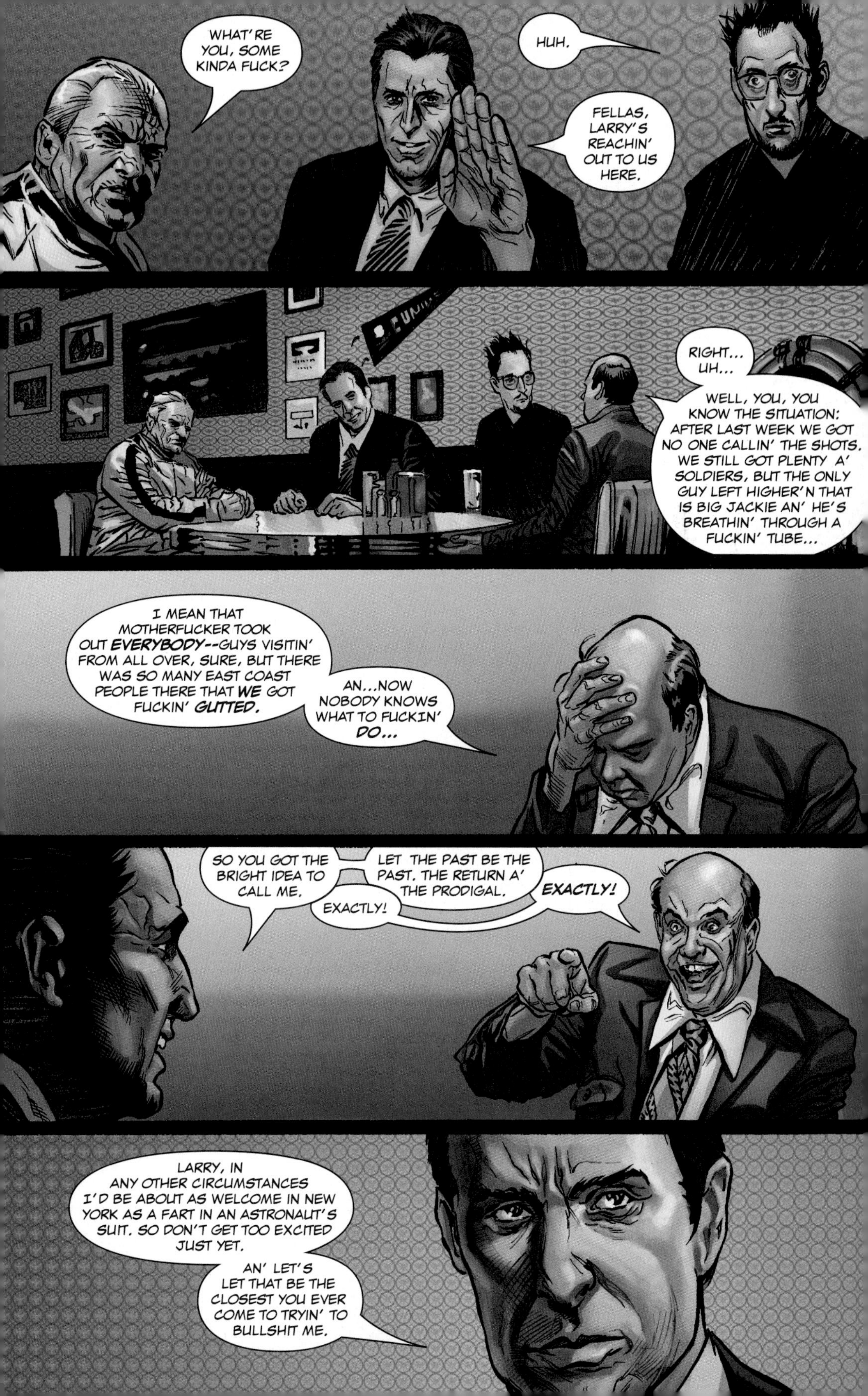
WHAT'RE YOU, SOME KINDA FUCK?
HUH.
FELLAS, LARRY'S REACHIN' OUT TO US HERE.
RIGHT... UH...
WELL, YOU, YOU KNOW THE SITUATION: AFTER LAST WEEK WE GOT NO ONE CALLIN' THE SHOTS. WE STILL GOT PLENTY A' SOLDIERS, BUT THE ONLY GUY LEFT HIGHER'N THAT IS BIG JACKIE AN' HE'S BREATHIN' THROUGH A FUCKIN' TUBE...
I MEAN THAT MOTHERFUCKER TOOK OUT EVERYBODY--GUYS VISITIN' FROM ALL OVER, SURE, BUT THERE WAS SO MANY EAST COAST PEOPLE THERE THAT WE GOT FUCKIN' GUTTED.
AN...NOW NOBODY KNOWS WHAT TO FUCKIN' DO...
SO YOU GOT THE BRIGHT IDEA TO CALL ME.
EXACTLY!
LET THE PAST BE THE PAST. THE RETURN A' THE PRODIGAL.
EXACTLY!
LARRY, IN ANY OTHER CIRCUMSTANCES I'D BE ABOUT AS WELCOME IN NEW YORK AS A FART IN AN ASTRONAUT'S SUIT. SO DON'T GET TOO EXCITED JUST YET.
AN' LET'S LET THAT BE THE CLOSEST YOU EVER COME TO TRYIN' TO BULLSHIT ME.

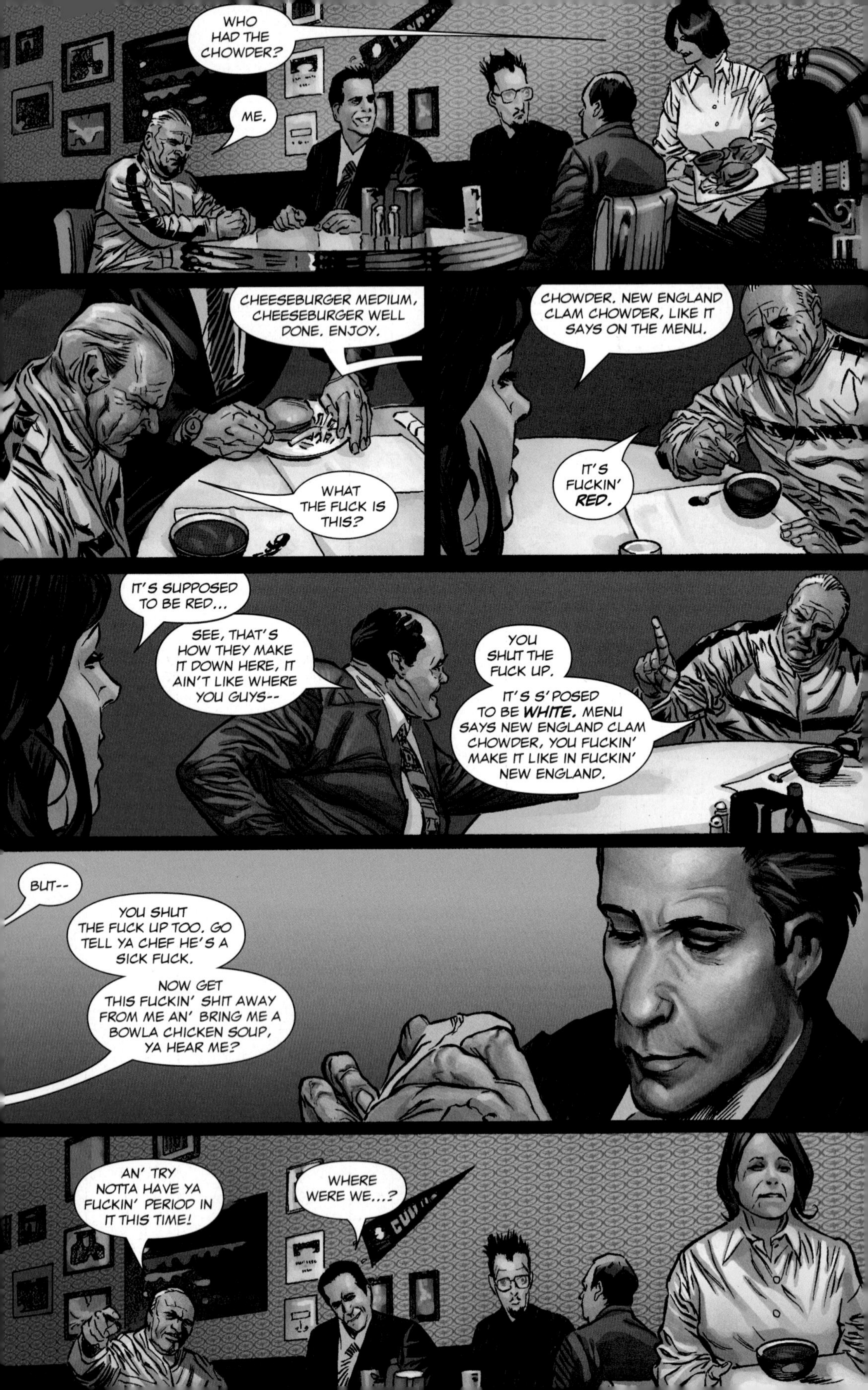
WHO HAD THE CHOWDER?
ME.
CHEESEBURGER MEDIUM, CHEESEBURGER WELL DONE. ENJOY.
WHAT THE FUCK IS THIS?
CHOWDER. NEW ENGLAND CLAM CHOWDER, LIKE IT SAYS ON THE MENU.
IT'S FUCKIN' RED.
IT'S SUPPOSED TO BE RED...
SEE, THAT'S HOW THEY MAKE IT DOWN HERE, IT AIN'T LIKE WHERE YOU GUYS--
YOU SHUT THE FUCK UP.
IT'S S'POSED TO BE WHITE. MENU SAYS NEW ENGLAND CLAM CHOWDER, YOU FUCKIN' MAKE IT LIKE IN FUCKIN' NEW ENGLAND.
BUT--
YOU SHUT THE FUCK UP TOO. GO TELL YA CHEF HE'S A SICK FUCK.
NOW GET THIS FUCKIN' SHIT AWAY FROM ME AN' BRING ME A BOWLA CHICKEN SOUP, YA HEAR ME?
AN' TRY NOTTA HAVE YA FUCKIN' PERIOD IN IT THIS TIME!
WHERE WERE WE...?

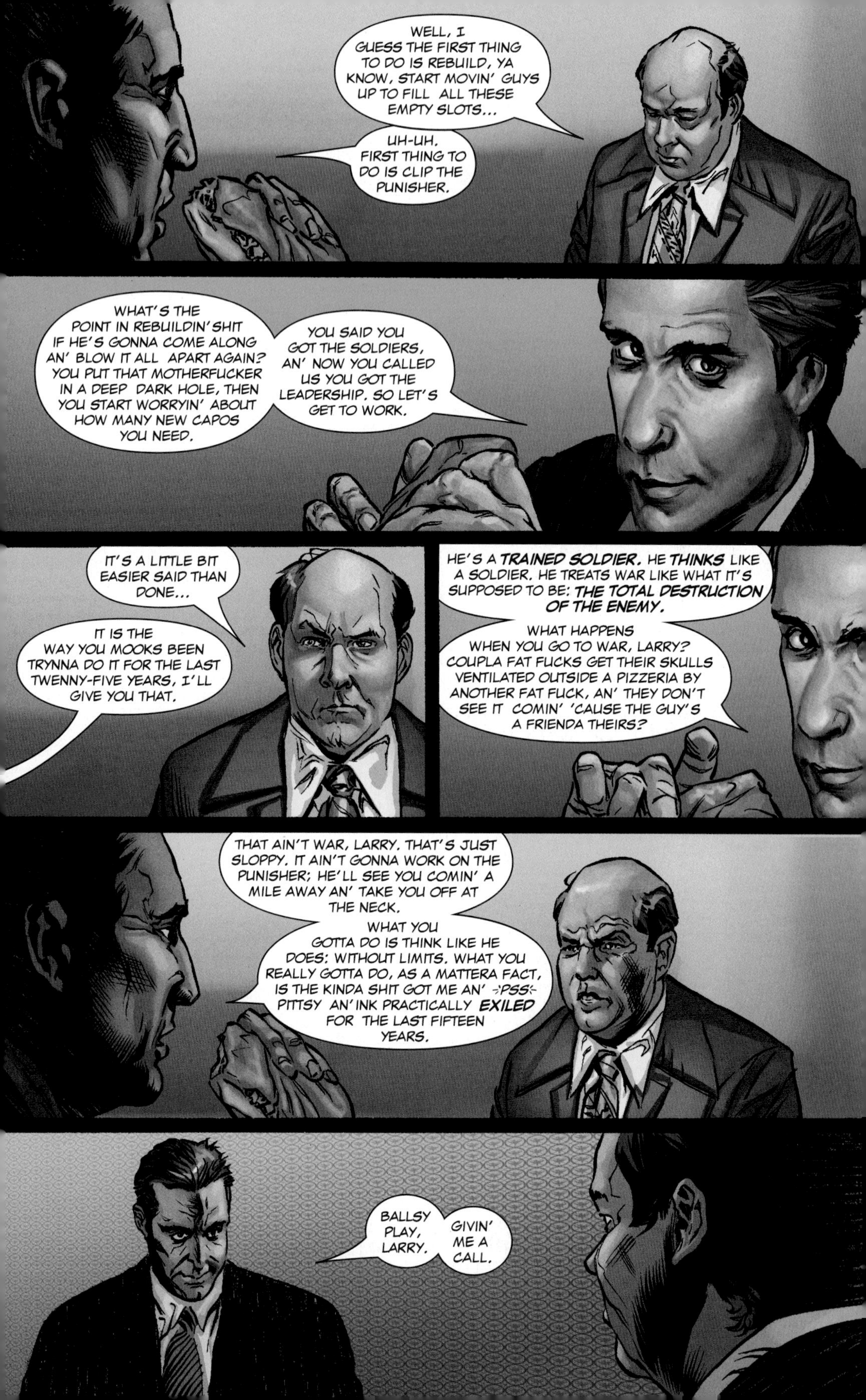
WELL, I GUESS THE FIRST THING TO DO IS REBUILD, YA KNOW, START MOVIN' GUYS UP TO FILL ALL THESE EMPTY SLOTS...
UH-UH. FIRST THING TO DO IS CLIP THE PUNISHER.
WHAT'S THE POINT IN REBUILDIN' SHIT IF HE'S GONNA COME ALONG AN' BLOW IT ALL APART AGAIN? YOU PUT THAT MOTHERFUCKER IN A DEEP DARK HOLE, THEN YOU START WORRYIN' ABOUT HOW MANY NEW CAPOS YOU NEED.
YOU SAID YOU GOT THE SOLDIERS, AN' NOW YOU CALLED US YOU GOT THE LEADERSHIP. SO LET'S GET TO WORK.
IT'S A LITTLE BIT EASIER SAID THAN DONE...
IT IS THE WAY YOU MOOKS BEEN TRYNNA DO IT FOR THE LAST TWENNY-FIVE YEARS, I'LL GIVE YOU THAT.
HE'S A **TRAINED SOLDIER.** HE **THINKS** LIKE A SOLDIER. HE TREATS WAR LIKE WHAT IT'S SUPPOSED TO BE: **THE TOTAL DESTRUCTION OF THE ENEMY.**
WHAT HAPPENS WHEN YOU GO TO WAR, LARRY? COUPLA FAT FUCKS GET THEIR SKULLS VENTILATED OUTSIDE A PIZZERIA BY ANOTHER FAT FUCK, AN' THEY DON'T SEE IT COMIN' 'CAUSE THE GUY'S A FRIENDA THEIRS?
THAT AIN'T WAR, LARRY. THAT'S JUST SLOPPY. IT AIN'T GONNA WORK ON THE PUNISHER; HE'LL SEE YOU COMIN' A MILE AWAY AN' TAKE YOU OFF AT THE NECK.
WHAT YOU GOTTA DO IS THINK LIKE HE DOES: WITHOUT LIMITS. WHAT YOU REALLY GOTTA DO, AS A MATTERA FACT, IS THE KINDA SHIT GOT ME AN' -PSS- PITTSY AN' INK PRACTICALLY **EXILED** FOR THE LAST FIFTEEN YEARS.
BALLSY PLAY, LARRY.
GIVIN' ME A CALL.

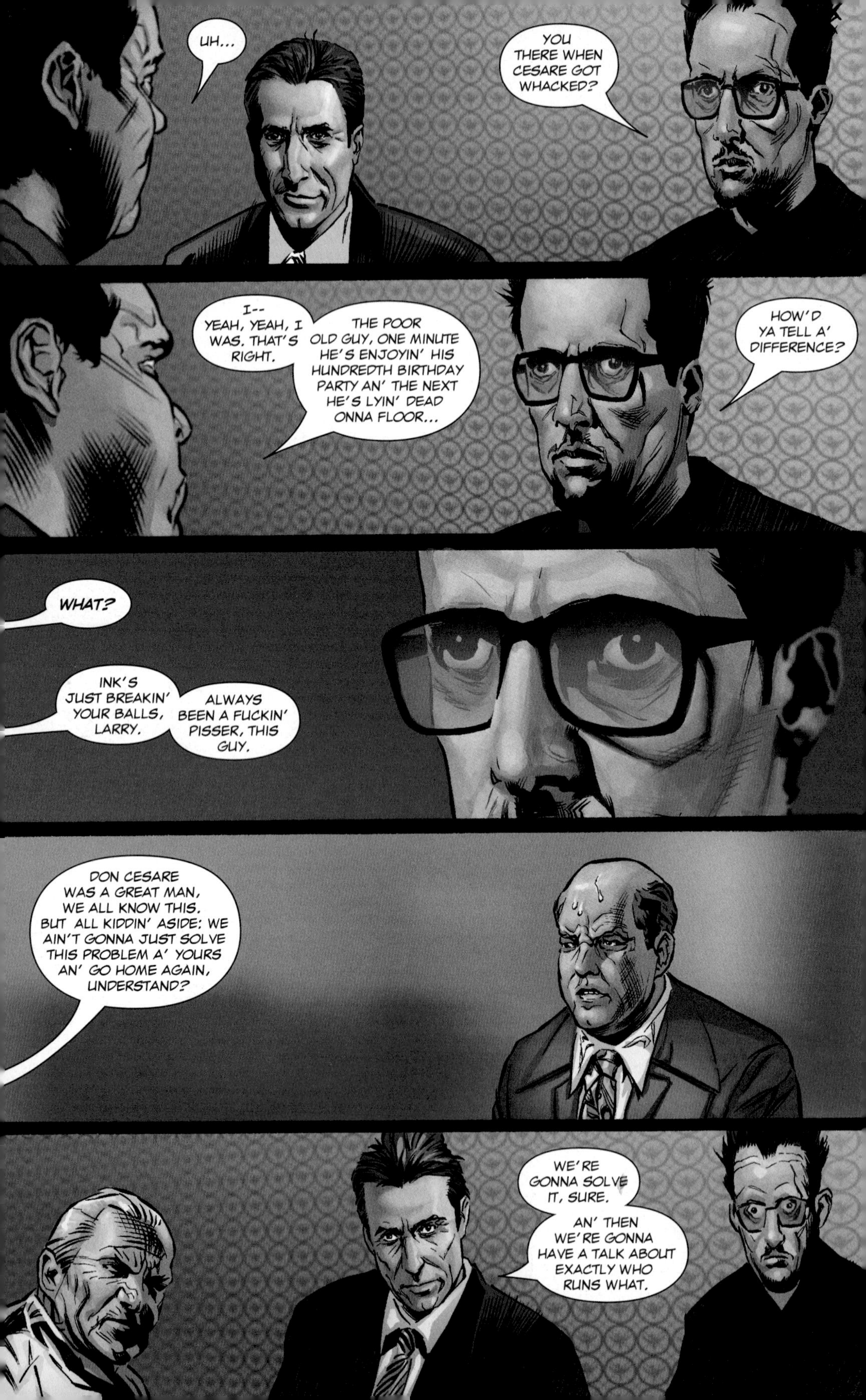
UH...
YOU THERE WHEN CESARE GOT WHACKED?
I-- YEAH, YEAH, I WAS. THAT'S RIGHT.
THE POOR OLD GUY, ONE MINUTE HE'S ENJOYIN' HIS HUNDREDTH BIRTHDAY PARTY AN' THE NEXT HE'S LYIN' DEAD ONNA FLOOR...
HOW'D YA TELL A' DIFFERENCE?
WHAT?
INK'S JUST BREAKIN' YOUR BALLS, LARRY.
ALWAYS BEEN A FUCKIN' PISSER, THIS GUY.
DON CESARE WAS A GREAT MAN, WE ALL KNOW THIS. BUT ALL KIDDIN' ASIDE: WE AIN'T GONNA JUST SOLVE THIS PROBLEM A' YOURS AN' GO HOME AGAIN, UNDERSTAND?
WE'RE GONNA SOLVE IT, SURE.
AN' THEN WE'RE GONNA HAVE A TALK ABOUT EXACTLY WHO RUNS WHAT.

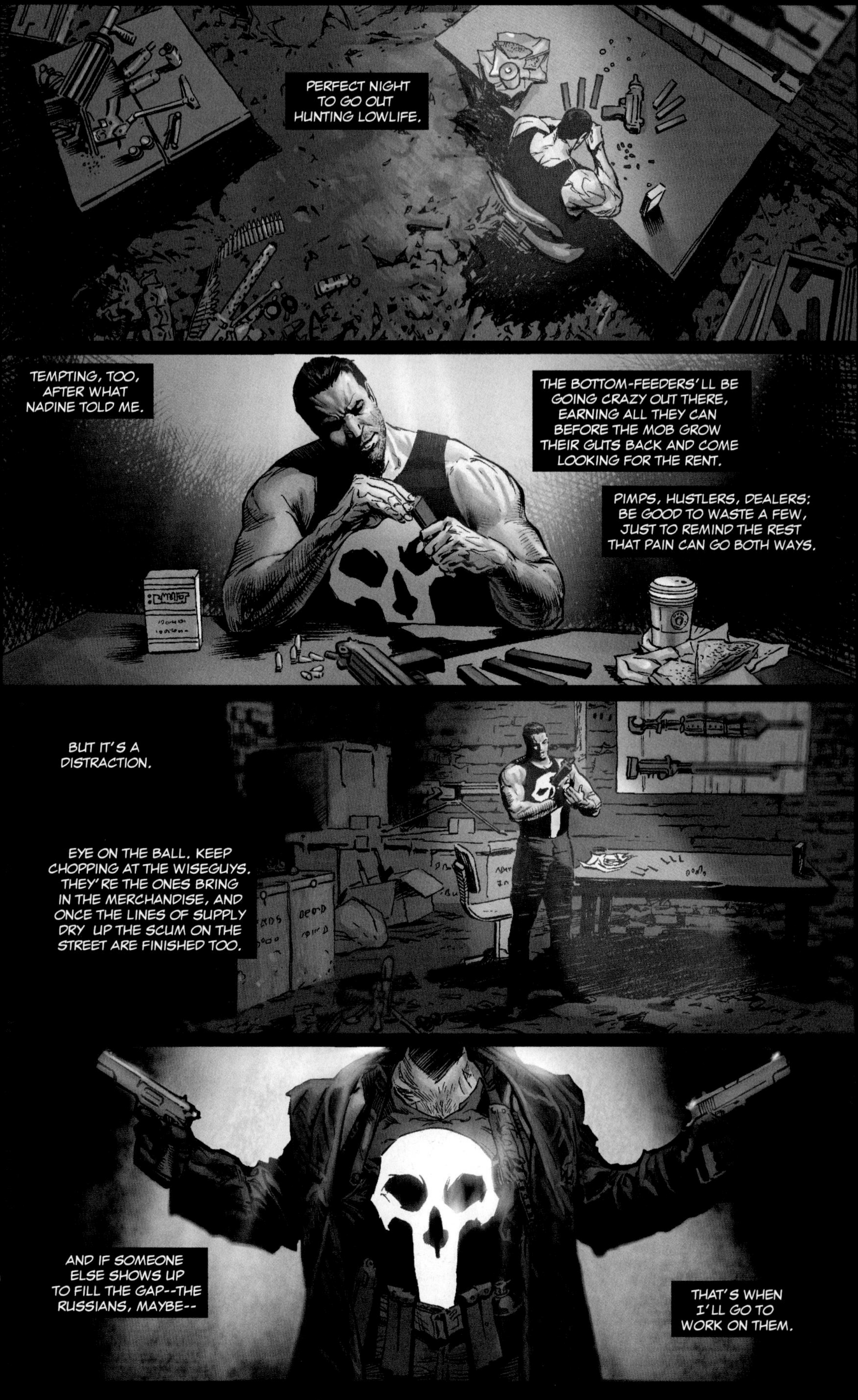
PERFECT NIGHT TO GO OUT HUNTING LOWLIFE.
TEMPTING, TOO, AFTER WHAT NADINE TOLD ME.
THE BOTTOM-FEEDERS'LL BE GOING CRAZY OUT THERE, EARNING ALL THEY CAN BEFORE THE MOB GROW THEIR GUTS BACK AND COME LOOKING FOR THE RENT.
PIMPS, HUSTLERS, DEALERS: BE GOOD TO WASTE A FEW, JUST TO REMIND THE REST THAT PAIN CAN GO BOTH WAYS.
BUT IT'S A DISTRACTION.
EYE ON THE BALL. KEEP CHOPPING AT THE WISEGUYS. THEY'RE THE ONES BRING IN THE MERCHANDISE, AND ONCE THE LINES OF SUPPLY DRY UP THE SCUM ON THE STREET ARE FINISHED TOO.
AND IF SOMEONE ELSE SHOWS UP TO FILL THE GAP--THE RUSSIANS, MAYBE--
THAT'S WHEN I'LL GO TO WORK ON THEM.

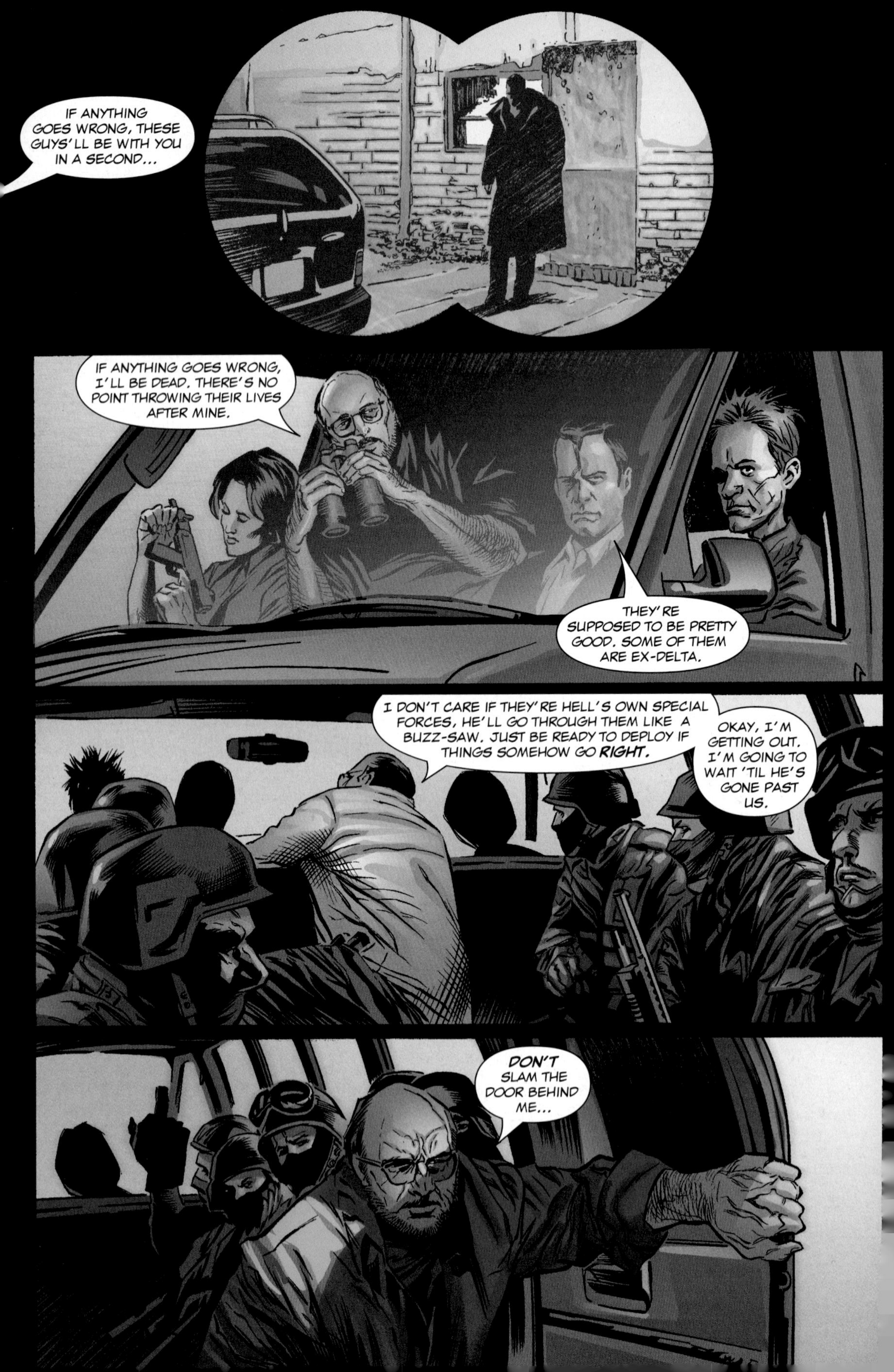
IF ANYTHING GOES WRONG, THESE GUYS'LL BE WITH YOU IN A SECOND...
IF ANYTHING GOES WRONG, I'LL BE DEAD. THERE'S NO POINT THROWING THEIR LIVES AFTER MINE.
THEY'RE SUPPOSED TO BE PRETTY GOOD. SOME OF THEM ARE EX-DELTA.
I DON'T CARE IF THEY'RE HELL'S OWN SPECIAL FORCES, HE'LL GO THROUGH THEM LIKE A BUZZ-SAW. JUST BE READY TO DEPLOY IF THINGS SOMEHOW GO RIGHT.
OKAY, I'M GETTING OUT. I'M GOING TO WAIT 'TIL HE'S GONE PAST US.
DON'T SLAM THE DOOR BEHIND ME...

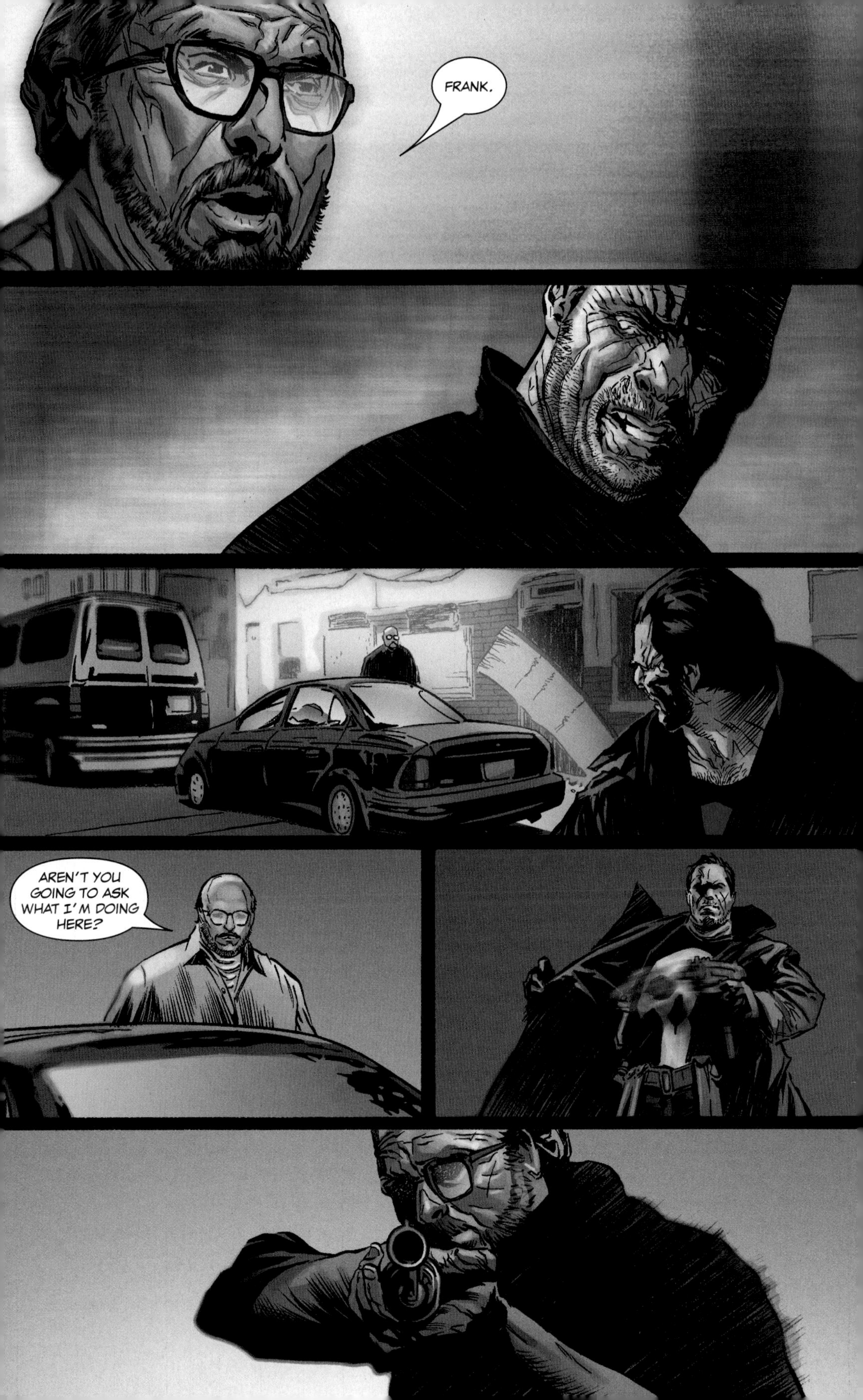
FRANK.
AREN'T YOU GOING TO ASK WHAT I'M DOING HERE?

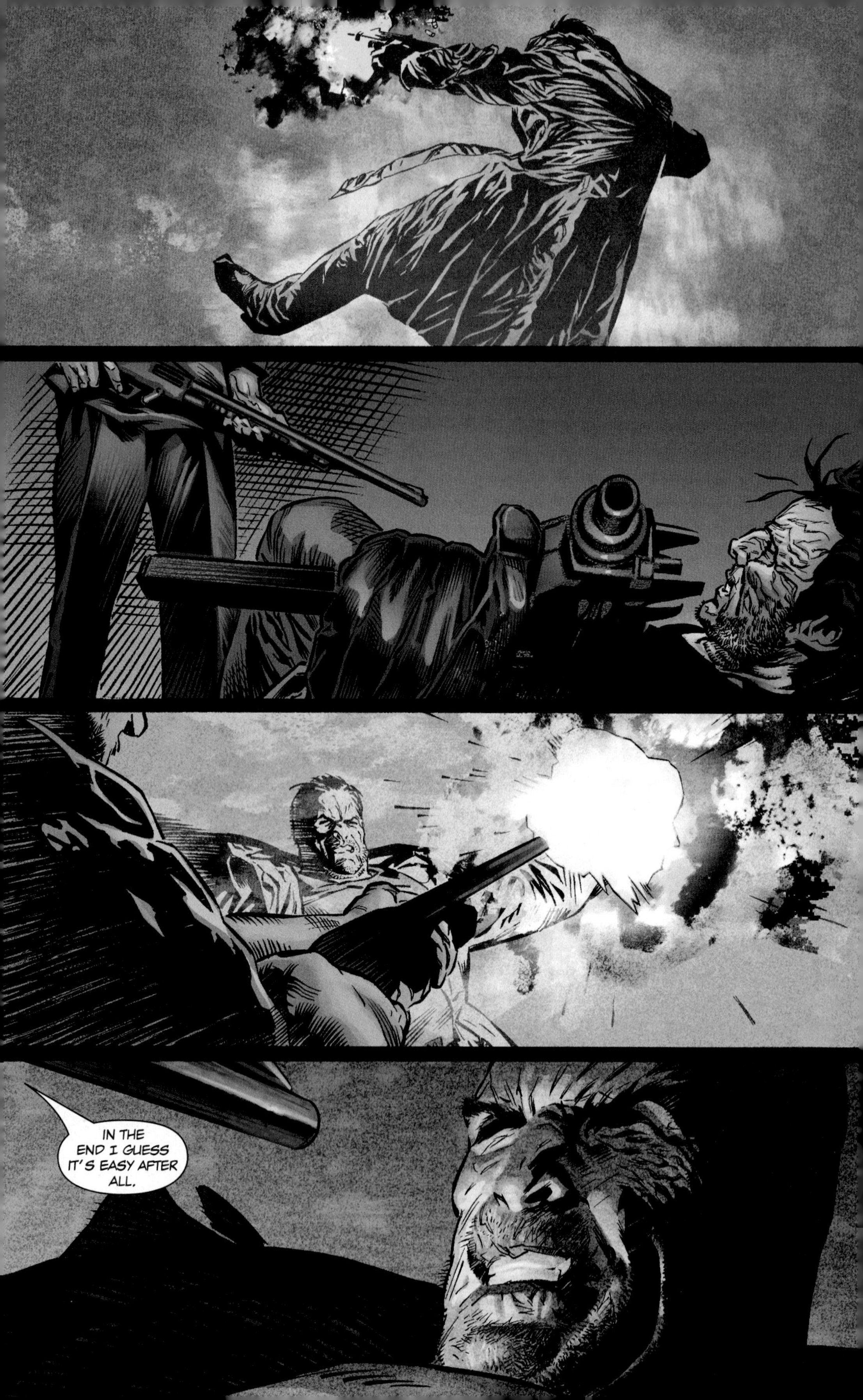
IN THE
END I GUESS
IT'S EASY AFTER
ALL.

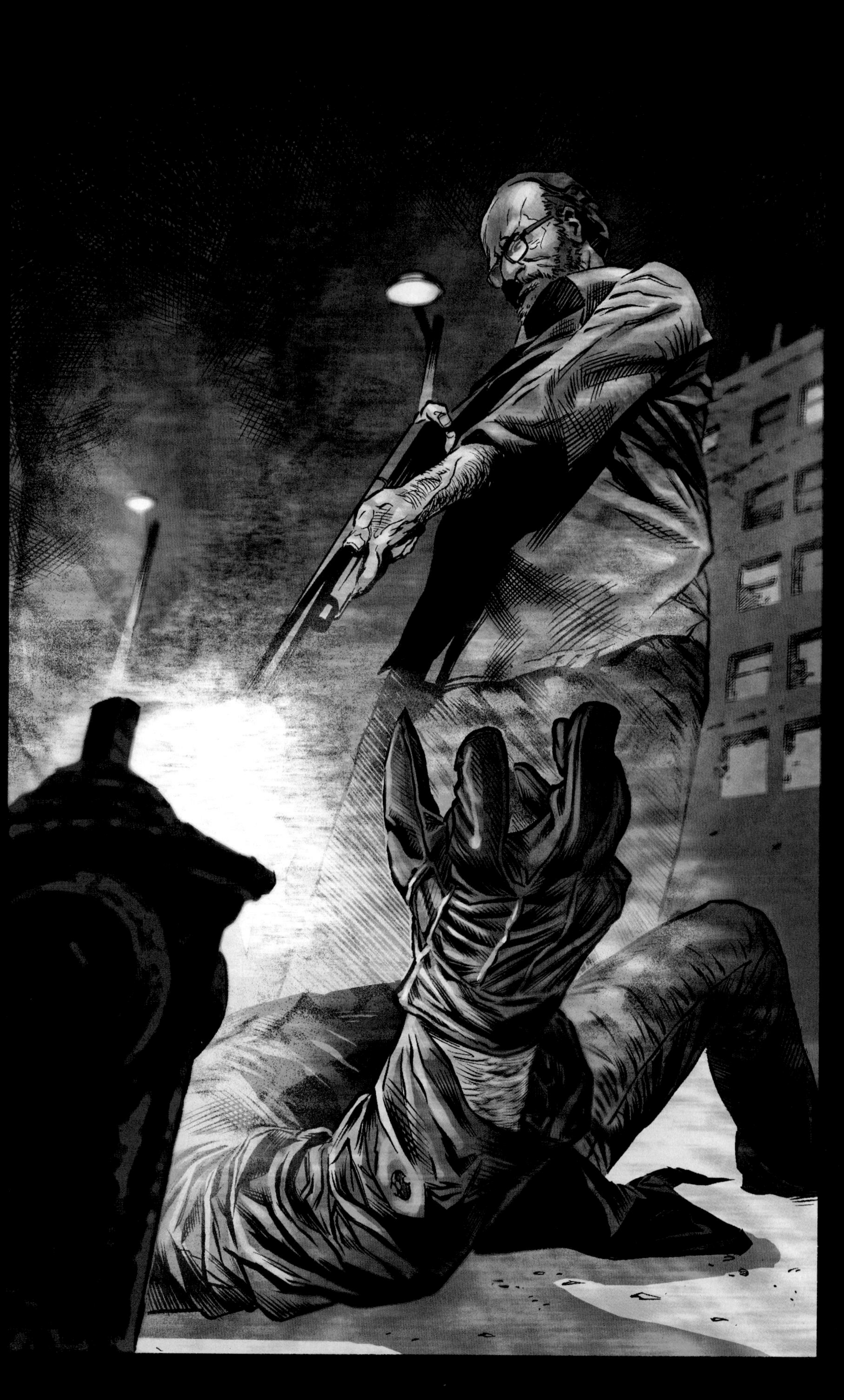

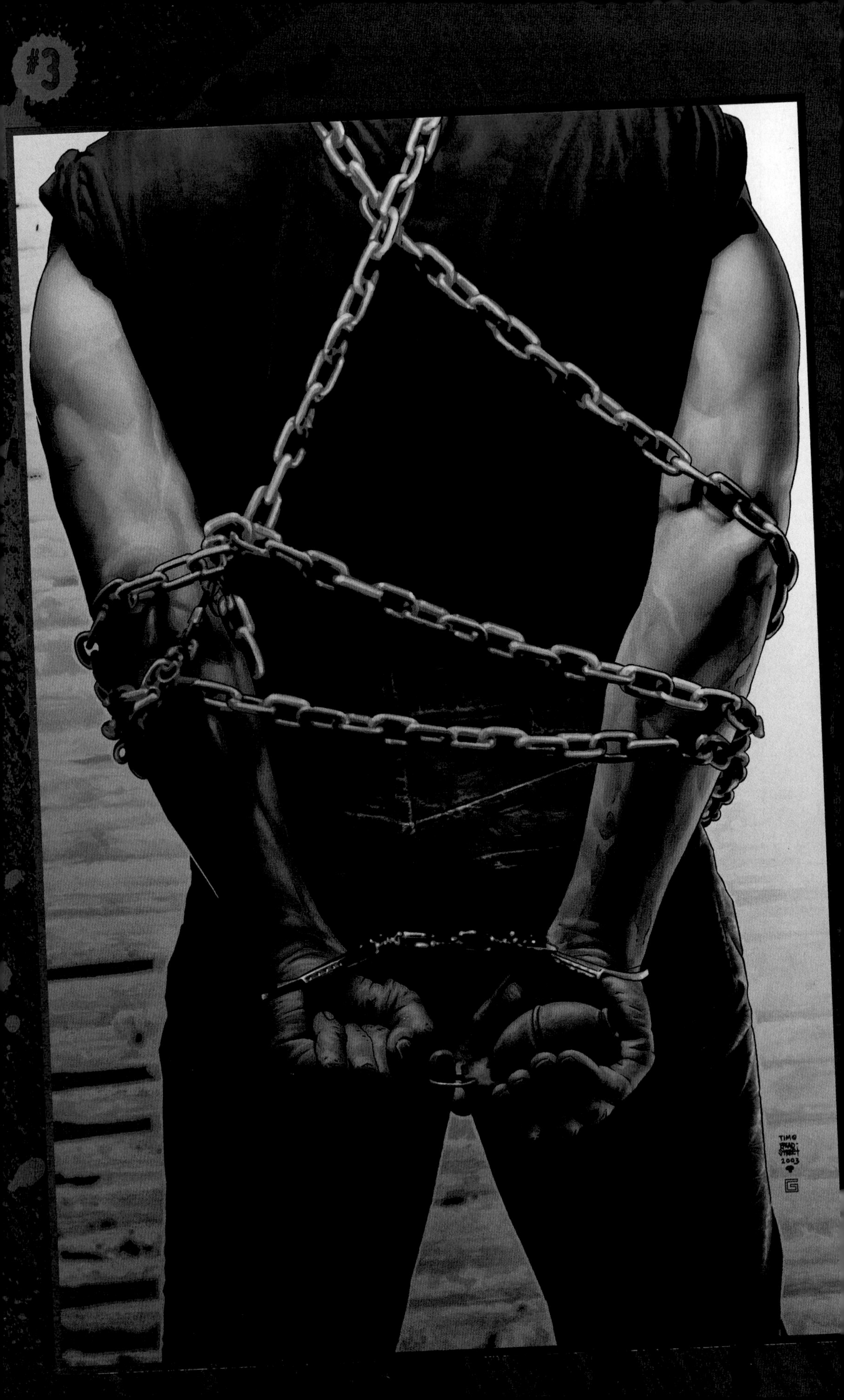
#3

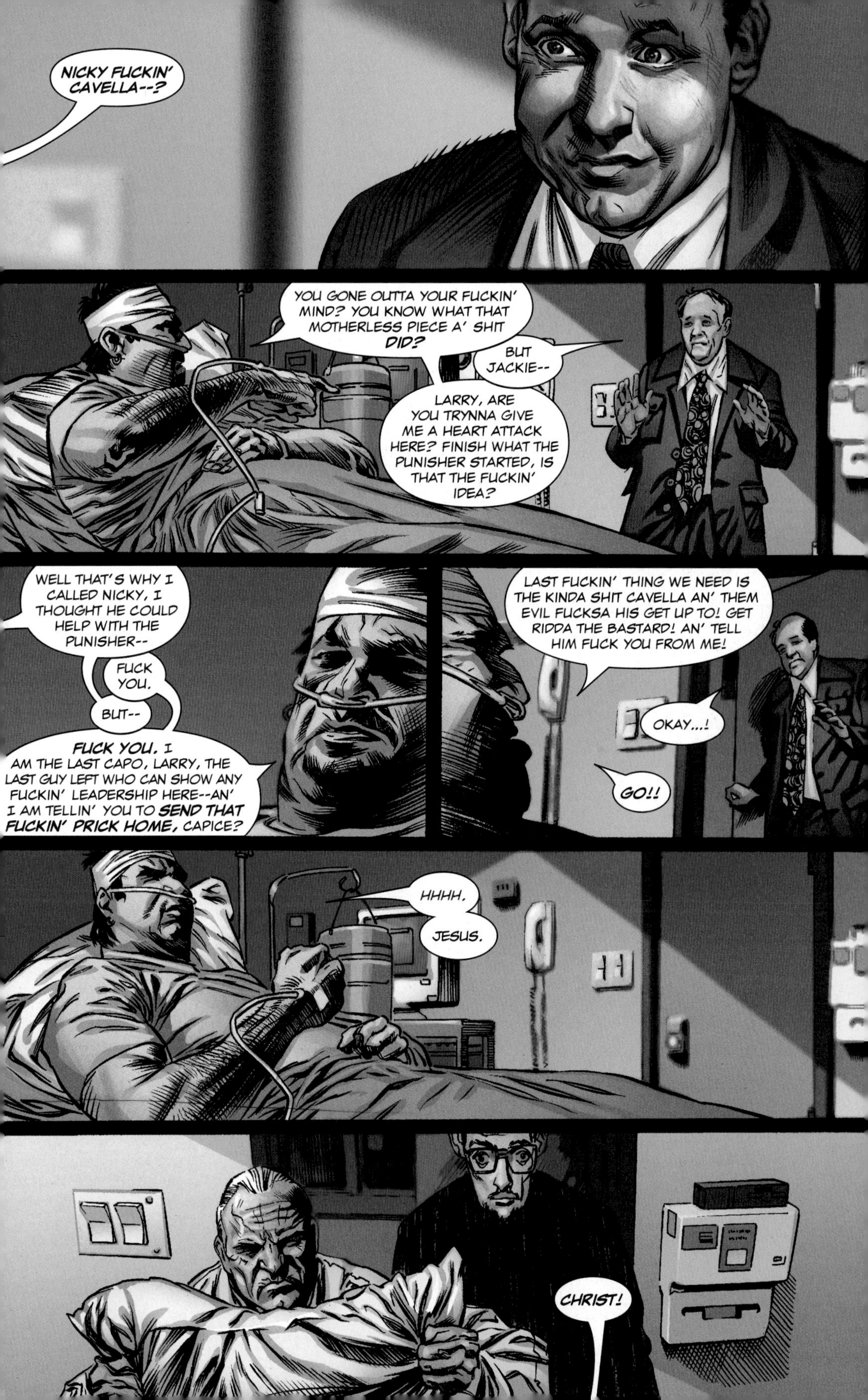
NICKY FUCKIN' CAVELLA--?
YOU GONE OUTTA YOUR FUCKIN' MIND? YOU KNOW WHAT THAT MOTHERLESS PIECE A' SHIT DID?
BUT JACKIE--
LARRY, ARE YOU TRYNNA GIVE ME A HEART ATTACK HERE? FINISH WHAT THE PUNISHER STARTED, IS THAT THE FUCKIN' IDEA?
WELL THAT'S WHY I CALLED NICKY, I THOUGHT HE COULD HELP WITH THE PUNISHER--
FUCK YOU.
BUT--
FUCK YOU. I AM THE LAST CAPO, LARRY, THE LAST GUY LEFT WHO CAN SHOW ANY FUCKIN' LEADERSHIP HERE--AN' I AM TELLIN' YOU TO SEND THAT FUCKIN' PRICK HOME, CAPICE?
LAST FUCKIN' THING WE NEED IS THE KINDA SHIT CAVELLA AN' THEM EVIL FUCKSA HIS GET UP TO! GET RIDDA THE BASTARD! AN' TELL HIM FUCK YOU FROM ME!
OKAY...!
GO!!
HHHH.
JESUS.
CHRIST!

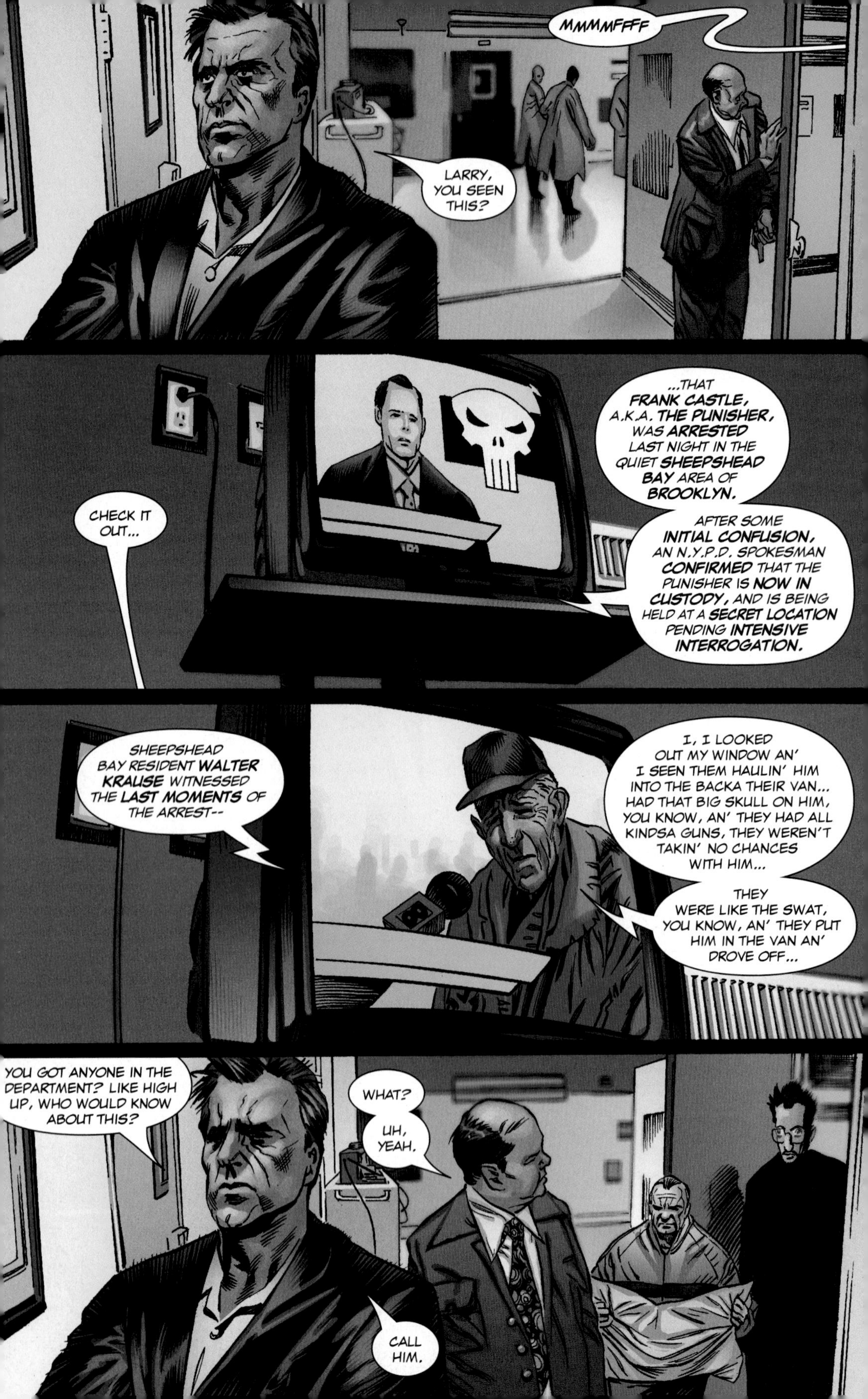
MMMMFFFF
LARRY, YOU SEEN THIS?
CHECK IT OUT...
...THAT FRANK CASTLE, A.K.A. THE PUNISHER, WAS ARRESTED LAST NIGHT IN THE QUIET SHEEPSHEAD BAY AREA OF BROOKLYN.
AFTER SOME INITIAL CONFUSION, AN N.Y.P.D. SPOKESMAN CONFIRMED THAT THE PUNISHER IS NOW IN CUSTODY, AND IS BEING HELD AT A SECRET LOCATION PENDING INTENSIVE INTERROGATION.
SHEEPSHEAD BAY RESIDENT WALTER KRAUSE WITNESSED THE LAST MOMENTS OF THE ARREST--
I, I LOOKED OUT MY WINDOW AN' I SEEN THEM HAULIN' HIM INTO THE BACKA THEIR VAN... HAD THAT BIG SKULL ON HIM, YOU KNOW, AN' THEY HAD ALL KINDSA GUNS, THEY WEREN'T TAKIN' NO CHANCES WITH HIM...
THEY WERE LIKE THE SWAT, YOU KNOW, AN' THEY PUT HIM IN THE VAN AN' DROVE OFF...
YOU GOT ANYONE IN THE DEPARTMENT? LIKE HIGH UP, WHO WOULD KNOW ABOUT THIS?
WHAT?
UH, YEAH.
CALL HIM.

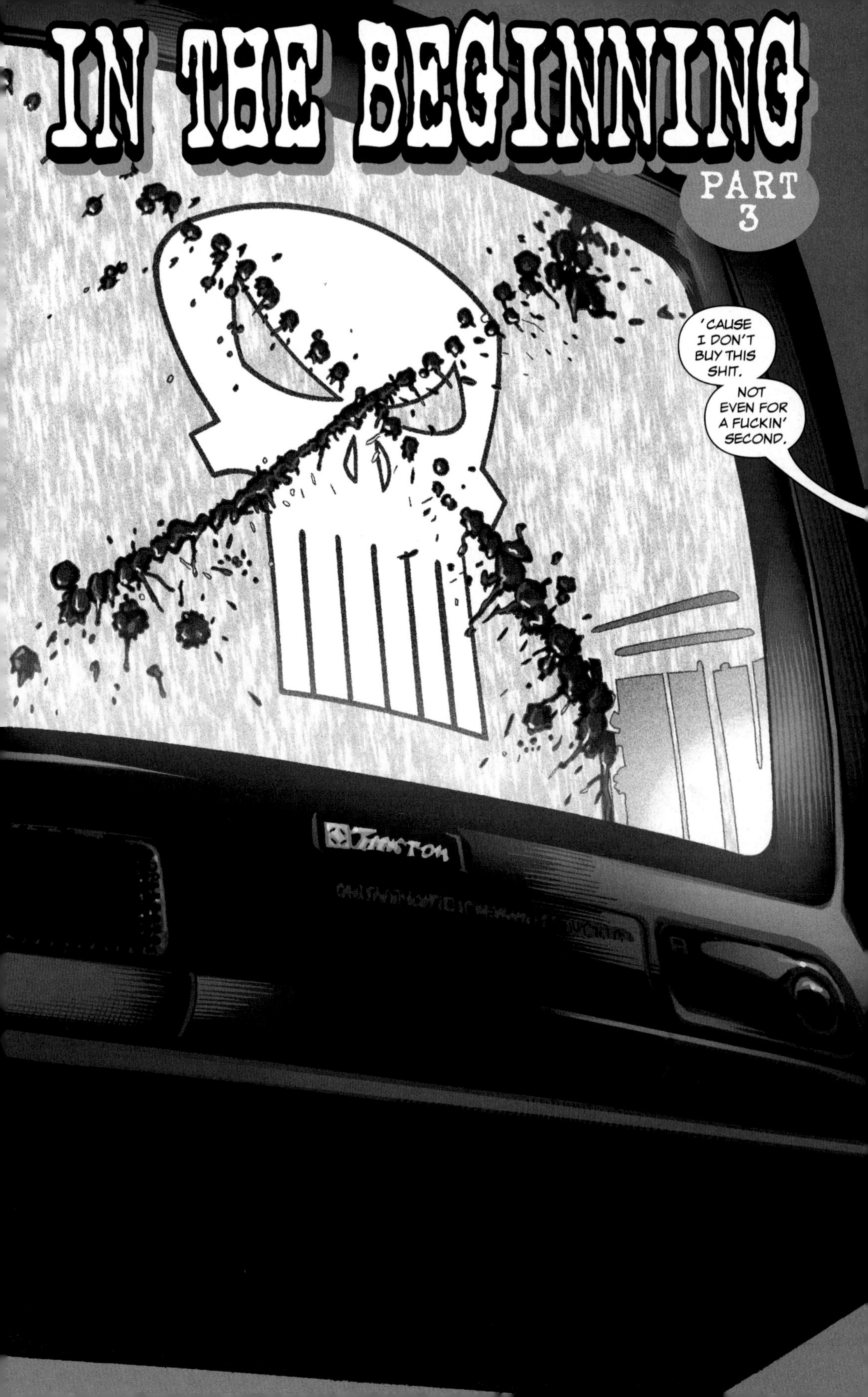
IN THE BEGINNING
PART 3
'CAUSE I DON'T BUY THIS SHIT.
NOT EVEN FOR A FUCKIN' SECOND.

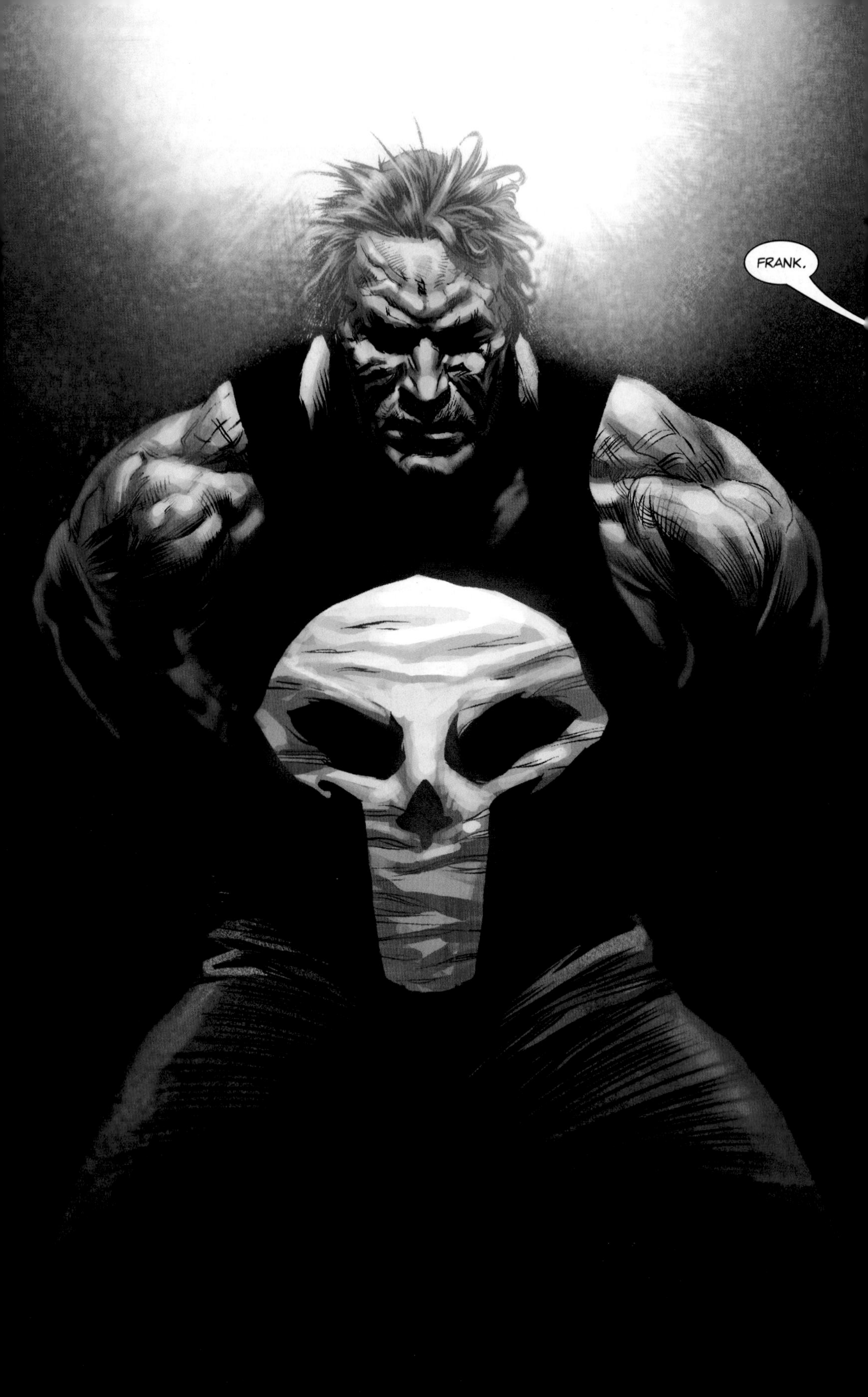
FRANK.

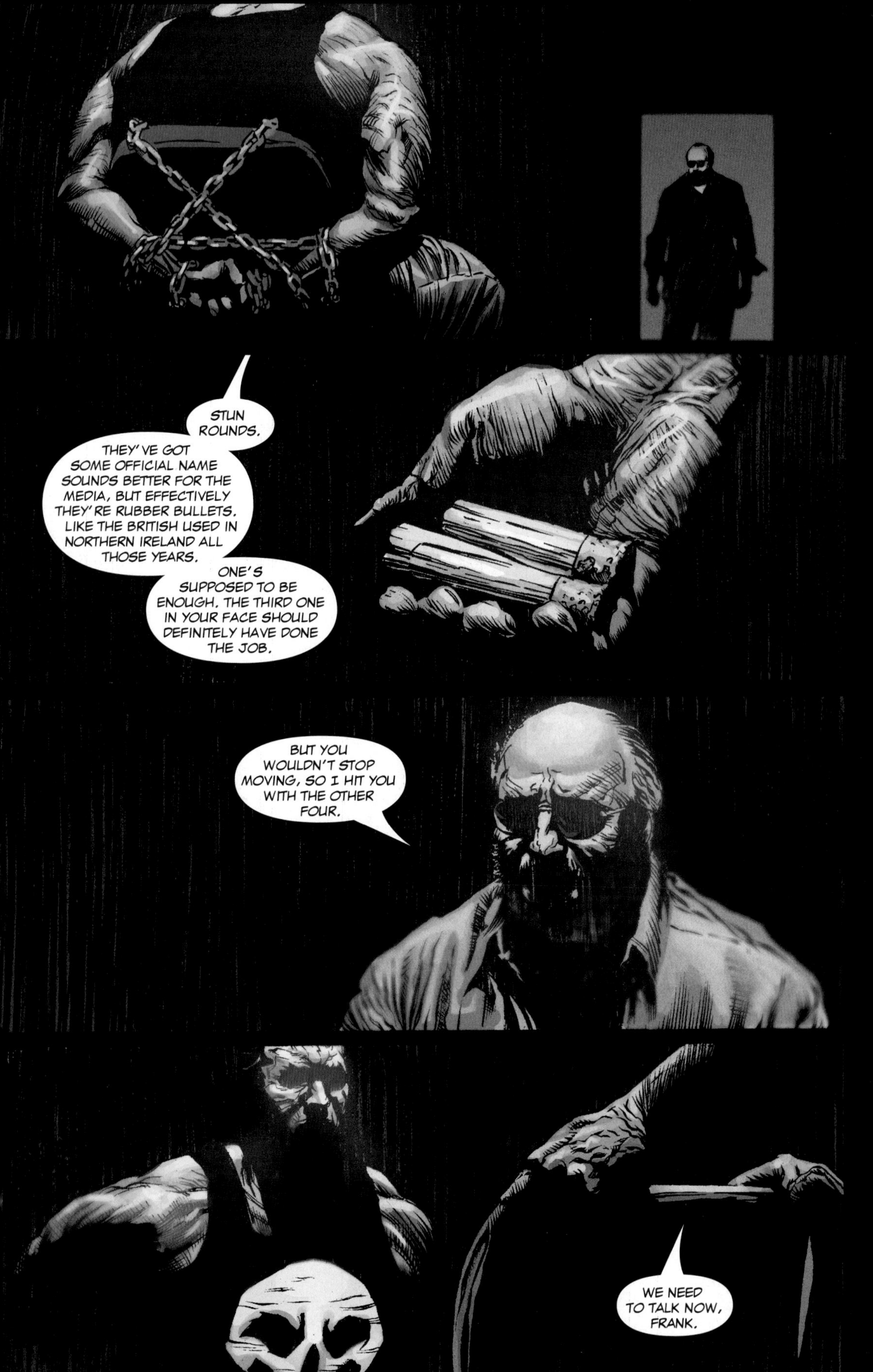
STUN ROUNDS.
THEY'VE GOT SOME OFFICIAL NAME SOUNDS BETTER FOR THE MEDIA, BUT EFFECTIVELY THEY'RE RUBBER BULLETS. LIKE THE BRITISH USED IN NORTHERN IRELAND ALL THOSE YEARS.
ONE'S SUPPOSED TO BE ENOUGH. THE THIRD ONE IN YOUR FACE SHOULD DEFINITELY HAVE DONE THE JOB.
BUT YOU WOULDN'T STOP MOVING, SO I HIT YOU WITH THE OTHER FOUR.
WE NEED TO TALK NOW, FRANK.

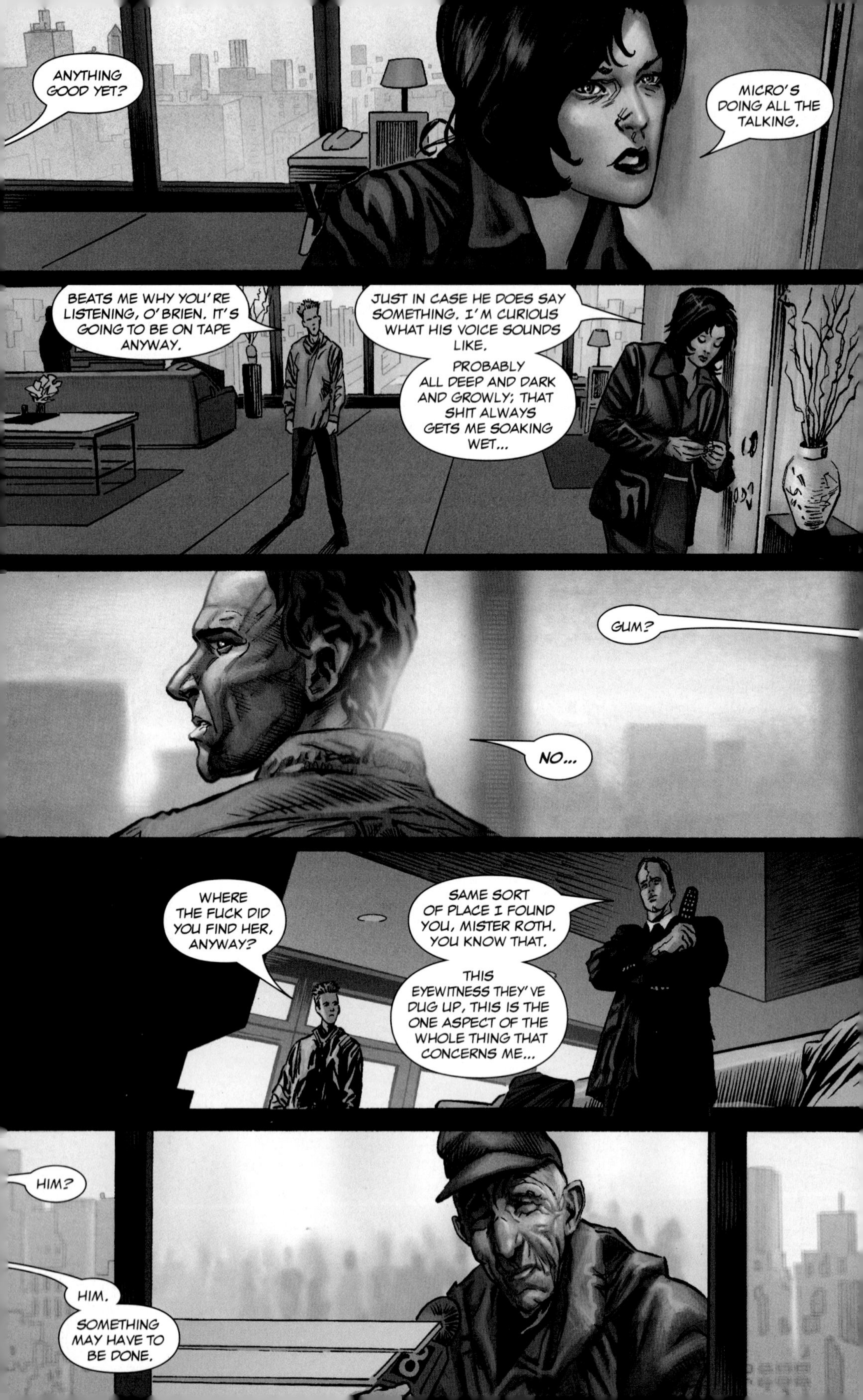
ANYTHING GOOD YET?
MICRO'S DOING ALL THE TALKING.
BEATS ME WHY YOU'RE LISTENING, O'BRIEN. IT'S GOING TO BE ON TAPE ANYWAY.
JUST IN CASE HE DOES SAY SOMETHING. I'M CURIOUS WHAT HIS VOICE SOUNDS LIKE.
PROBABLY ALL DEEP AND DARK AND GROWLY; THAT SHIT ALWAYS GETS ME SOAKING WET...
GUM?
NO...
WHERE THE FUCK DID YOU FIND HER, ANYWAY?
SAME SORT OF PLACE I FOUND YOU, MISTER ROTH. YOU KNOW THAT.
THIS EYEWITNESS THEY'VE DUG UP, THIS IS THE ONE ASPECT OF THE WHOLE THING THAT CONCERNS ME...
HIM?
HIM.
SOMETHING MAY HAVE TO BE DONE.

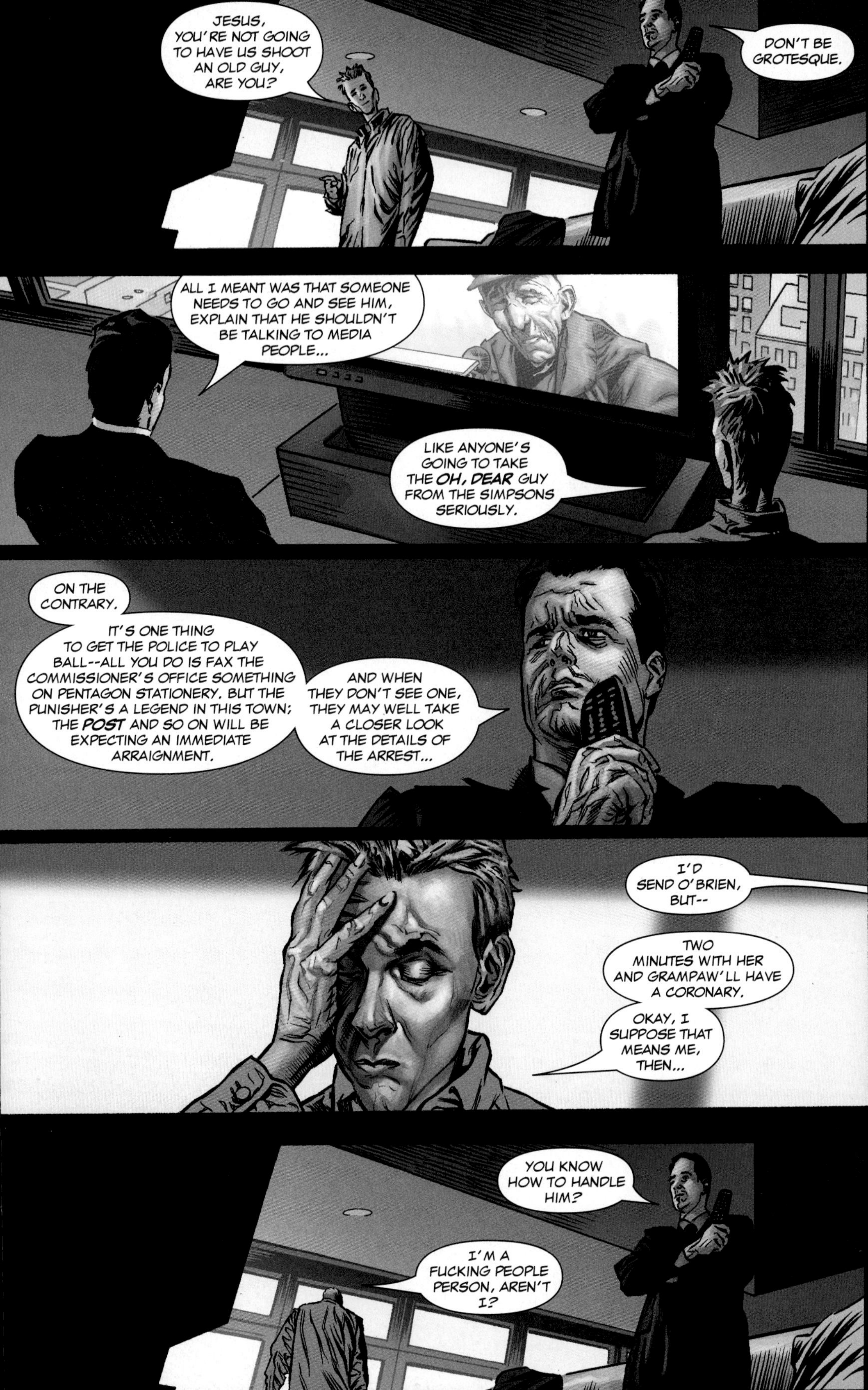
JESUS, YOU'RE NOT GOING TO HAVE US SHOOT AN OLD GUY, ARE YOU?
DON'T BE GROTESQUE.
ALL I MEANT WAS THAT SOMEONE NEEDS TO GO AND SEE HIM, EXPLAIN THAT HE SHOULDN'T BE TALKING TO MEDIA PEOPLE...
LIKE ANYONE'S GOING TO TAKE THE *OH, DEAR* GUY FROM THE SIMPSONS SERIOUSLY.
ON THE CONTRARY.
IT'S ONE THING TO GET THE POLICE TO PLAY BALL--ALL YOU DO IS FAX THE COMMISSIONER'S OFFICE SOMETHING ON PENTAGON STATIONERY. BUT THE PUNISHER'S A LEGEND IN THIS TOWN; THE *POST* AND SO ON WILL BE EXPECTING AN IMMEDIATE ARRAIGNMENT.
AND WHEN THEY DON'T SEE ONE, THEY MAY WELL TAKE A CLOSER LOOK AT THE DETAILS OF THE ARREST...
I'D SEND O'BRIEN, BUT--
TWO MINUTES WITH HER AND GRAMPAW'LL HAVE A CORONARY.
OKAY, I SUPPOSE THAT MEANS ME, THEN...
YOU KNOW HOW TO HANDLE HIM?
I'M A FUCKING PEOPLE PERSON, AREN'T I?

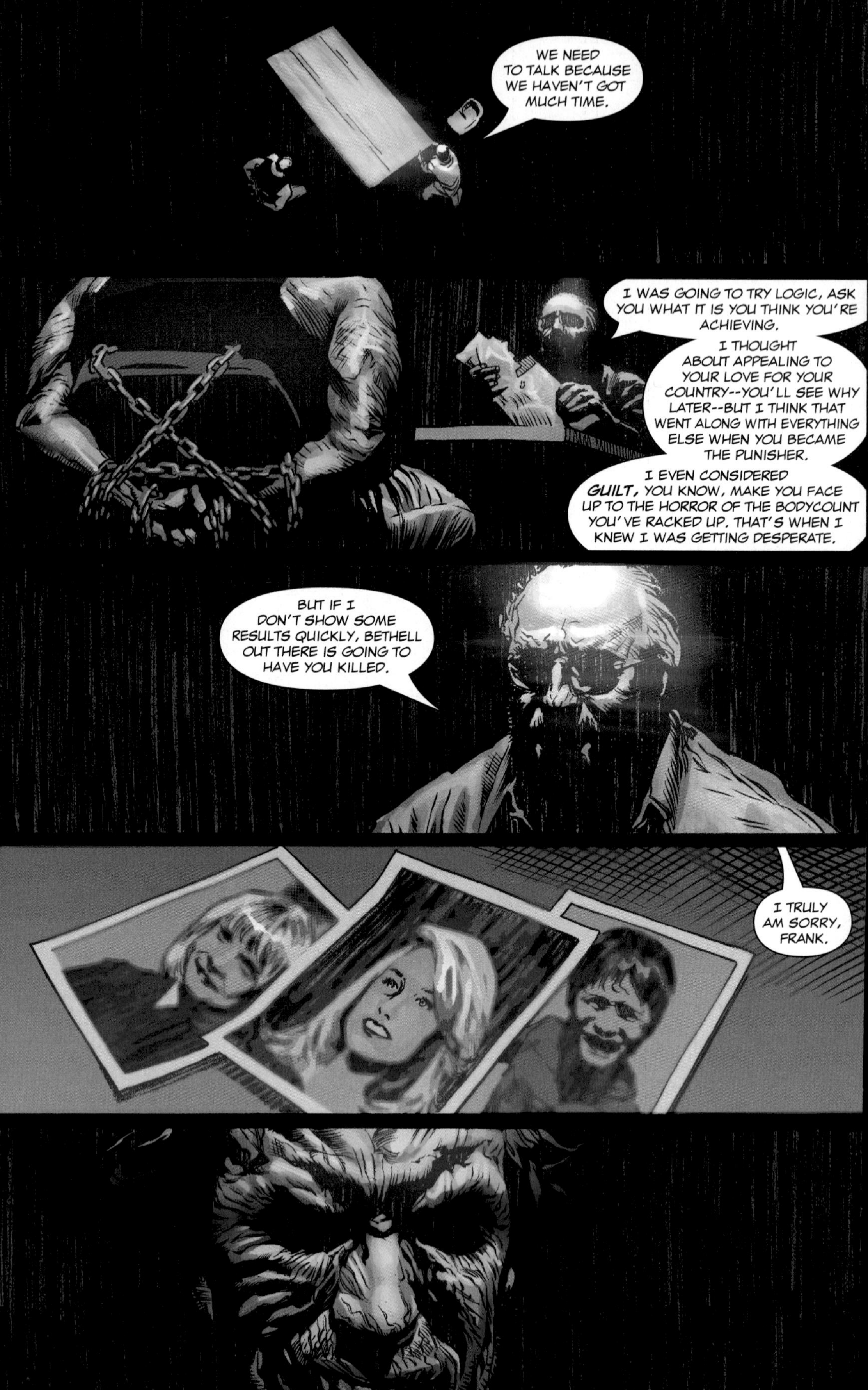
WE NEED TO TALK BECAUSE WE HAVEN'T GOT MUCH TIME.
I WAS GOING TO TRY LOGIC, ASK YOU WHAT IT IS YOU THINK YOU'RE ACHIEVING.
I THOUGHT ABOUT APPEALING TO YOUR LOVE FOR YOUR COUNTRY--YOU'LL SEE WHY LATER--BUT I THINK THAT WENT ALONG WITH EVERYTHING ELSE WHEN YOU BECAME THE PUNISHER.
I EVEN CONSIDERED GUILT, YOU KNOW, MAKE YOU FACE UP TO THE HORROR OF THE BODYCOUNT YOU'VE RACKED UP. THAT'S WHEN I KNEW I WAS GETTING DESPERATE.
BUT IF I DON'T SHOW SOME RESULTS QUICKLY, BETHELL OUT THERE IS GOING TO HAVE YOU KILLED.
I TRULY AM SORRY, FRANK.

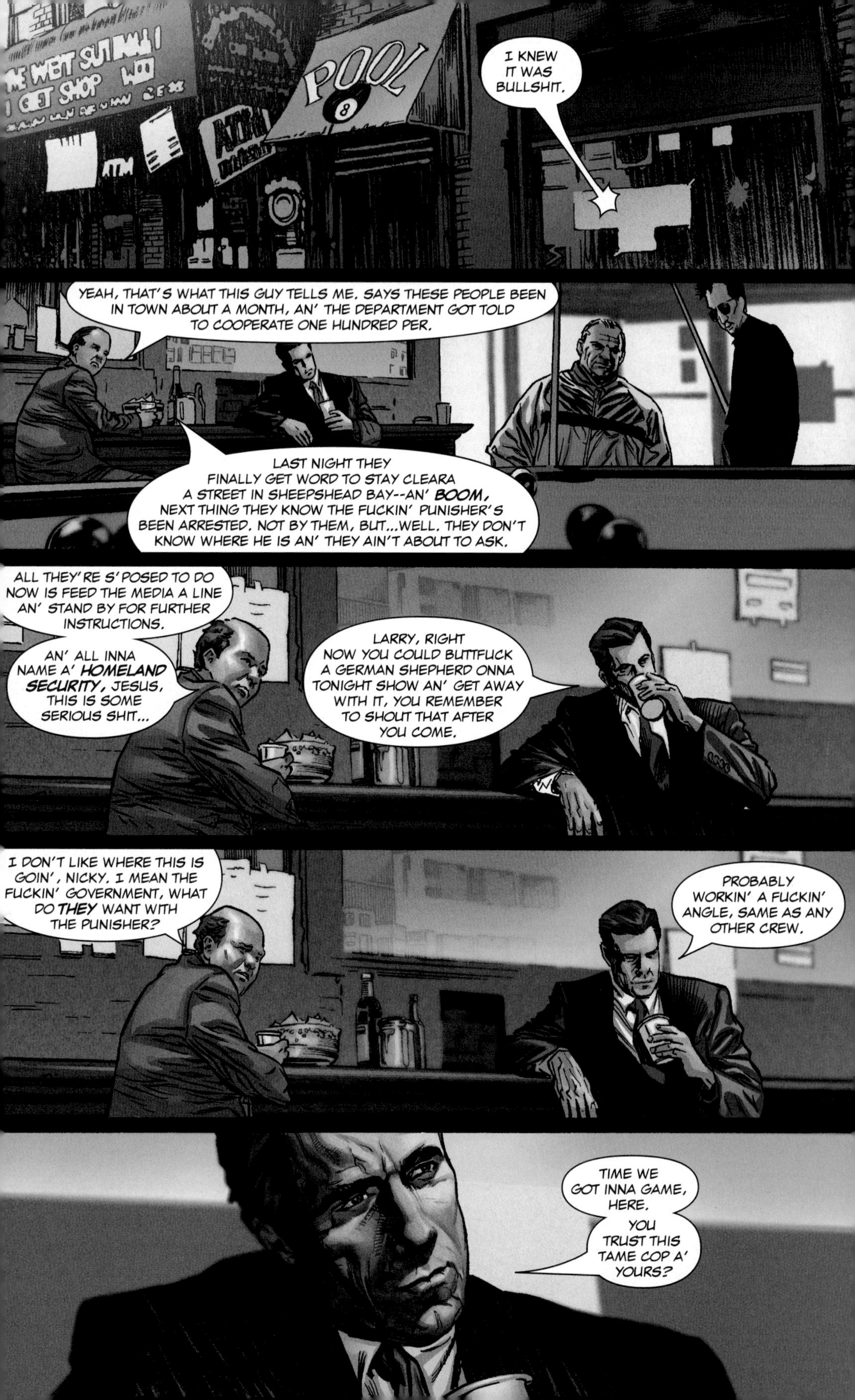
I KNEW IT WAS BULLSHIT.
POOL
ATM
YEAH, THAT'S WHAT THIS GUY TELLS ME. SAYS THESE PEOPLE BEEN IN TOWN ABOUT A MONTH, AN' THE DEPARTMENT GOT TOLD TO COOPERATE ONE HUNDRED PER.
LAST NIGHT THEY FINALLY GET WORD TO STAY CLEARA A STREET IN SHEEPSHEAD BAY--AN' BOOM, NEXT THING THEY KNOW THE FUCKIN' PUNISHER'S BEEN ARRESTED. NOT BY THEM, BUT...WELL. THEY DON'T KNOW WHERE HE IS AN' THEY AIN'T ABOUT TO ASK.
ALL THEY'RE S'POSED TO DO NOW IS FEED THE MEDIA A LINE AN' STAND BY FOR FURTHER INSTRUCTIONS.
AN' ALL INNA NAME A' HOMELAND SECURITY, JESUS, THIS IS SOME SERIOUS SHIT...
LARRY, RIGHT NOW YOU COULD BUTTFUCK A GERMAN SHEPHERD ONNA TONIGHT SHOW AN' GET AWAY WITH IT, YOU REMEMBER TO SHOUT THAT AFTER YOU COME.
I DON'T LIKE WHERE THIS IS GOIN', NICKY. I MEAN THE FUCKIN' GOVERNMENT, WHAT DO THEY WANT WITH THE PUNISHER?
PROBABLY WORKIN' A FUCKIN' ANGLE, SAME AS ANY OTHER CREW.
TIME WE GOT INNA GAME, HERE.
YOU TRUST THIS TAME COP A' YOURS?

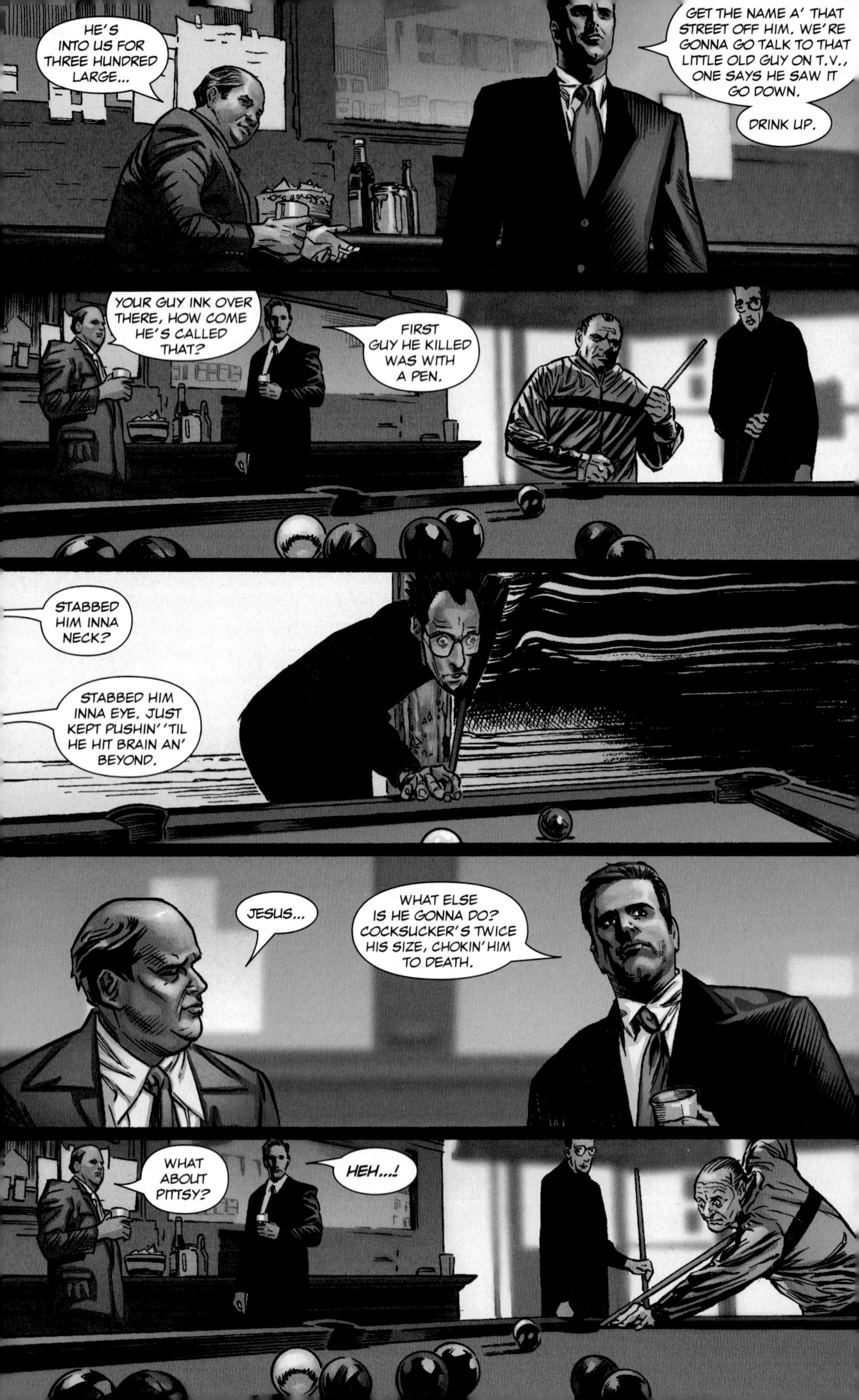
HE'S INTO US FOR THREE HUNDRED LARGE...
GET THE NAME A' THAT STREET OFF HIM. WE'RE GONNA GO TALK TO THAT LITTLE OLD GUY ON T.V., ONE SAYS HE SAW IT GO DOWN.
DRINK UP.
YOUR GUY INK OVER THERE, HOW COME HE'S CALLED THAT?
FIRST GUY HE KILLED WAS WITH A PEN.
STABBED HIM INNA NECK?
STABBED HIM INNA EYE. JUST KEPT PUSHIN' 'TIL HE HIT BRAIN AN' BEYOND.
JESUS...
WHAT ELSE IS HE GONNA DO? COCKSUCKER'S TWICE HIS SIZE, CHOKIN' HIM TO DEATH.
WHAT ABOUT PITTSY?
HEH...!

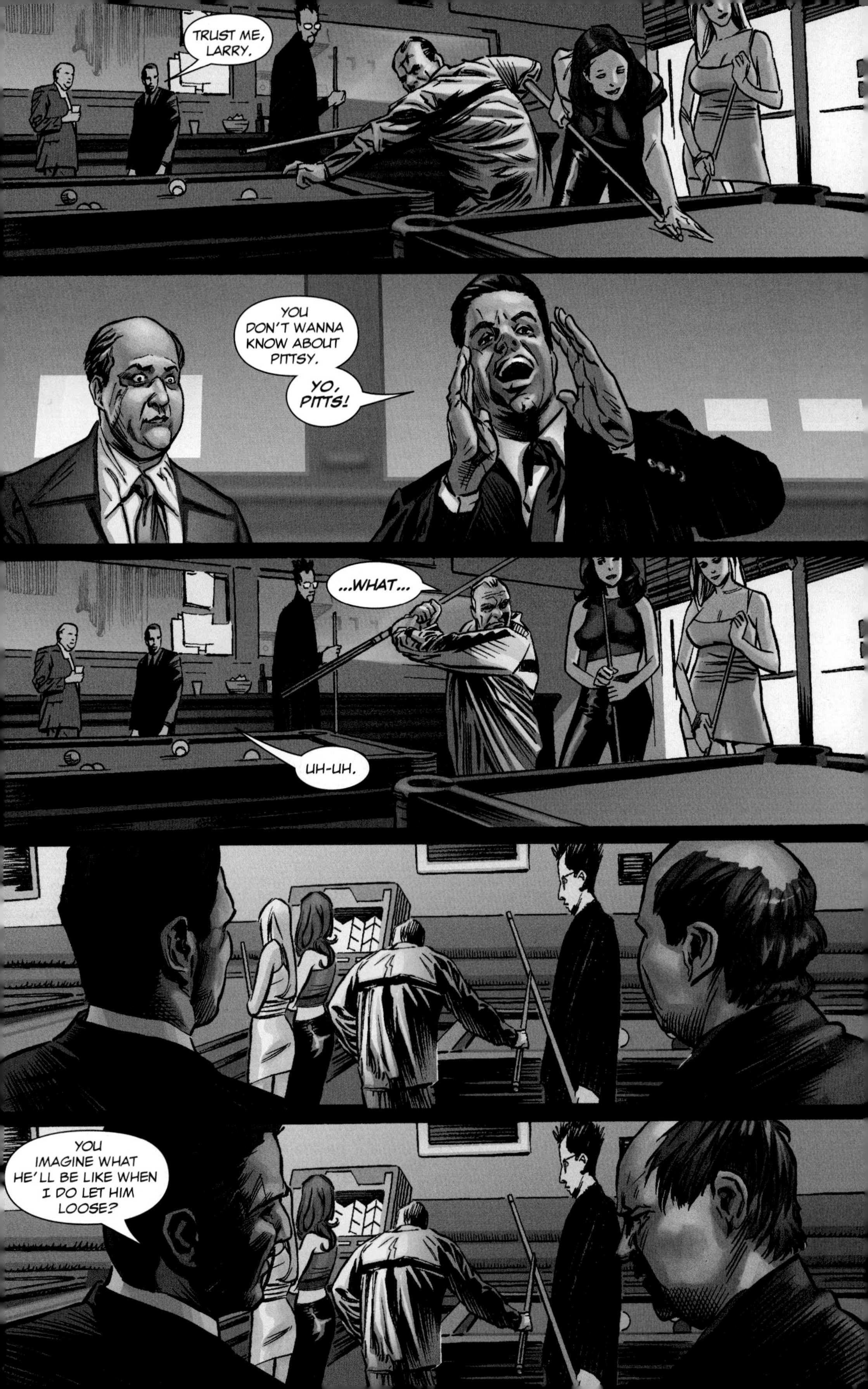
TRUST ME, LARRY.
YOU DON'T WANNA KNOW ABOUT PITTSY.
YO, PITTS!
...WHAT...
UH-UH.
YOU IMAGINE WHAT HE'LL BE LIKE WHEN I DO LET HIM LOOSE?

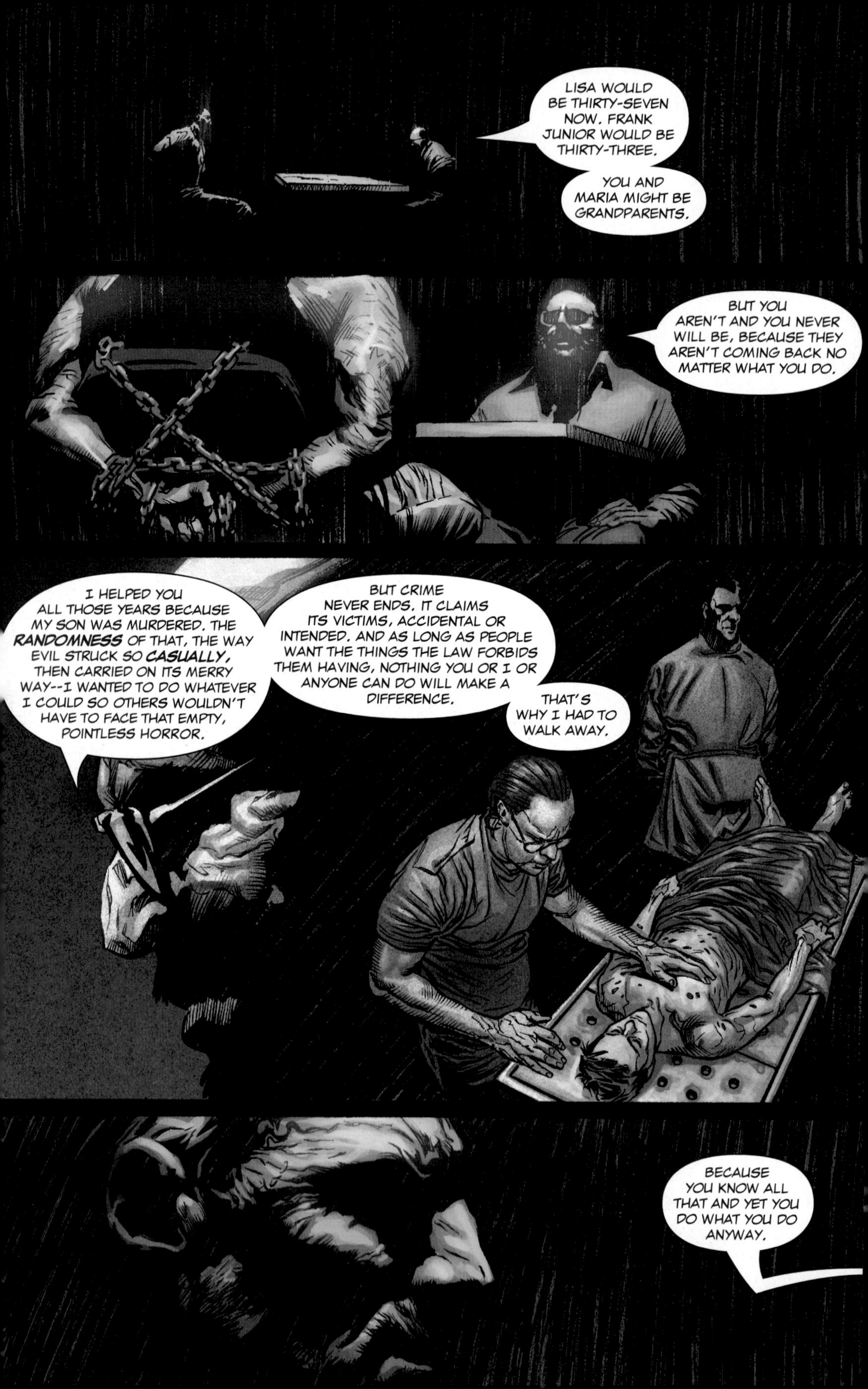

LISA WOULD BE THIRTY-SEVEN NOW. FRANK JUNIOR WOULD BE THIRTY-THREE.
YOU AND MARIA MIGHT BE GRANDPARENTS.
BUT YOU AREN'T AND YOU NEVER WILL BE, BECAUSE THEY AREN'T COMING BACK NO MATTER WHAT YOU DO.
I HELPED YOU ALL THOSE YEARS BECAUSE MY SON WAS MURDERED. THE RANDOMNESS OF THAT, THE WAY EVIL STRUCK SO CASUALLY, THEN CARRIED ON ITS MERRY WAY--I WANTED TO DO WHATEVER I COULD SO OTHERS WOULDN'T HAVE TO FACE THAT EMPTY, POINTLESS HORROR.
BUT CRIME NEVER ENDS. IT CLAIMS ITS VICTIMS, ACCIDENTAL OR INTENDED. AND AS LONG AS PEOPLE WANT THE THINGS THE LAW FORBIDS THEM HAVING, NOTHING YOU OR I OR ANYONE CAN DO WILL MAKE A DIFFERENCE.
THAT'S WHY I HAD TO WALK AWAY.
BECAUSE YOU KNOW ALL THAT AND YET YOU DO WHAT YOU DO ANYWAY.

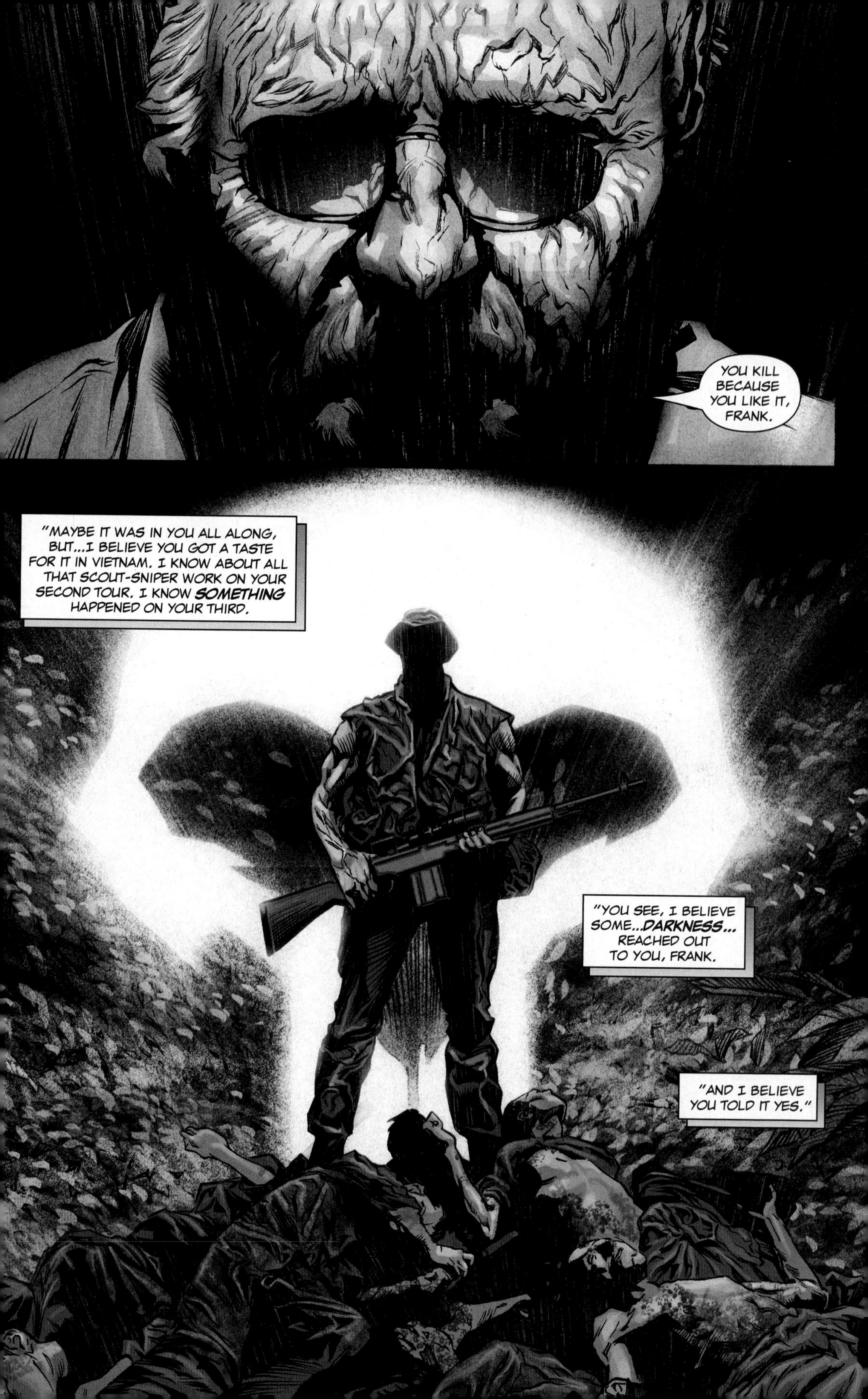
YOU KILL BECAUSE YOU LIKE IT, FRANK.
"MAYBE IT WAS IN YOU ALL ALONG, BUT...I BELIEVE YOU GOT A TASTE FOR IT IN VIETNAM. I KNOW ABOUT ALL THAT SCOUT-SNIPER WORK ON YOUR SECOND TOUR. I KNOW SOMETHING HAPPENED ON YOUR THIRD.
"YOU SEE, I BELIEVE SOME...DARKNESS... REACHED OUT TO YOU, FRANK.
"AND I BELIEVE YOU TOLD IT YES."

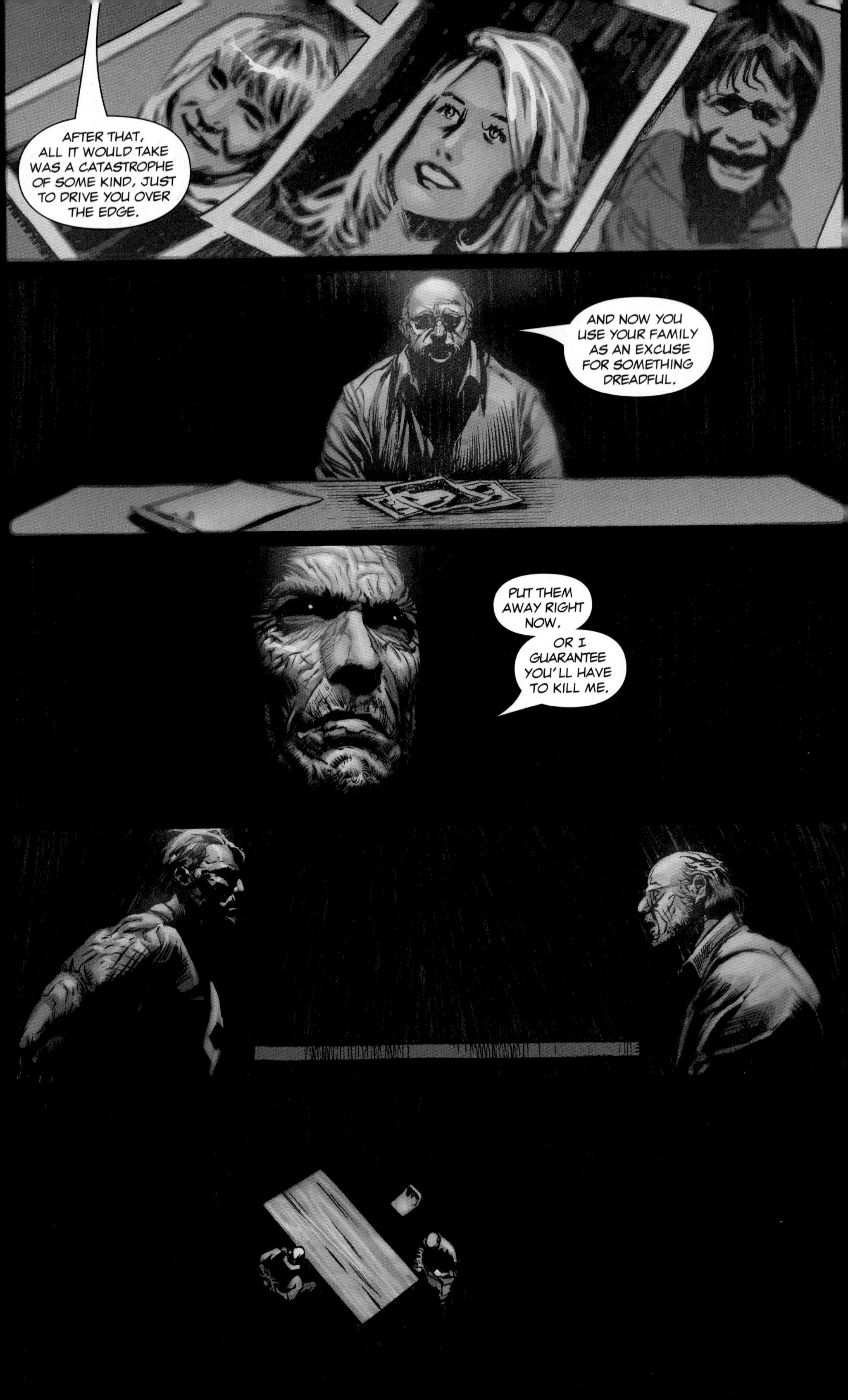
AFTER THAT, ALL IT WOULD TAKE WAS A CATASTROPHE OF SOME KIND, JUST TO DRIVE YOU OVER THE EDGE.
AND NOW YOU USE YOUR FAMILY AS AN EXCUSE FOR SOMETHING DREADFUL.
PUT THEM AWAY RIGHT NOW.
OR I GUARANTEE YOU'LL HAVE TO KILL ME.

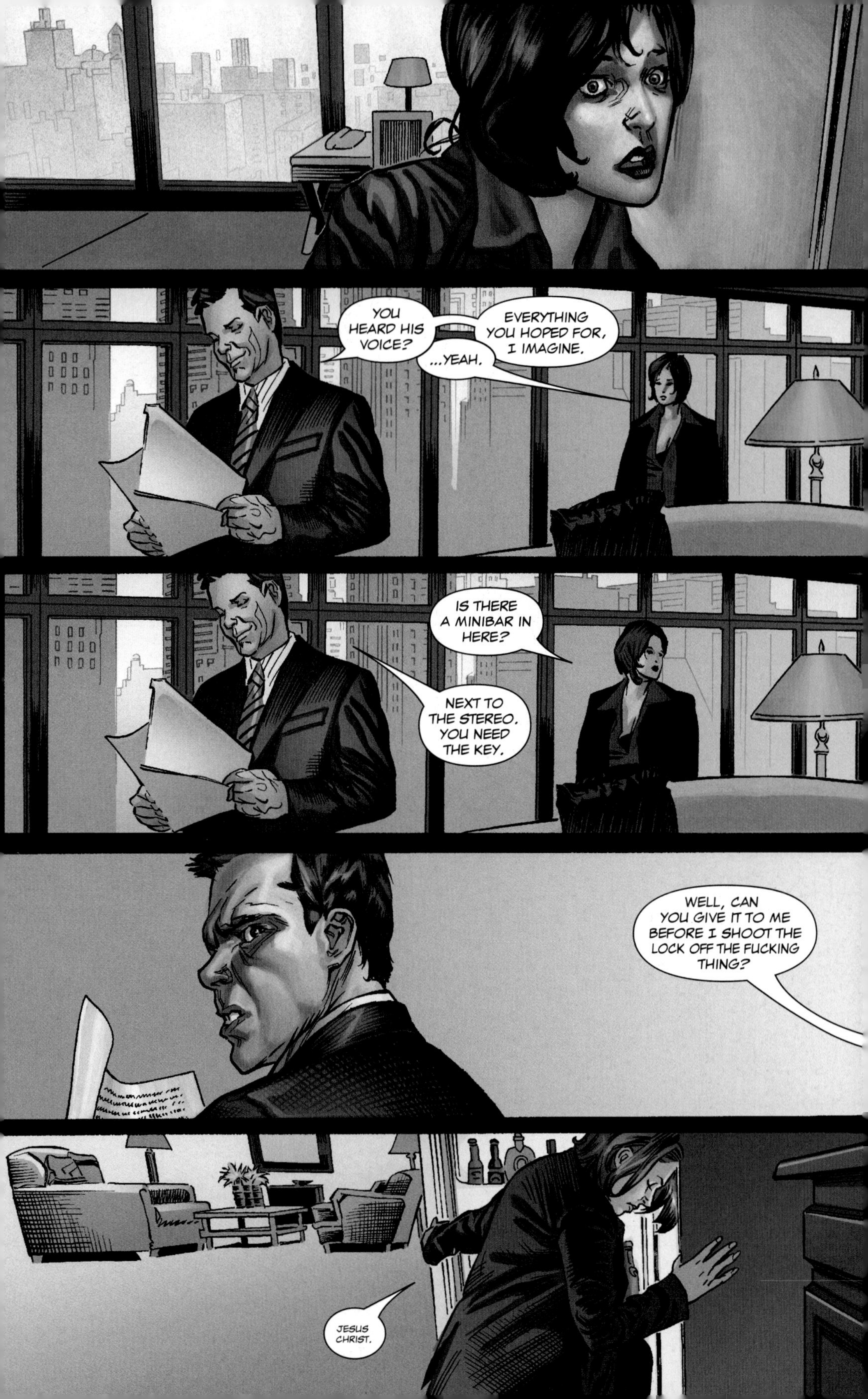
YOU HEARD HIS VOICE?
EVERYTHING YOU HOPED FOR, I IMAGINE.
...YEAH.
IS THERE A MINIBAR IN HERE?
NEXT TO THE STEREO. YOU NEED THE KEY.
WELL, CAN YOU GIVE IT TO ME BEFORE I SHOOT THE LOCK OFF THE FUCKING THING?
JESUS CHRIST.

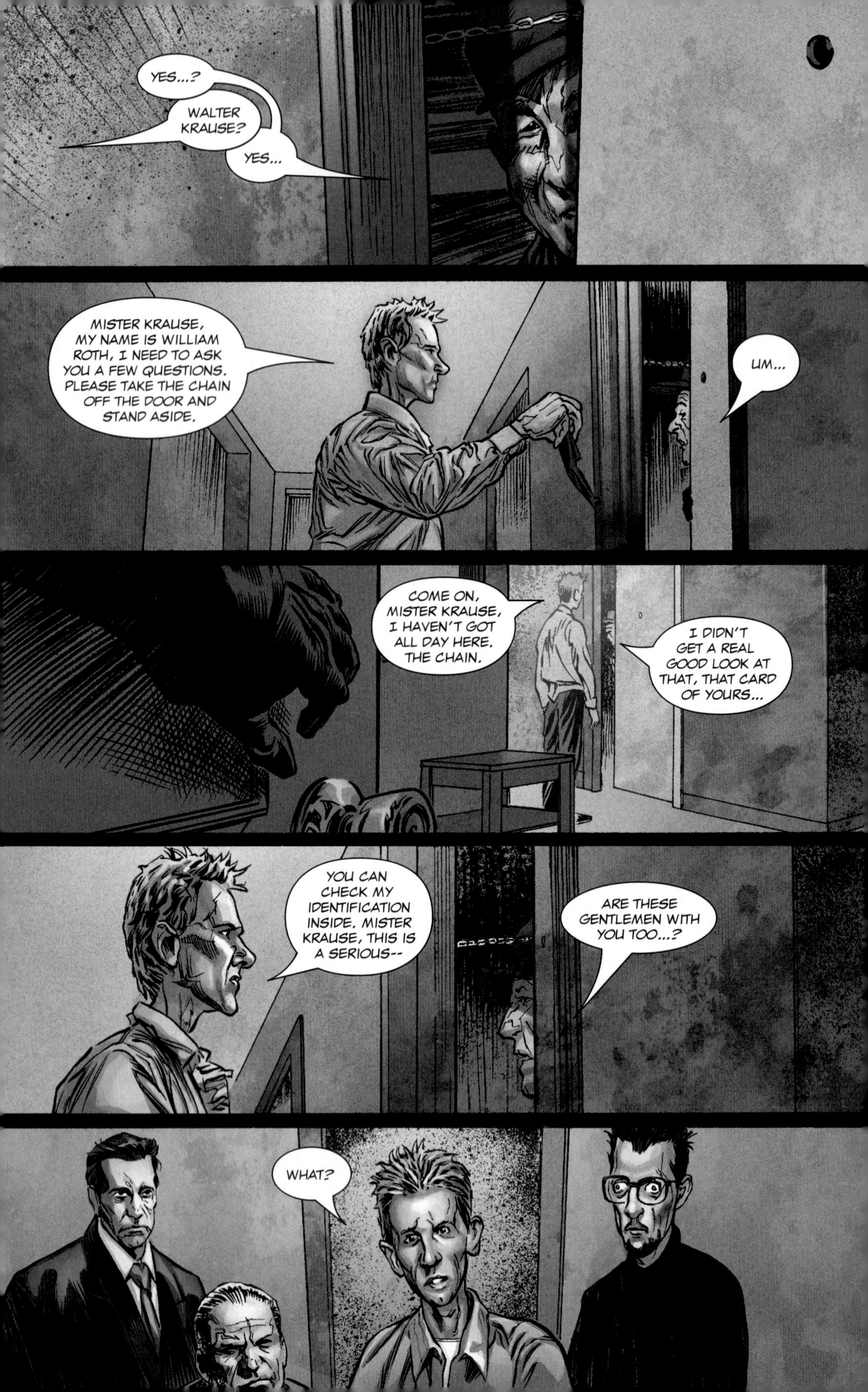
YES...?
WALTER KRAUSE?
YES...
MISTER KRAUSE, MY NAME IS WILLIAM ROTH, I NEED TO ASK YOU A FEW QUESTIONS. PLEASE TAKE THE CHAIN OFF THE DOOR AND STAND ASIDE.
UM...
COME ON, MISTER KRAUSE, I HAVEN'T GOT ALL DAY HERE. THE CHAIN.
I DIDN'T GET A REAL GOOD LOOK AT THAT, THAT CARD OF YOURS...
YOU CAN CHECK MY IDENTIFICATION INSIDE. MISTER KRAUSE, THIS IS A SERIOUS--
ARE THESE GENTLEMEN WITH YOU TOO...?
WHAT?

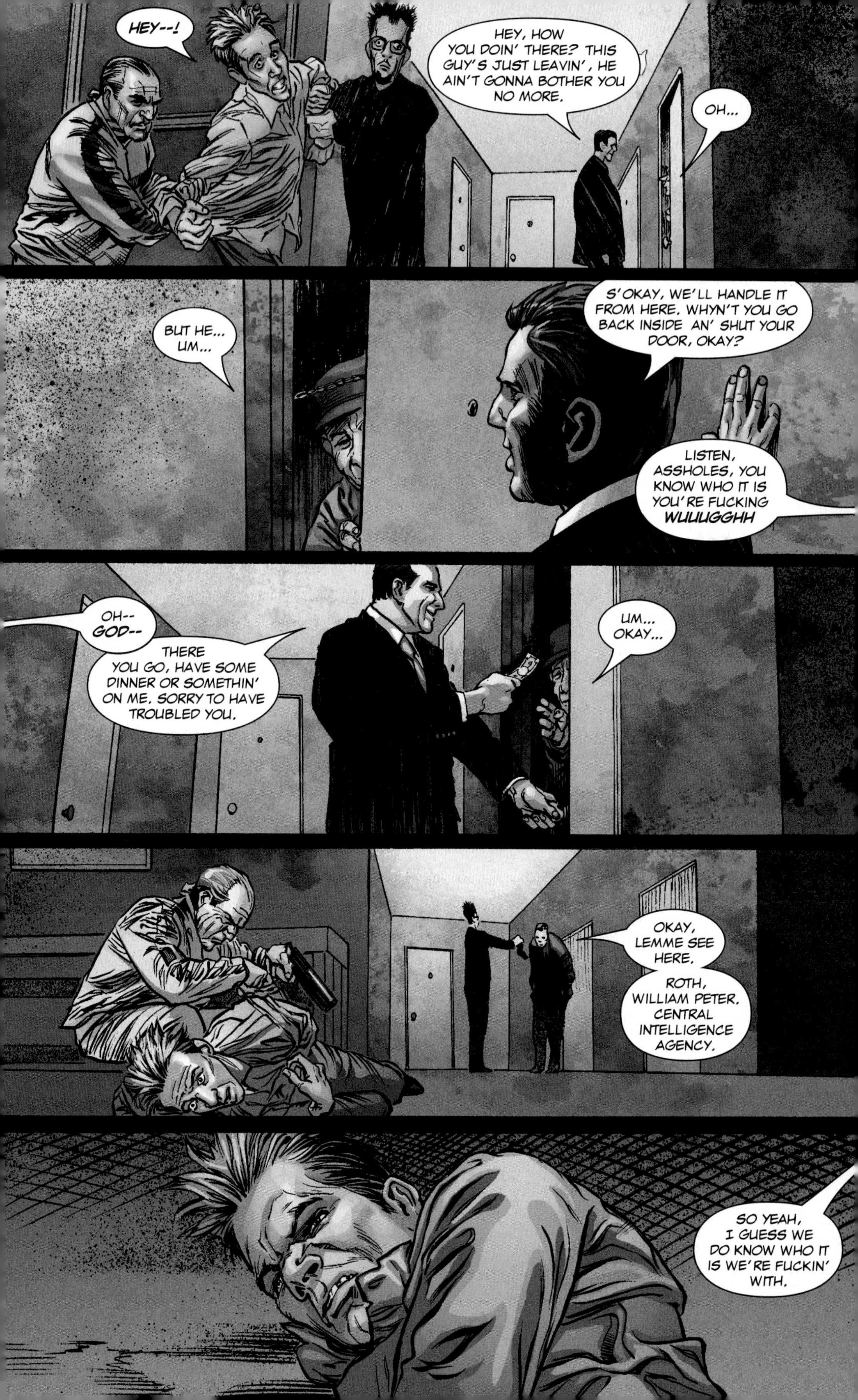
HEY--!
HEY, HOW YOU DOIN' THERE? THIS GUY'S JUST LEAVIN', HE AIN'T GONNA BOTHER YOU NO MORE.
OH...
BUT HE... UM...
S'OKAY, WE'LL HANDLE IT FROM HERE. WHYN'T YOU GO BACK INSIDE AN' SHUT YOUR DOOR, OKAY?
LISTEN, ASSHOLES, YOU KNOW WHO IT IS YOU'RE FUCKING **WUUUGGHH**
OH-- **GOD--**
THERE YOU GO, HAVE SOME DINNER OR SOMETHIN' ON ME. SORRY TO HAVE TROUBLED YOU.
UM... OKAY...
OKAY, LEMME SEE HERE.
ROTH, WILLIAM PETER. CENTRAL INTELLIGENCE AGENCY.
SO YEAH, I GUESS WE DO KNOW WHO IT IS WE'RE FUCKIN' WITH.

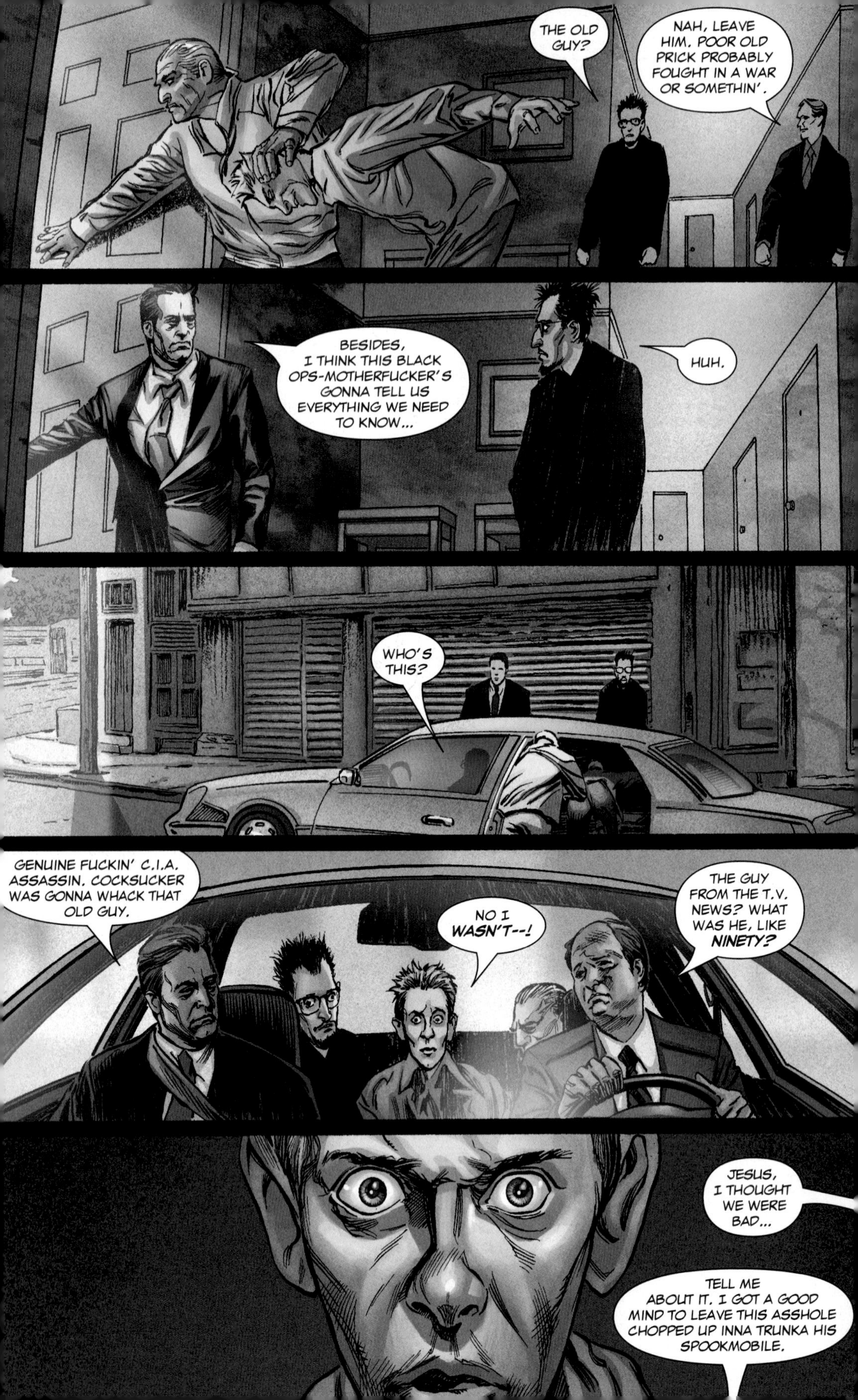
THE OLD GUY?
NAH, LEAVE HIM. POOR OLD PRICK PROBABLY FOUGHT IN A WAR OR SOMETHIN'.
BESIDES, I THINK THIS BLACK OPS-MOTHERFUCKER'S GONNA TELL US EVERYTHING WE NEED TO KNOW...
HUH.
WHO'S THIS?
GENUINE FUCKIN' C.I.A. ASSASSIN. COCKSUCKER WAS GONNA WHACK THAT OLD GUY.
NO I WASN'T--!
THE GUY FROM THE T.V. NEWS? WHAT WAS HE, LIKE NINETY?
JESUS, I THOUGHT WE WERE BAD...
TELL ME ABOUT IT. I GOT A GOOD MIND TO LEAVE THIS ASSHOLE CHOPPED UP INNA TRUNKA HIS SPOOKMOBILE.

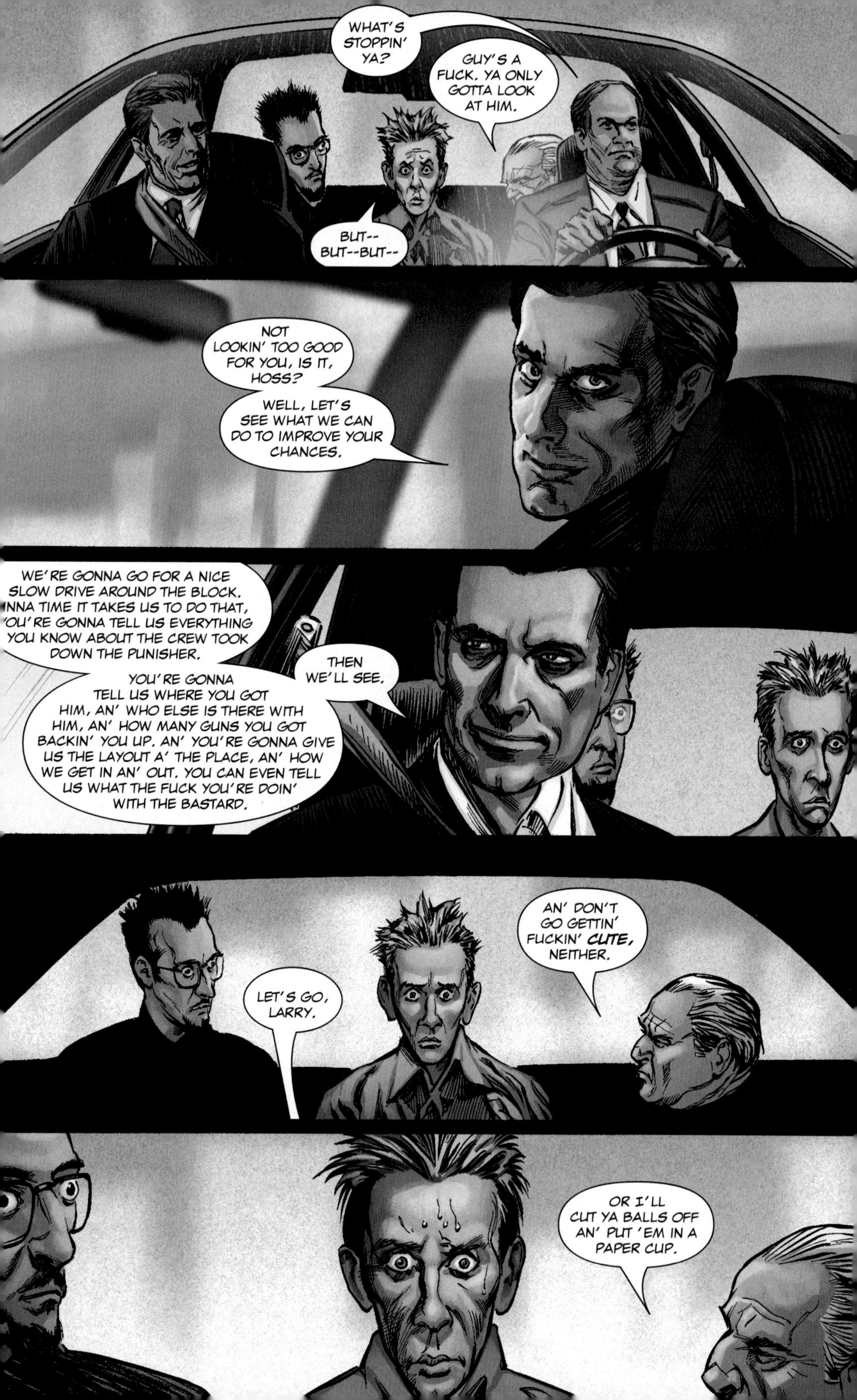
WHAT'S STOPPIN' YA?
GUY'S A FUCK. YA ONLY GOTTA LOOK AT HIM.
BUT-- BUT--BUT--
NOT LOOKIN' TOO GOOD FOR YOU, IS IT, HOSS?
WELL, LET'S SEE WHAT WE CAN DO TO IMPROVE YOUR CHANCES.
WE'RE GONNA GO FOR A NICE SLOW DRIVE AROUND THE BLOCK. INNA TIME IT TAKES US TO DO THAT, 'OU'RE GONNA TELL US EVERYTHING YOU KNOW ABOUT THE CREW TOOK DOWN THE PUNISHER.
YOU'RE GONNA TELL US WHERE YOU GOT HIM, AN' WHO ELSE IS THERE WITH HIM, AN' HOW MANY GUNS YOU GOT BACKIN' YOU UP. AN' YOU'RE GONNA GIVE US THE LAYOUT A' THE PLACE, AN' HOW WE GET IN AN' OUT. YOU CAN EVEN TELL US WHAT THE FUCK YOU'RE DOIN' WITH THE BASTARD.
THEN WE'LL SEE.
LET'S GO, LARRY.
AN' DON'T GO GETTIN' FUCKIN' CUTE, NEITHER.
OR I'LL CUT YA BALLS OFF AN' PUT 'EM IN A PAPER CUP.

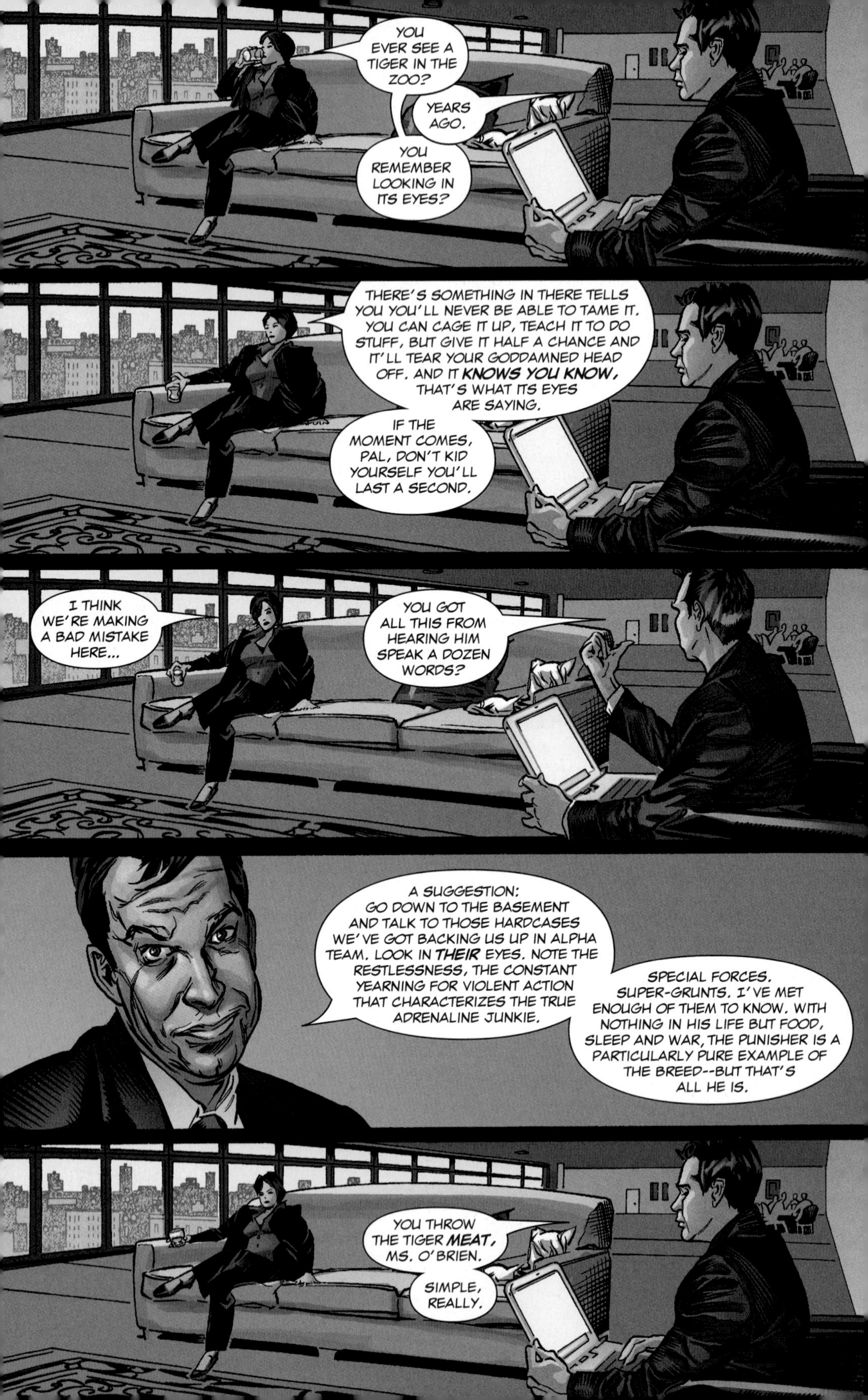
YOU EVER SEE A TIGER IN THE ZOO?
YEARS AGO.
YOU REMEMBER LOOKING IN ITS EYES?
THERE'S SOMETHING IN THERE TELLS YOU YOU'LL NEVER BE ABLE TO TAME IT. YOU CAN CAGE IT UP, TEACH IT TO DO STUFF, BUT GIVE IT HALF A CHANCE AND IT'LL TEAR YOUR GODDAMNED HEAD OFF. AND IT KNOWS YOU KNOW. THAT'S WHAT ITS EYES ARE SAYING.
IF THE MOMENT COMES, PAL, DON'T KID YOURSELF YOU'LL LAST A SECOND.
I THINK WE'RE MAKING A BAD MISTAKE HERE...
YOU GOT ALL THIS FROM HEARING HIM SPEAK A DOZEN WORDS?
A SUGGESTION: GO DOWN TO THE BASEMENT AND TALK TO THOSE HARDCASES WE'VE GOT BACKING US UP IN ALPHA TEAM. LOOK IN THEIR EYES. NOTE THE RESTLESSNESS, THE CONSTANT YEARNING FOR VIOLENT ACTION THAT CHARACTERIZES THE TRUE ADRENALINE JUNKIE.
SPECIAL FORCES. SUPER-GRUNTS. I'VE MET ENOUGH OF THEM TO KNOW. WITH NOTHING IN HIS LIFE BUT FOOD, SLEEP AND WAR, THE PUNISHER IS A PARTICULARLY PURE EXAMPLE OF THE BREED--BUT THAT'S ALL HE IS.
YOU THROW THE TIGER MEAT, MS. O'BRIEN.
SIMPLE, REALLY.

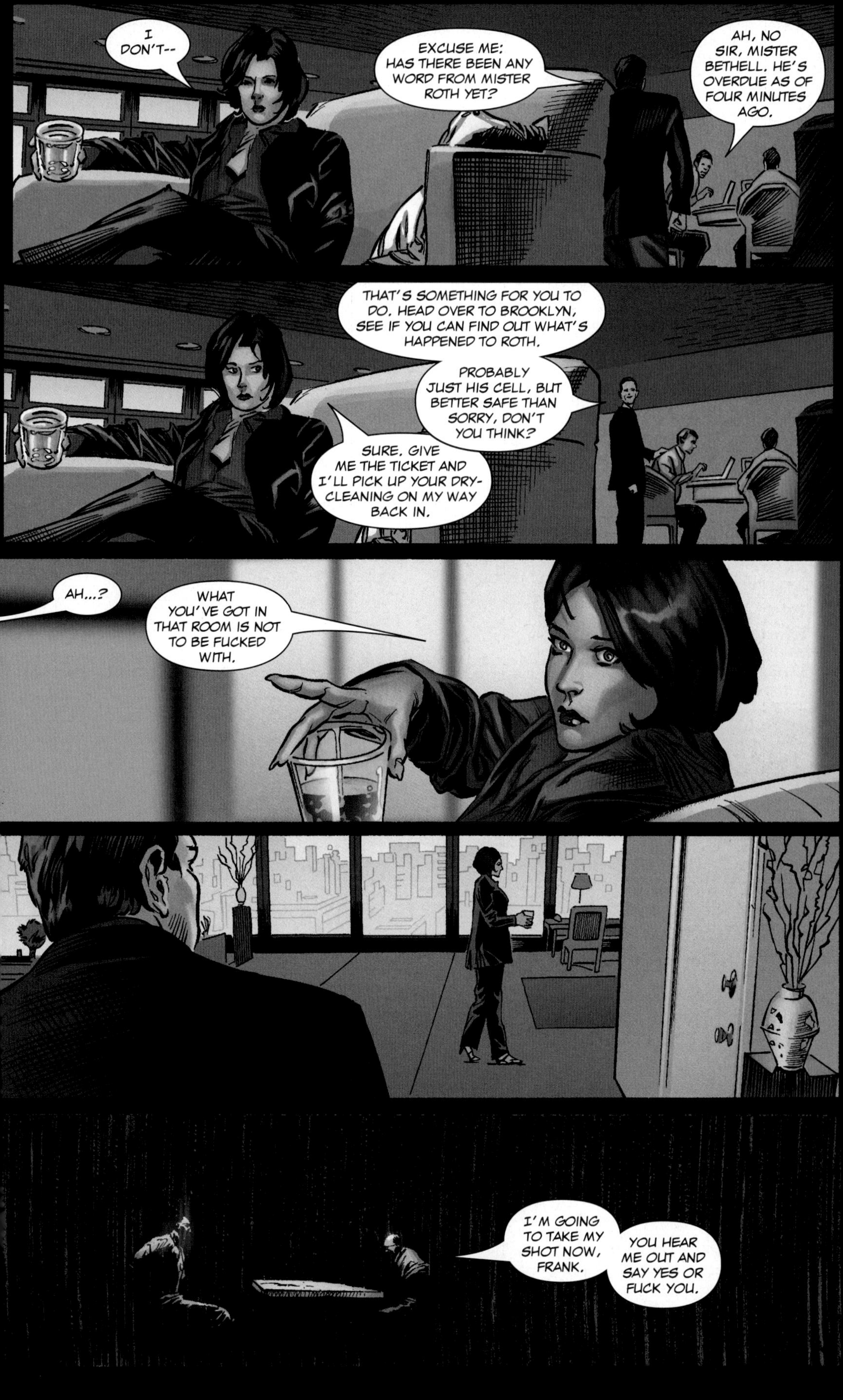
I DON'T--
EXCUSE ME: HAS THERE BEEN ANY WORD FROM MISTER ROTH YET?
AH, NO SIR, MISTER BETHELL. HE'S OVERDUE AS OF FOUR MINUTES AGO.
THAT'S SOMETHING FOR YOU TO DO. HEAD OVER TO BROOKLYN, SEE IF YOU CAN FIND OUT WHAT'S HAPPENED TO ROTH.
PROBABLY JUST HIS CELL, BUT BETTER SAFE THAN SORRY, DON'T YOU THINK?
SURE. GIVE ME THE TICKET AND I'LL PICK UP YOUR DRY-CLEANING ON MY WAY BACK IN.
AH...?
WHAT YOU'VE GOT IN THAT ROOM IS NOT TO BE FUCKED WITH.
I'M GOING TO TAKE MY SHOT NOW, FRANK.
YOU HEAR ME OUT AND SAY YES OR FUCK YOU.

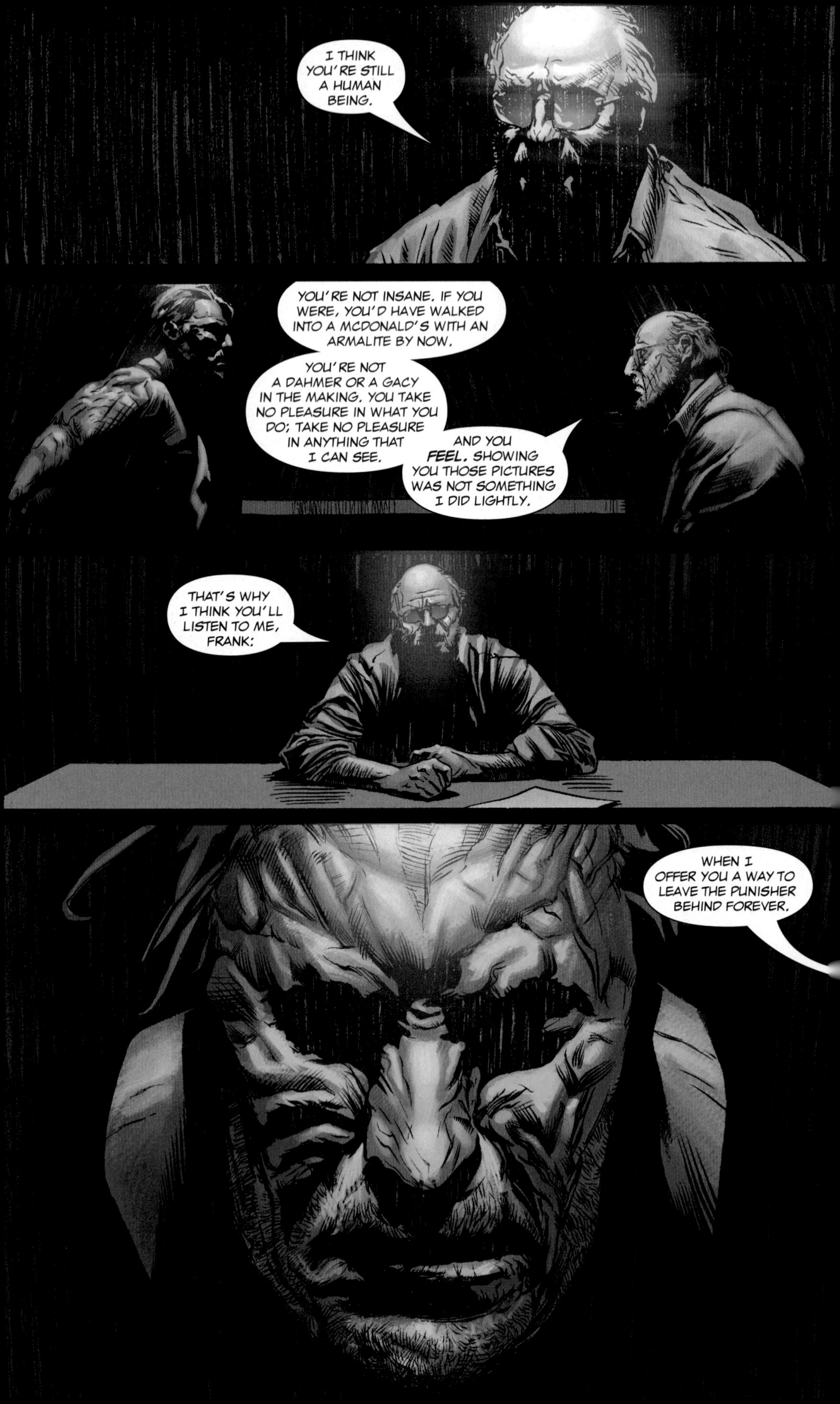
I THINK YOU'RE STILL A HUMAN BEING.
YOU'RE NOT INSANE. IF YOU WERE, YOU'D HAVE WALKED INTO A MCDONALD'S WITH AN ARMALITE BY NOW.
YOU'RE NOT A DAHMER OR A GACY IN THE MAKING. YOU TAKE NO PLEASURE IN WHAT YOU DO; TAKE NO PLEASURE IN ANYTHING THAT I CAN SEE.
AND YOU FEEL. SHOWING YOU THOSE PICTURES WAS NOT SOMETHING I DID LIGHTLY.
THAT'S WHY I THINK YOU'LL LISTEN TO ME, FRANK:
WHEN I OFFER YOU A WAY TO LEAVE THE PUNISHER BEHIND FOREVER.

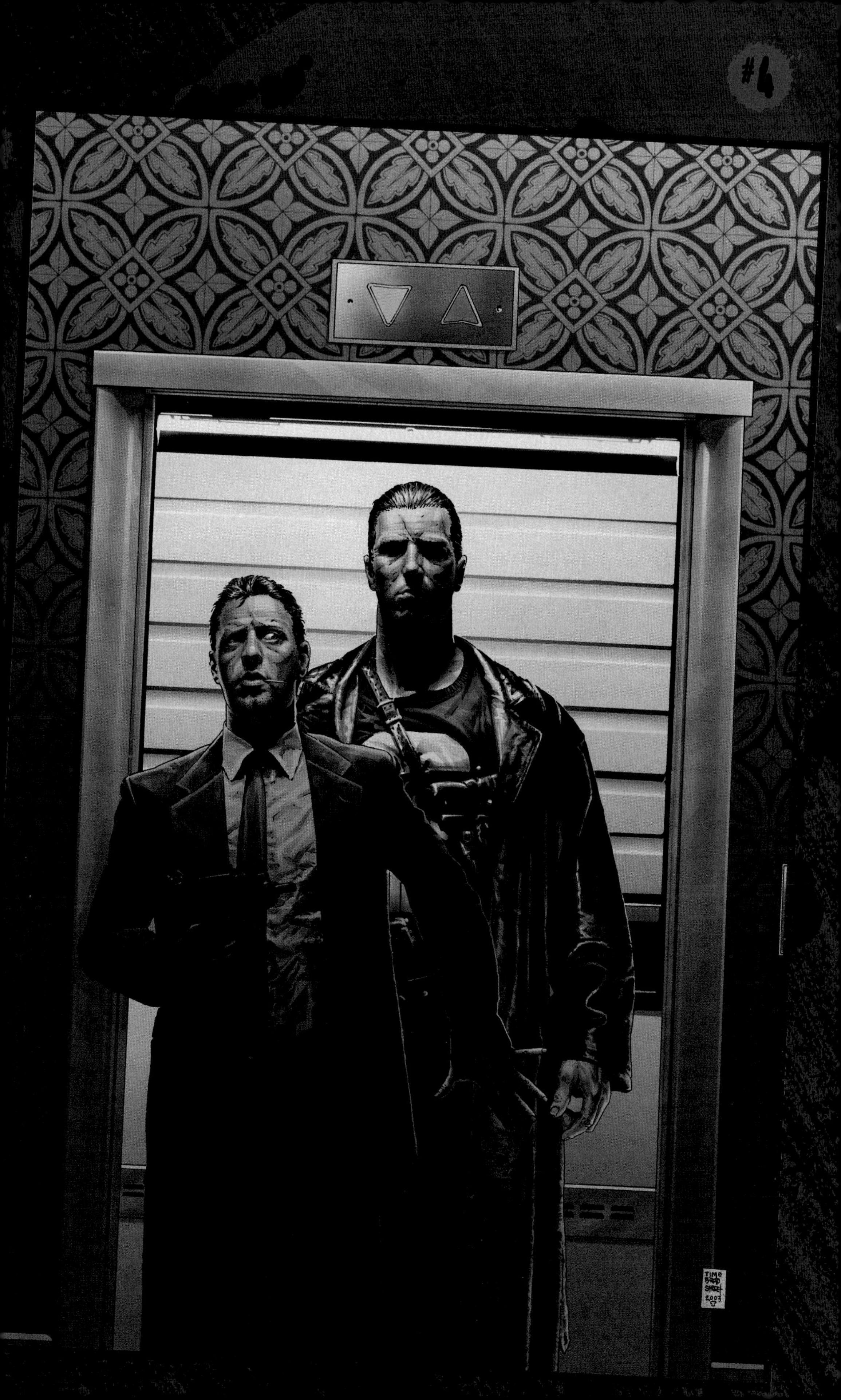
#4

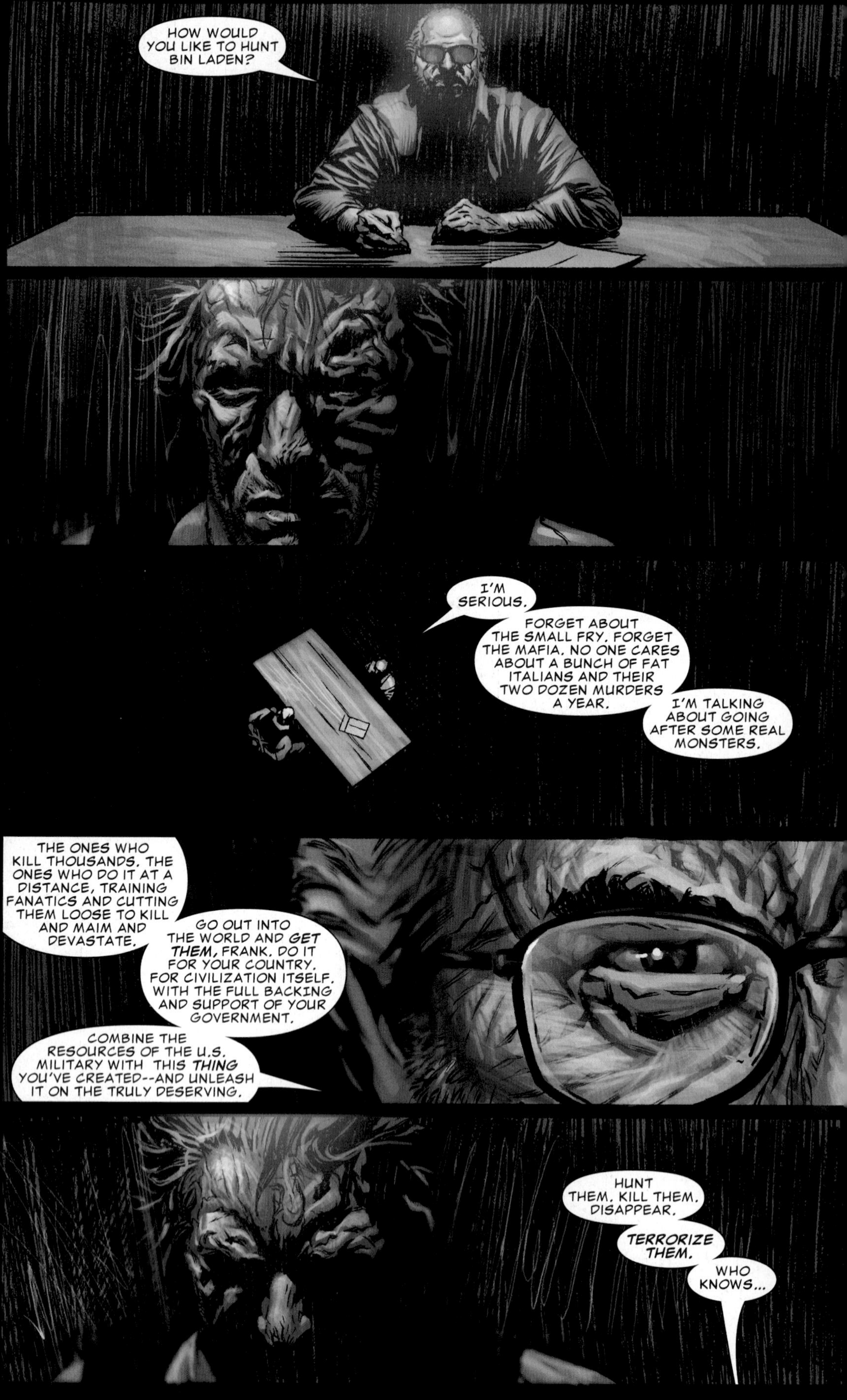

HOW WOULD YOU LIKE TO HUNT BIN LADEN?
I'M SERIOUS.
FORGET ABOUT THE SMALL FRY. FORGET THE MAFIA. NO ONE CARES ABOUT A BUNCH OF FAT ITALIANS AND THEIR TWO DOZEN MURDERS A YEAR.
I'M TALKING ABOUT GOING AFTER SOME REAL MONSTERS.
THE ONES WHO KILL THOUSANDS. THE ONES WHO DO IT AT A DISTANCE, TRAINING FANATICS AND CUTTING THEM LOOSE TO KILL AND MAIM AND DEVASTATE.
GO OUT INTO THE WORLD AND *GET THEM,* FRANK. DO IT FOR YOUR COUNTRY. FOR CIVILIZATION ITSELF. WITH THE FULL BACKING AND SUPPORT OF YOUR GOVERNMENT.
COMBINE THE RESOURCES OF THE U.S. MILITARY WITH THIS *THING* YOU'VE CREATED--AND UNLEASH IT ON THE TRULY DESERVING.
HUNT THEM. KILL THEM. DISAPPEAR.
TERRORIZE THEM.
WHO KNOWS...

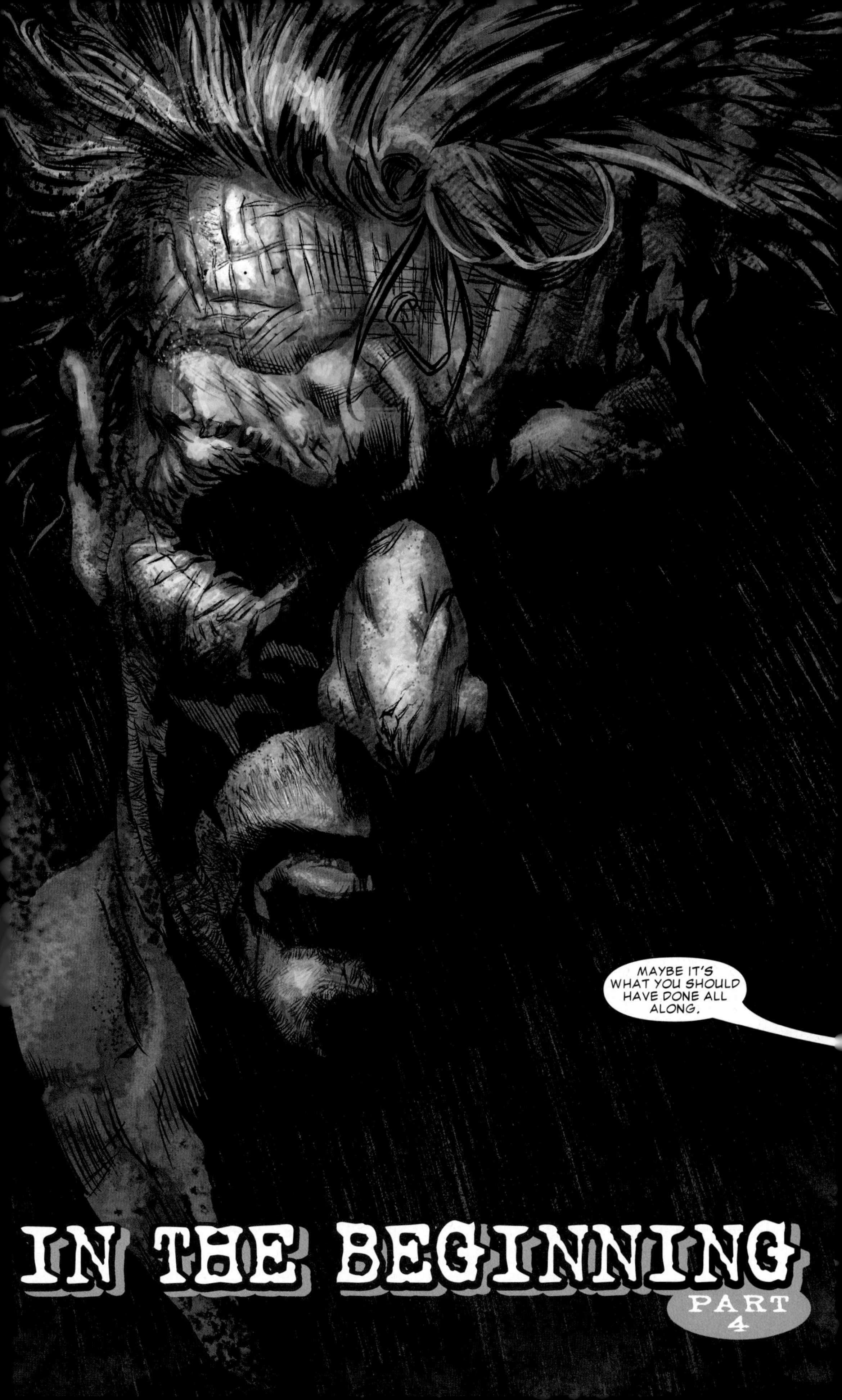
MAYBE IT'S WHAT YOU SHOULD HAVE DONE ALL ALONG.
IN THE BEGINNING
PART 4

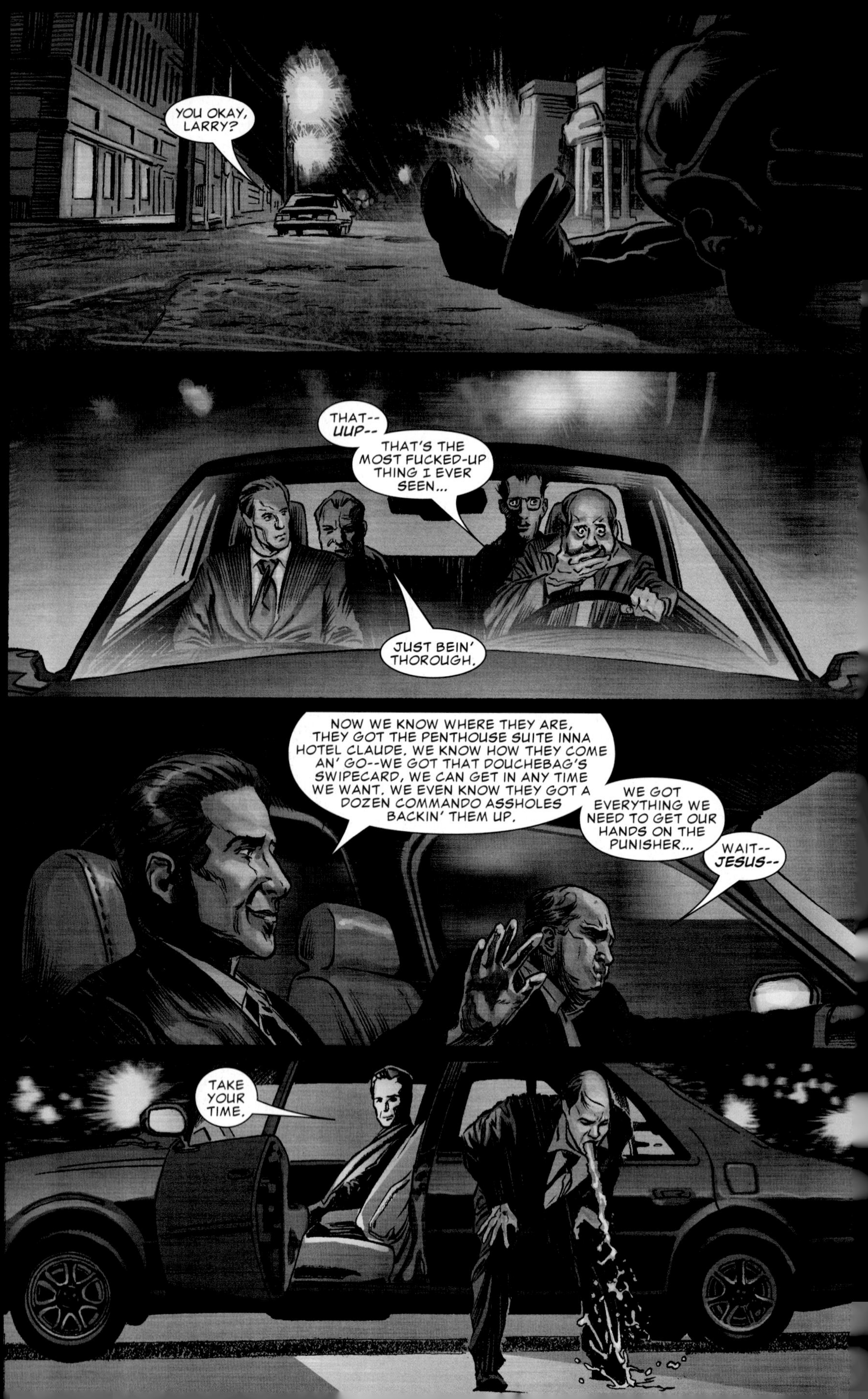
YOU OKAY, LARRY?
THAT-- UUP--
THAT'S THE MOST FUCKED-UP THING I EVER SEEN...
JUST BEIN' THOROUGH.
NOW WE KNOW WHERE THEY ARE, THEY GOT THE PENTHOUSE SUITE INNA HOTEL CLAUDE. WE KNOW HOW THEY COME AN' GO--WE GOT THAT DOUCHEBAG'S SWIPECARD, WE CAN GET IN ANY TIME WE WANT. WE EVEN KNOW THEY GOT A DOZEN COMMANDO ASSHOLES BACKIN' THEM UP.
WE GOT EVERYTHING WE NEED TO GET OUR HANDS ON THE PUNISHER...
WAIT-- JESUS--
TAKE YOUR TIME.

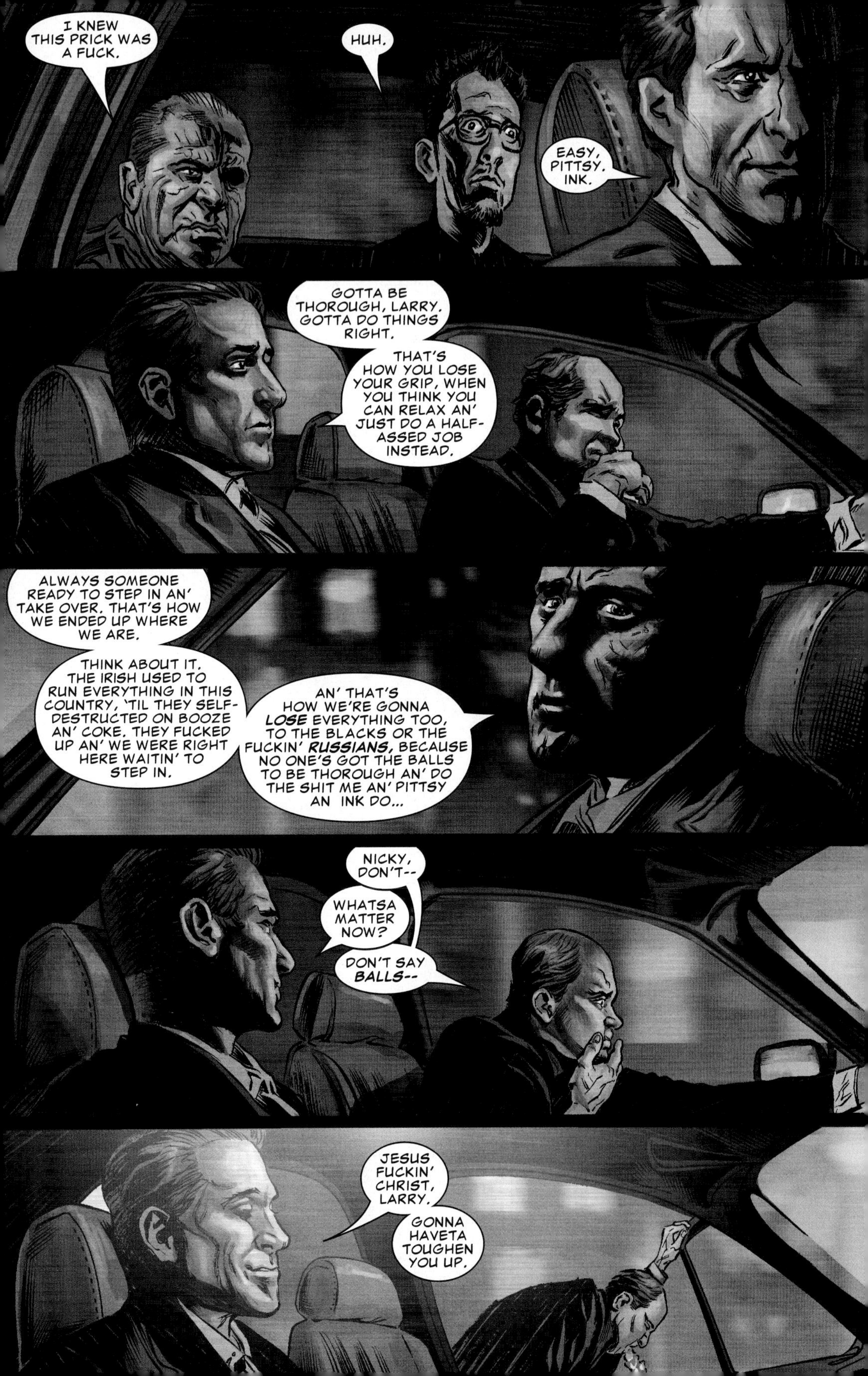
I KNEW THIS PRICK WAS A FUCK.
HUH.
EASY, PITTSY. INK.
GOTTA BE THOROUGH, LARRY. GOTTA DO THINGS RIGHT.
THAT'S HOW YOU LOSE YOUR GRIP, WHEN YOU THINK YOU CAN RELAX AN' JUST DO A HALF-ASSED JOB INSTEAD.
ALWAYS SOMEONE READY TO STEP IN AN' TAKE OVER. THAT'S HOW WE ENDED UP WHERE WE ARE.
THINK ABOUT IT. THE IRISH USED TO RUN EVERYTHING IN THIS COUNTRY, 'TIL THEY SELF-DESTRUCTED ON BOOZE AN' COKE. THEY FUCKED UP AN' WE WERE RIGHT HERE WAITIN' TO STEP IN.
AN' THAT'S HOW WE'RE GONNA *LOSE* EVERYTHING TOO, TO THE BLACKS OR THE FUCKIN' ***RUSSIANS,*** BECAUSE NO ONE'S GOT THE BALLS TO BE THOROUGH AN' DO THE SHIT ME AN' PITTSY AN INK DO...
NICKY, DON'T--
WHATSA MATTER NOW?
DON'T SAY ***BALLS--***
JESUS FUCKIN' CHRIST, LARRY.
GONNA HAVETA TOUGHEN YOU UP.

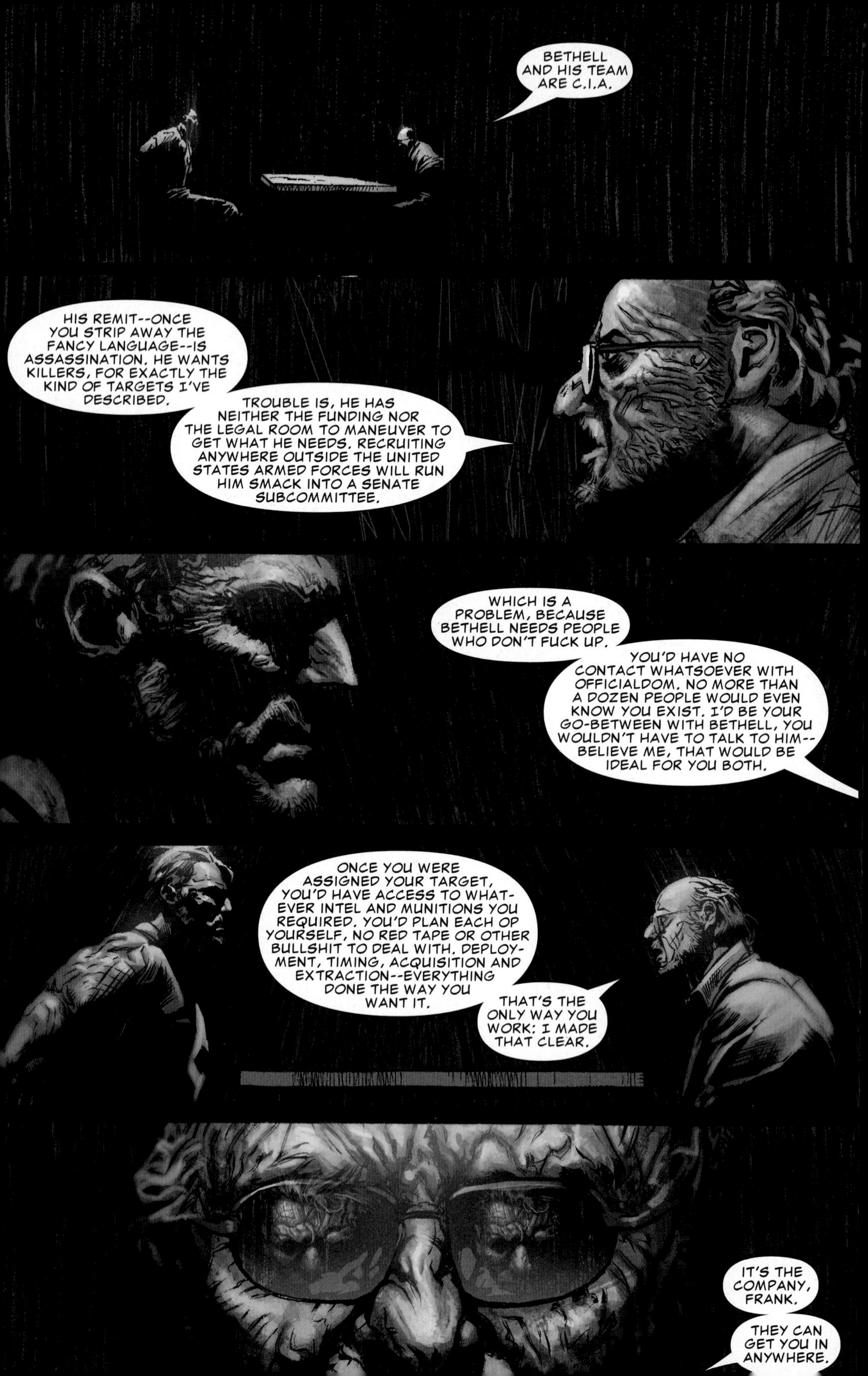
BETHELL AND HIS TEAM ARE C.I.A.
HIS REMIT--ONCE YOU STRIP AWAY THE FANCY LANGUAGE--IS ASSASSINATION. HE WANTS KILLERS, FOR EXACTLY THE KIND OF TARGETS I'VE DESCRIBED.
TROUBLE IS, HE HAS NEITHER THE FUNDING NOR THE LEGAL ROOM TO MANEUVER TO GET WHAT HE NEEDS. RECRUITING ANYWHERE OUTSIDE THE UNITED STATES ARMED FORCES WILL RUN HIM SMACK INTO A SENATE SUBCOMMITTEE.
WHICH IS A PROBLEM, BECAUSE BETHELL NEEDS PEOPLE WHO DON'T FUCK UP.
YOU'D HAVE NO CONTACT WHATSOEVER WITH OFFICIALDOM. NO MORE THAN A DOZEN PEOPLE WOULD EVEN KNOW YOU EXIST. I'D BE YOUR GO-BETWEEN WITH BETHELL, YOU WOULDN'T HAVE TO TALK TO HIM--BELIEVE ME, THAT WOULD BE IDEAL FOR YOU BOTH.
ONCE YOU WERE ASSIGNED YOUR TARGET, YOU'D HAVE ACCESS TO WHATEVER INTEL AND MUNITIONS YOU REQUIRED. YOU'D PLAN EACH OP YOURSELF, NO RED TAPE OR OTHER BULLSHIT TO DEAL WITH. DEPLOYMENT, TIMING, ACQUISITION AND EXTRACTION--EVERYTHING DONE THE WAY YOU WANT IT.
THAT'S THE ONLY WAY YOU WORK: I MADE THAT CLEAR.
IT'S THE COMPANY, FRANK.
THEY CAN GET YOU IN ANYWHERE.

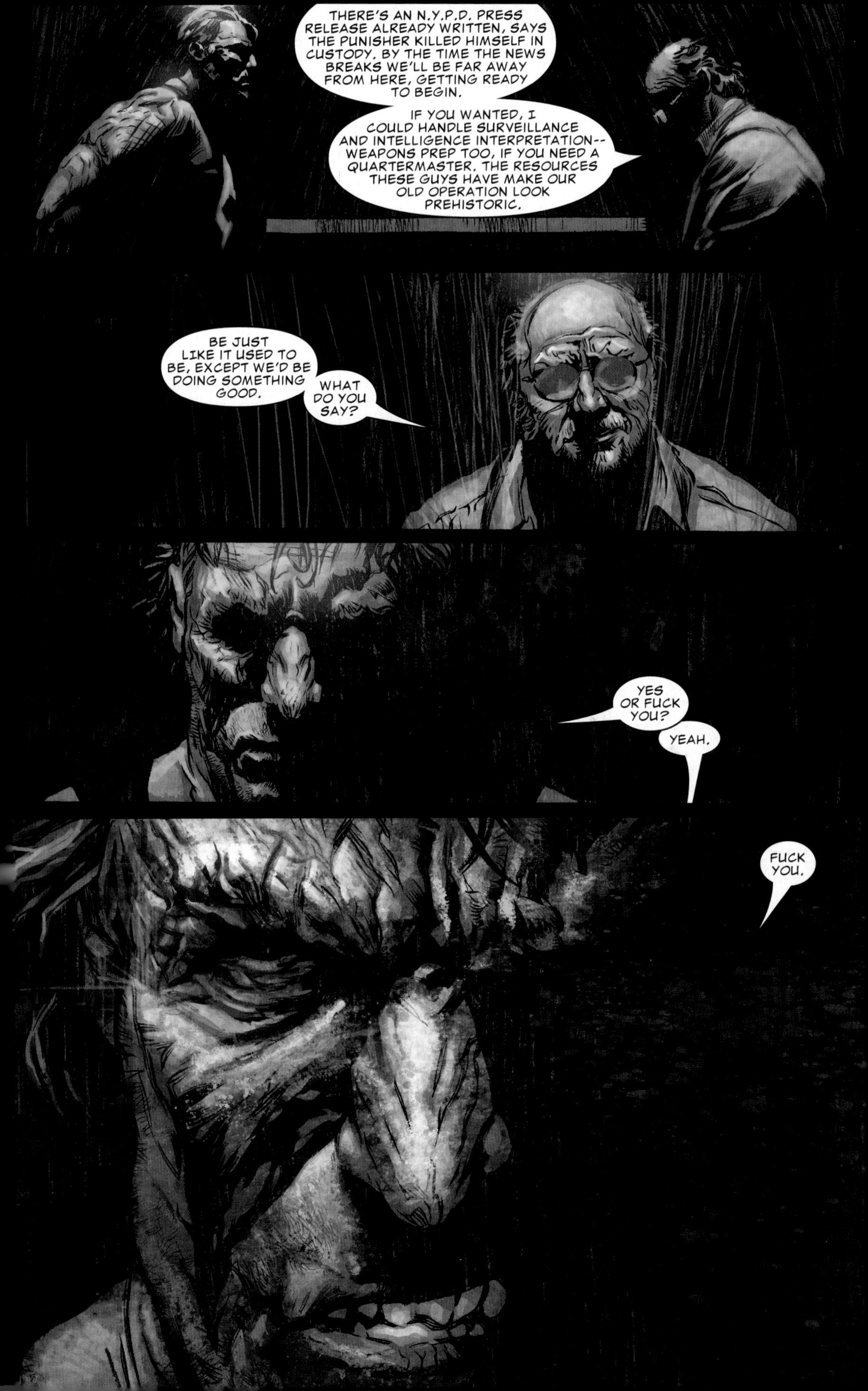
THERE'S AN N.Y.P.D. PRESS RELEASE ALREADY WRITTEN, SAYS THE PUNISHER KILLED HIMSELF IN CUSTODY. BY THE TIME THE NEWS BREAKS WE'LL BE FAR AWAY FROM HERE, GETTING READY TO BEGIN.
IF YOU WANTED, I COULD HANDLE SURVEILLANCE AND INTELLIGENCE INTERPRETATION-- WEAPONS PREP TOO, IF YOU NEED A QUARTERMASTER. THE RESOURCES THESE GUYS HAVE MAKE OUR OLD OPERATION LOOK PREHISTORIC.
BE JUST LIKE IT USED TO BE, EXCEPT WE'D BE DOING SOMETHING GOOD.
WHAT DO YOU SAY?
YES OR FUCK YOU?
YEAH.
FUCK YOU.

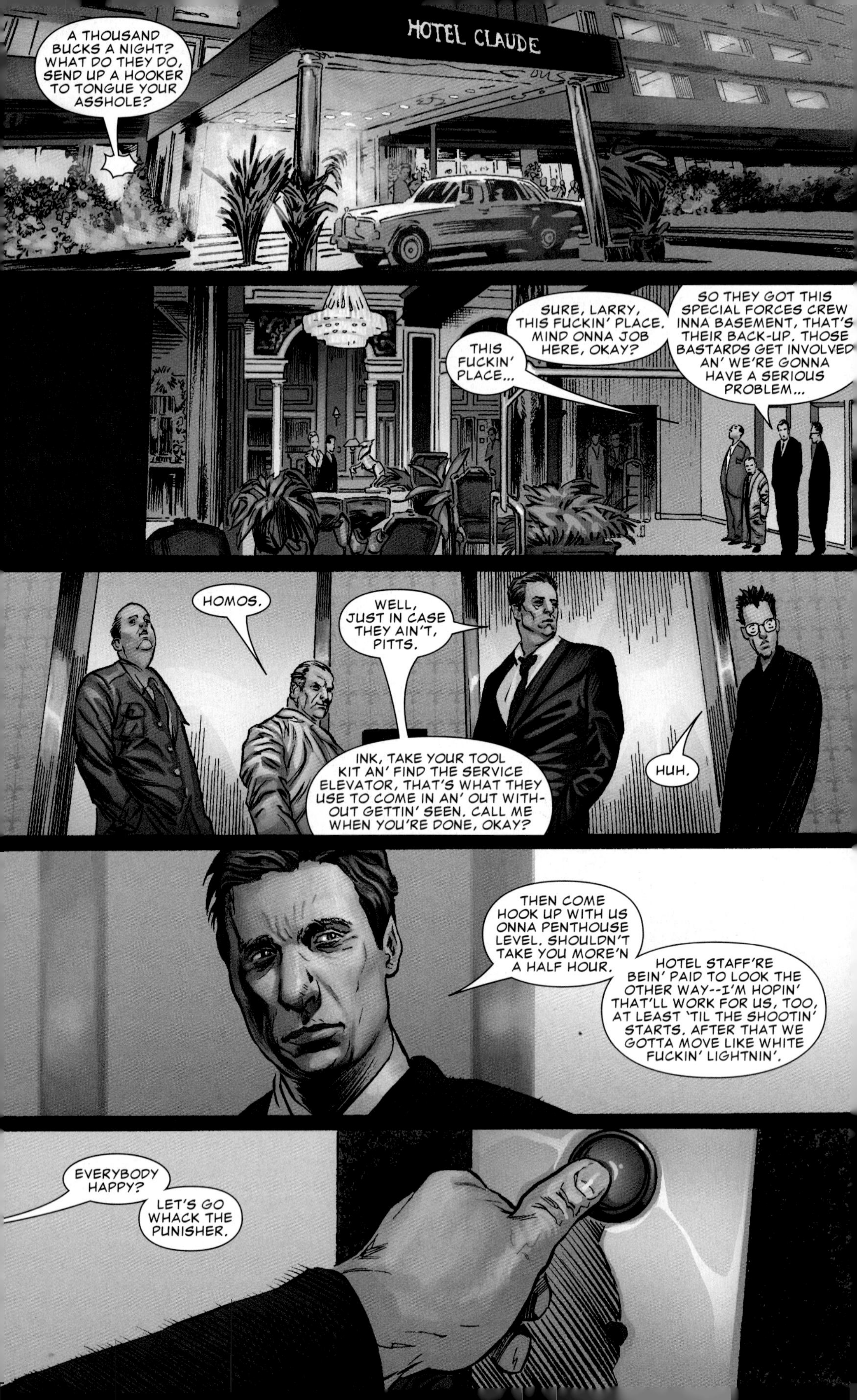
HOTEL CLAUDE
A THOUSAND BUCKS A NIGHT? WHAT DO THEY DO, SEND UP A HOOKER TO TONGUE YOUR ASSHOLE?
SO THEY GOT THIS SPECIAL FORCES CREW INNA BASEMENT, THAT'S THEIR BACK-UP. THOSE BASTARDS GET INVOLVED AN' WE'RE GONNA HAVE A SERIOUS PROBLEM...
SURE, LARRY, THIS FUCKIN' PLACE. MIND ONNA JOB HERE, OKAY?
THIS FUCKIN' PLACE...
HOMOS.
WELL, JUST IN CASE THEY AIN'T, PITTS.
INK, TAKE YOUR TOOL KIT AN' FIND THE SERVICE ELEVATOR, THAT'S WHAT THEY USE TO COME IN AN' OUT WITH-OUT GETTIN' SEEN. CALL ME WHEN YOU'RE DONE, OKAY?
HUH.
THEN COME HOOK UP WITH US ONNA PENTHOUSE LEVEL. SHOULDN'T TAKE YOU MORE'N A HALF HOUR.
HOTEL STAFF'RE BEIN' PAID TO LOOK THE OTHER WAY--I'M HOPIN' THAT'LL WORK FOR US, TOO, AT LEAST 'TIL THE SHOOTIN' STARTS. AFTER THAT WE GOTTA MOVE LIKE WHITE FUCKIN' LIGHTNIN'.
EVERYBODY HAPPY?
LET'S GO WHACK THE PUNISHER.

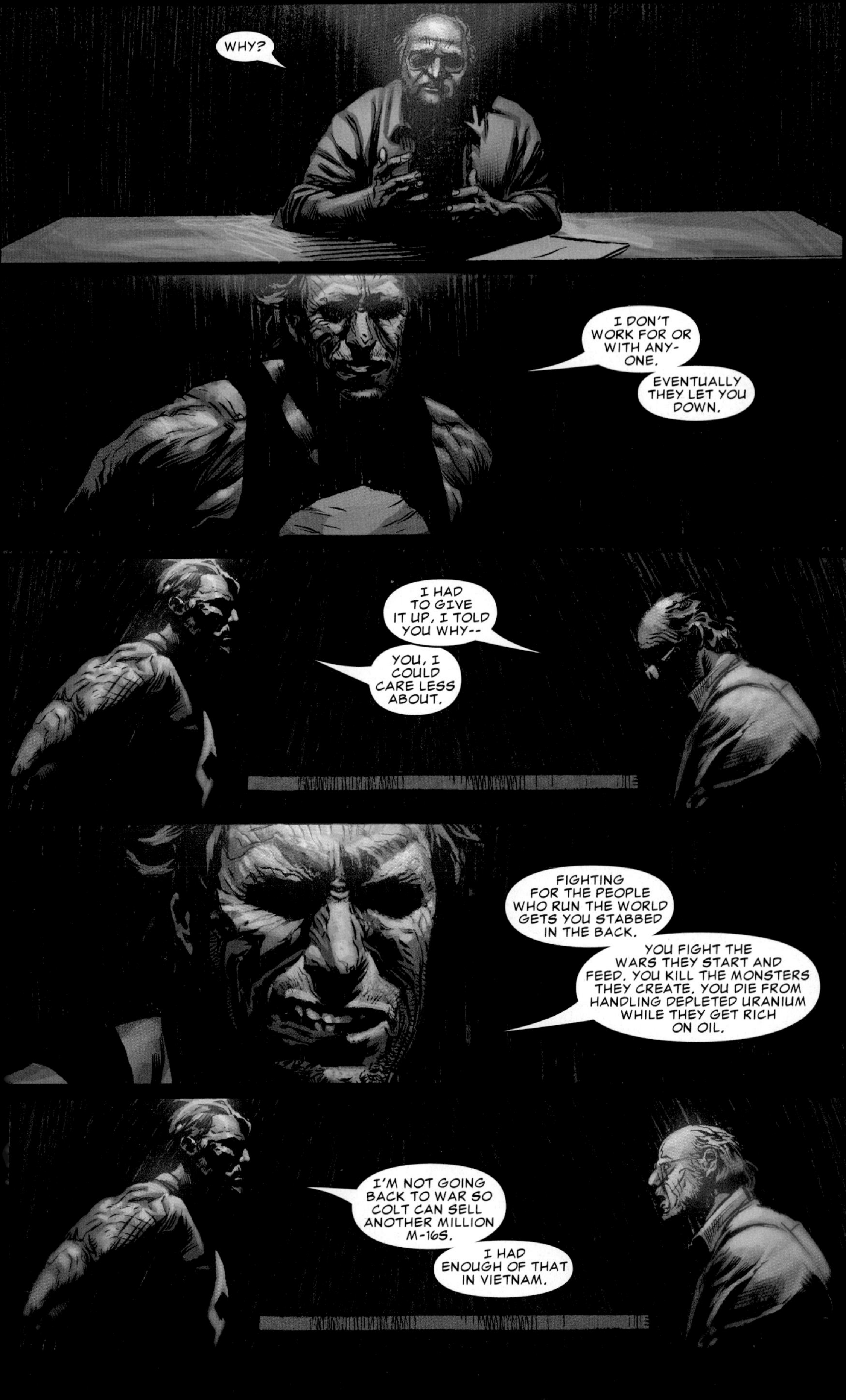
WHY?
I DON'T WORK FOR OR WITH ANY-ONE.
EVENTUALLY THEY LET YOU DOWN.
I HAD TO GIVE IT UP, I TOLD YOU WHY--
YOU, I COULD CARE LESS ABOUT.
FIGHTING FOR THE PEOPLE WHO RUN THE WORLD GETS YOU STABBED IN THE BACK.
YOU FIGHT THE WARS THEY START AND FEED. YOU KILL THE MONSTERS THEY CREATE. YOU DIE FROM HANDLING DEPLETED URANIUM WHILE THEY GET RICH ON OIL.
I'M NOT GOING BACK TO WAR SO COLT CAN SELL ANOTHER MILLION M-16S.
I HAD ENOUGH OF THAT IN VIETNAM.

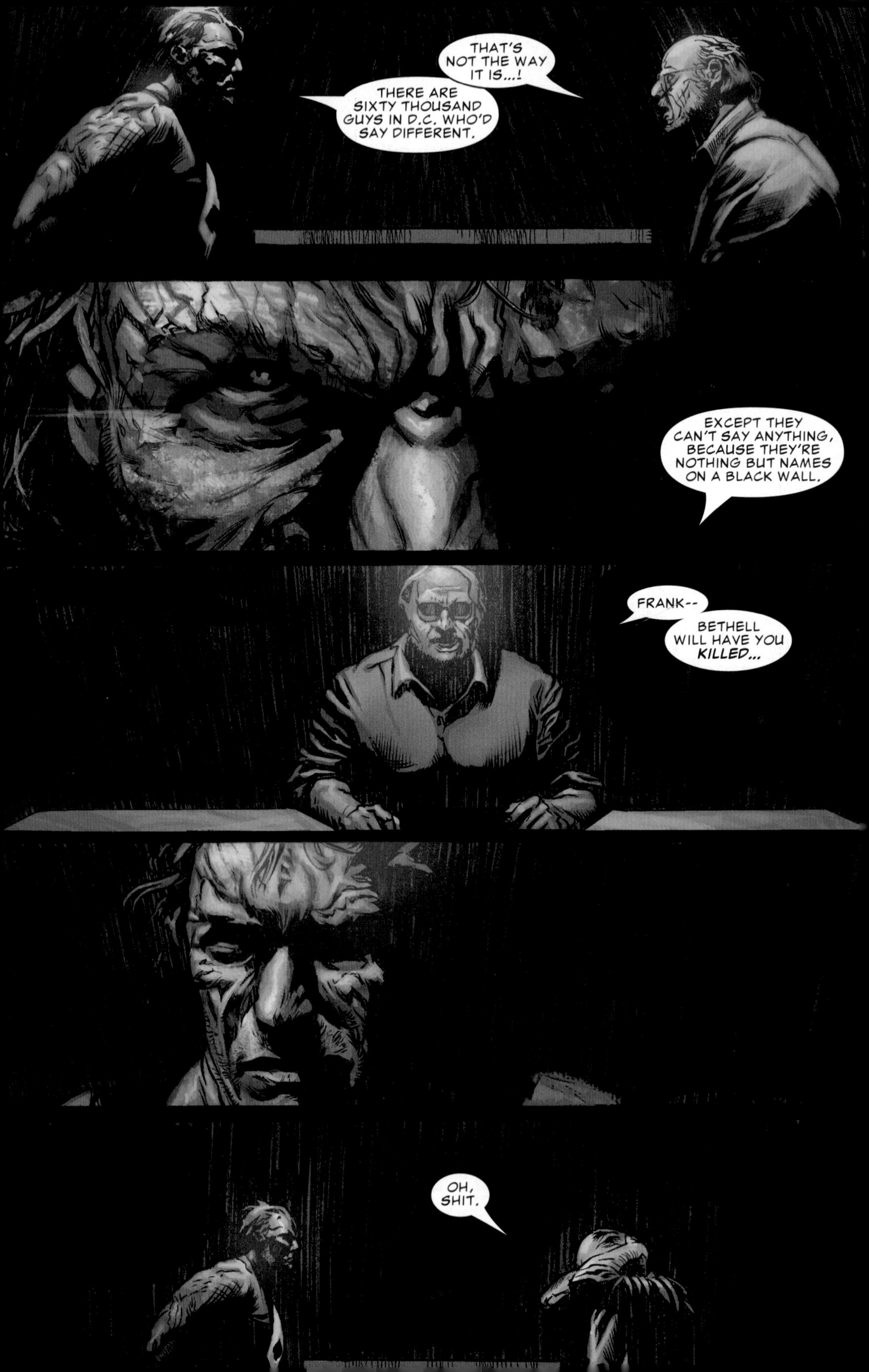
THAT'S NOT THE WAY IT IS...!
THERE ARE SIXTY THOUSAND GUYS IN D.C. WHO'D SAY DIFFERENT.
EXCEPT THEY CAN'T SAY ANYTHING, BECAUSE THEY'RE NOTHING BUT NAMES ON A BLACK WALL.
FRANK--
BETHELL WILL HAVE YOU *KILLED...*
OH, SHIT.

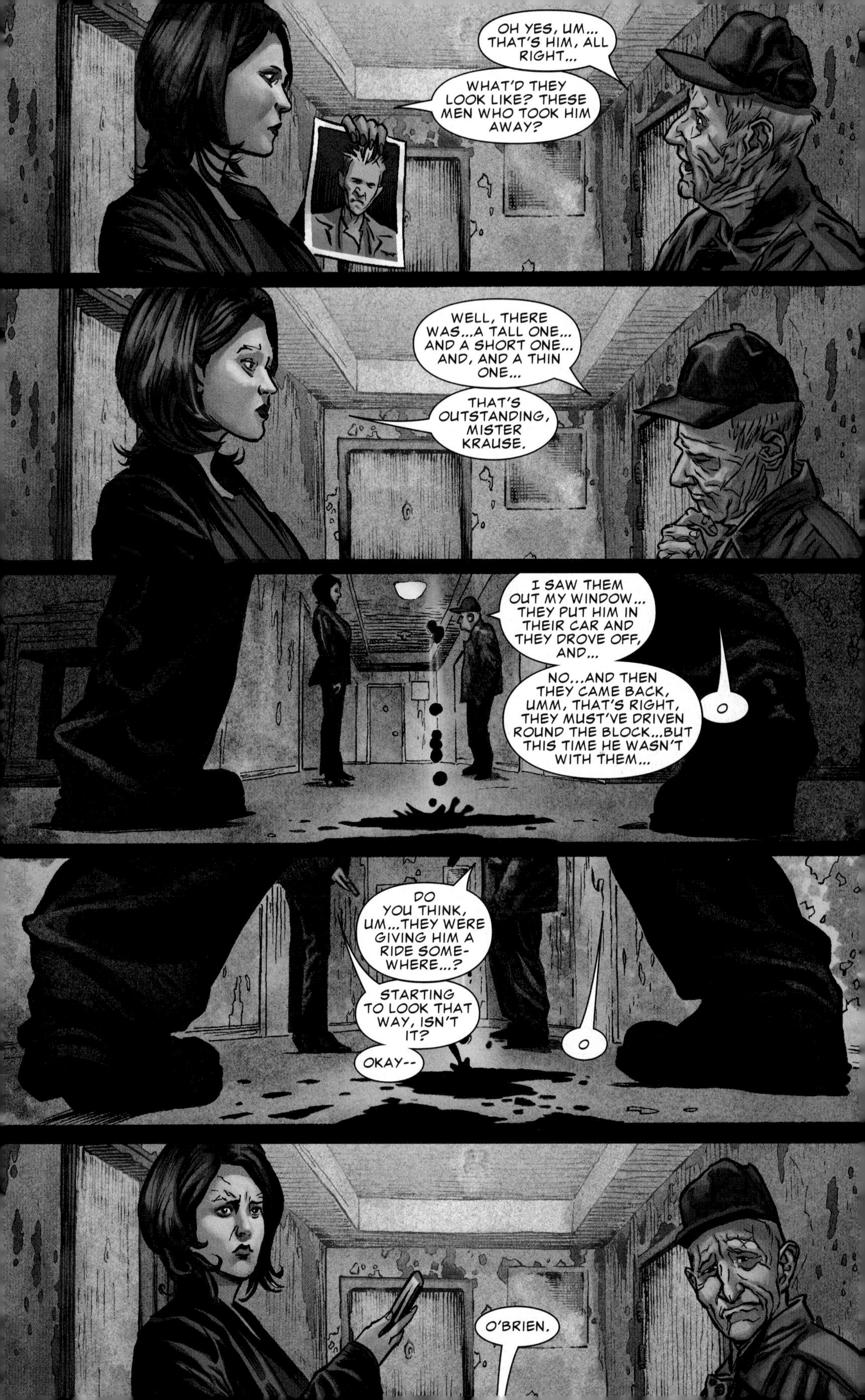
OH YES, UM... THAT'S HIM, ALL RIGHT...
WHAT'D THEY LOOK LIKE? THESE MEN WHO TOOK HIM AWAY?
WELL, THERE WAS...A TALL ONE... AND A SHORT ONE... AND, AND A THIN ONE...
THAT'S OUTSTANDING, MISTER KRAUSE.
I SAW THEM OUT MY WINDOW... THEY PUT HIM IN THEIR CAR AND THEY DROVE OFF, AND...
NO...AND THEN THEY CAME BACK, UMM, THAT'S RIGHT, THEY MUST'VE DRIVEN ROUND THE BLOCK...BUT THIS TIME HE WASN'T WITH THEM...
DO YOU THINK, UM...THEY WERE GIVING HIM A RIDE SOME-WHERE...?
STARTING TO LOOK THAT WAY, ISN'T IT?
OKAY--
O'BRIEN.

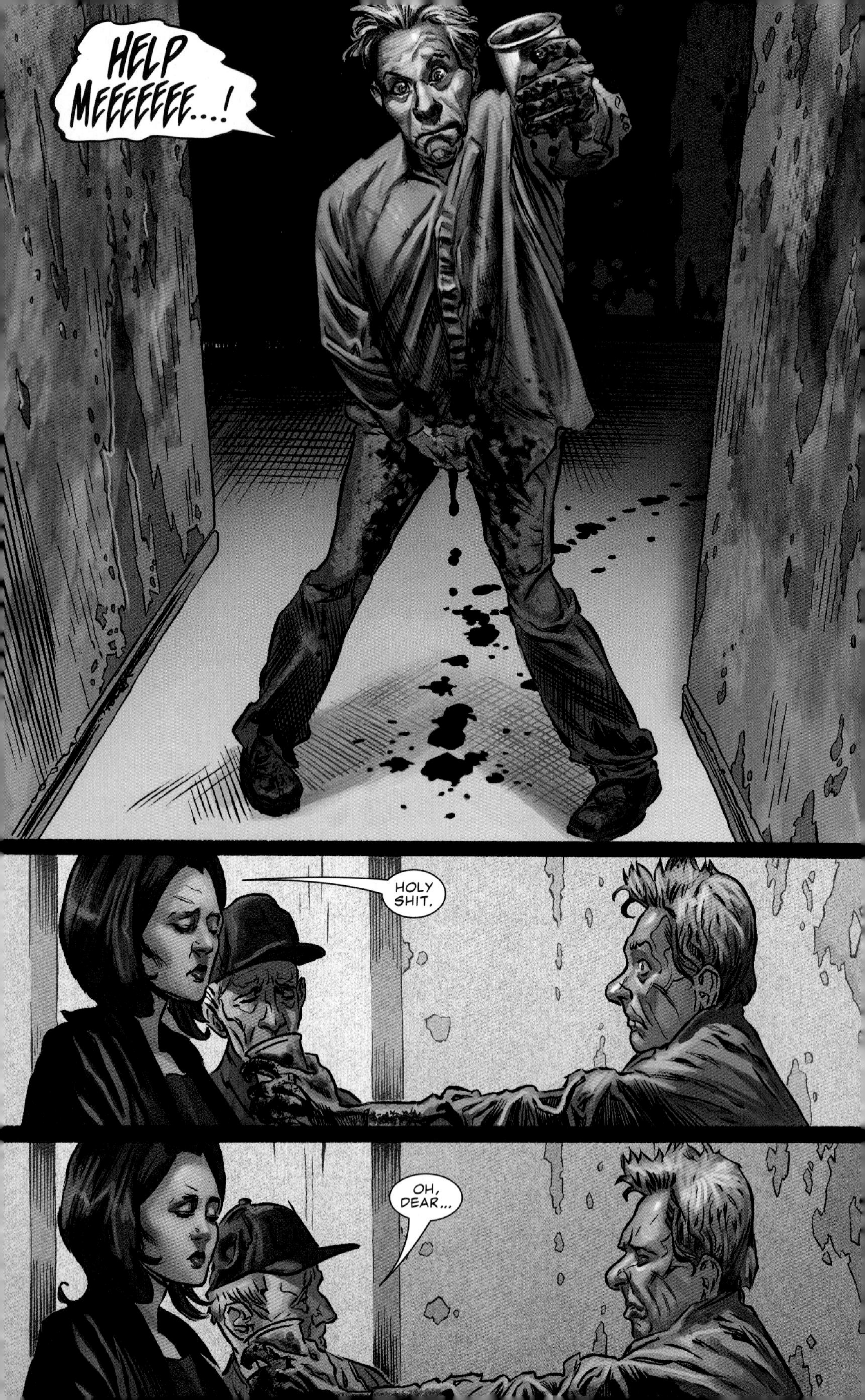
HELP MEEEEEEE...!
HOLY SHIT.
OH, DEAR...

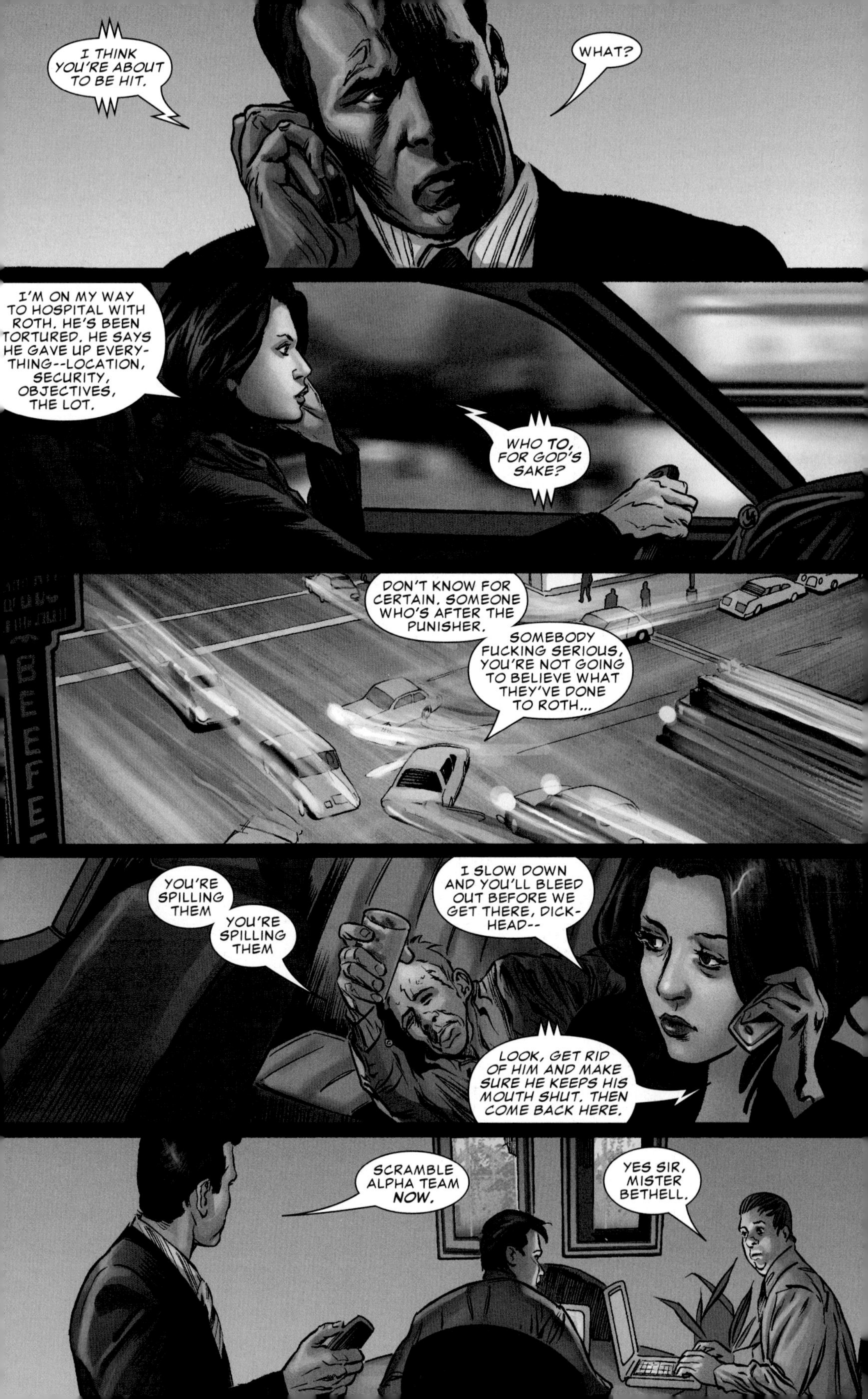
I THINK YOU'RE ABOUT TO BE HIT.
WHAT?
I'M ON MY WAY TO HOSPITAL WITH ROTH. HE'S BEEN TORTURED. HE SAYS HE GAVE UP EVERY-THING--LOCATION, SECURITY, OBJECTIVES, THE LOT.
WHO TO, FOR GOD'S SAKE?
DON'T KNOW FOR CERTAIN. SOMEONE WHO'S AFTER THE PUNISHER.
SOMEBODY FUCKING SERIOUS, YOU'RE NOT GOING TO BELIEVE WHAT THEY'VE DONE TO ROTH...
YOU'RE SPILLING THEM
YOU'RE SPILLING THEM
I SLOW DOWN AND YOU'LL BLEED OUT BEFORE WE GET THERE, DICK-HEAD--
LOOK, GET RID OF HIM AND MAKE SURE HE KEEPS HIS MOUTH SHUT. THEN COME BACK HERE.
SCRAMBLE ALPHA TEAM NOW.
YES SIR, MISTER BETHELL.

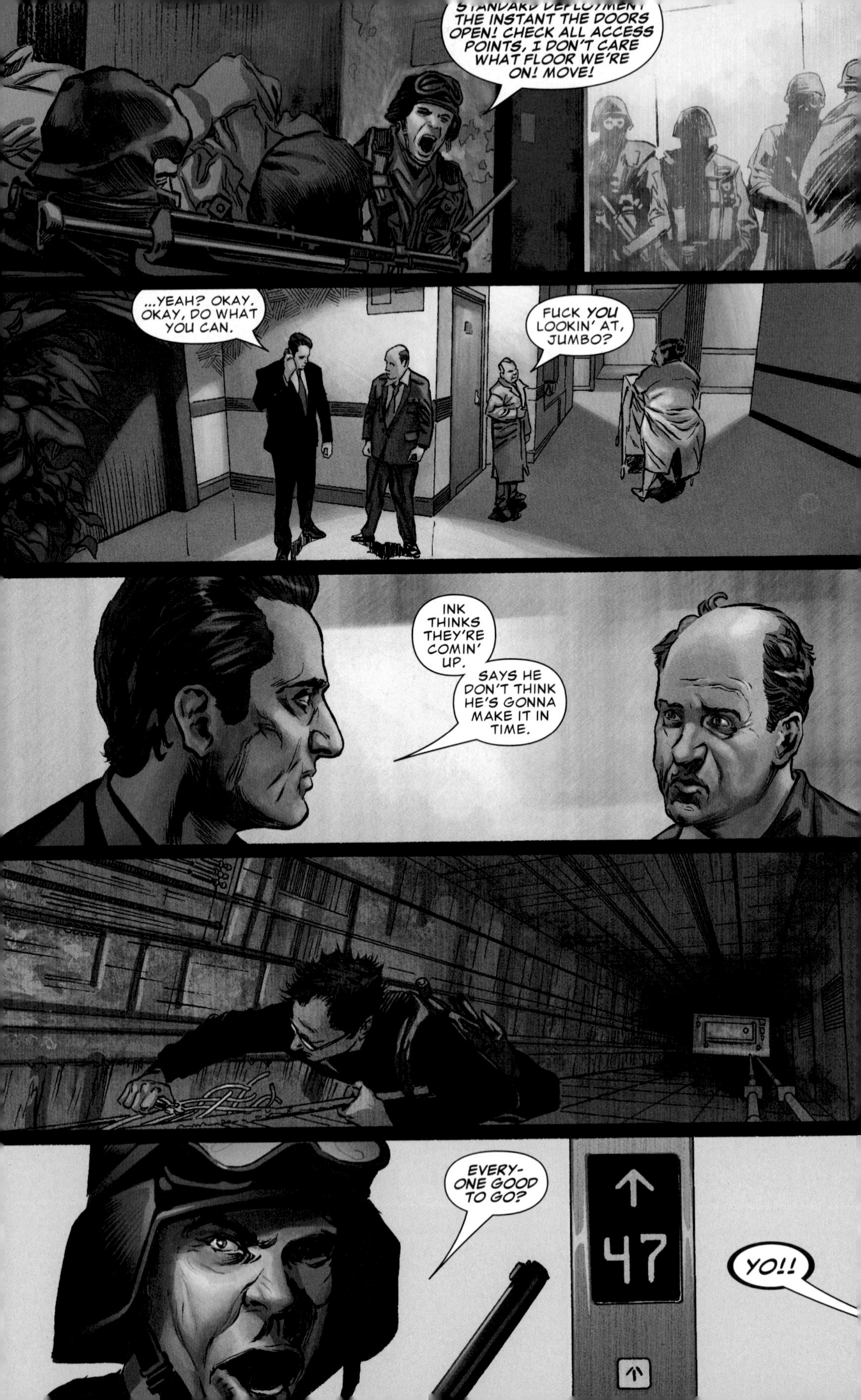
STANDARD DEPLOYMENT THE INSTANT THE DOORS OPEN! CHECK ALL ACCESS POINTS, I DON'T CARE WHAT FLOOR WE'RE ON! MOVE!
...YEAH? OKAY. OKAY, DO WHAT YOU CAN.
FUCK *YOU* LOOKIN' AT, JUMBO?
INK THINKS THEY'RE COMIN' UP.
SAYS HE DON'T THINK HE'S GONNA MAKE IT IN TIME.
EVERY-ONE GOOD TO GO?
47
YO!!

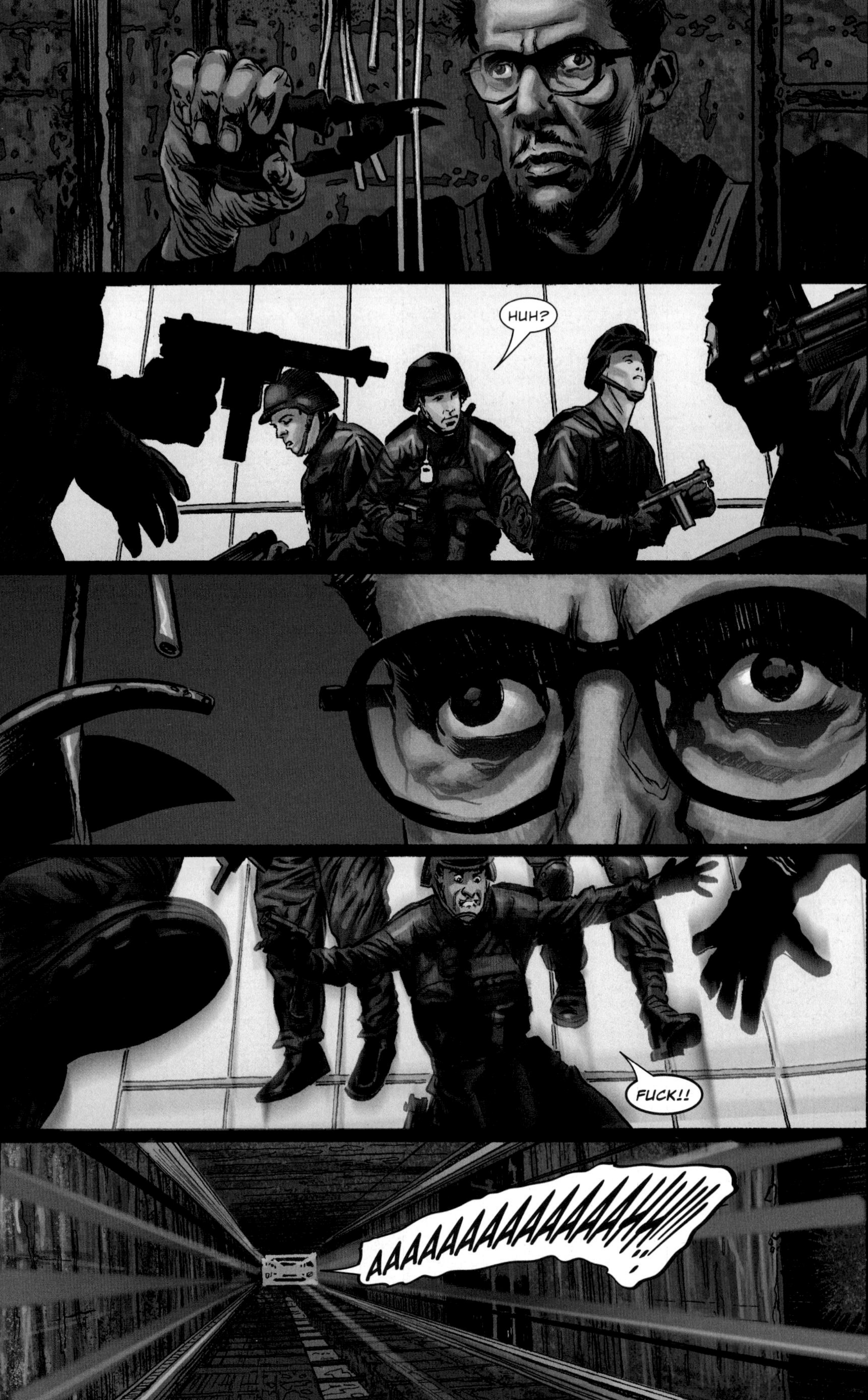
HUH?
FUCK!!
AAAAAAAAAAAAAAAAH!!!

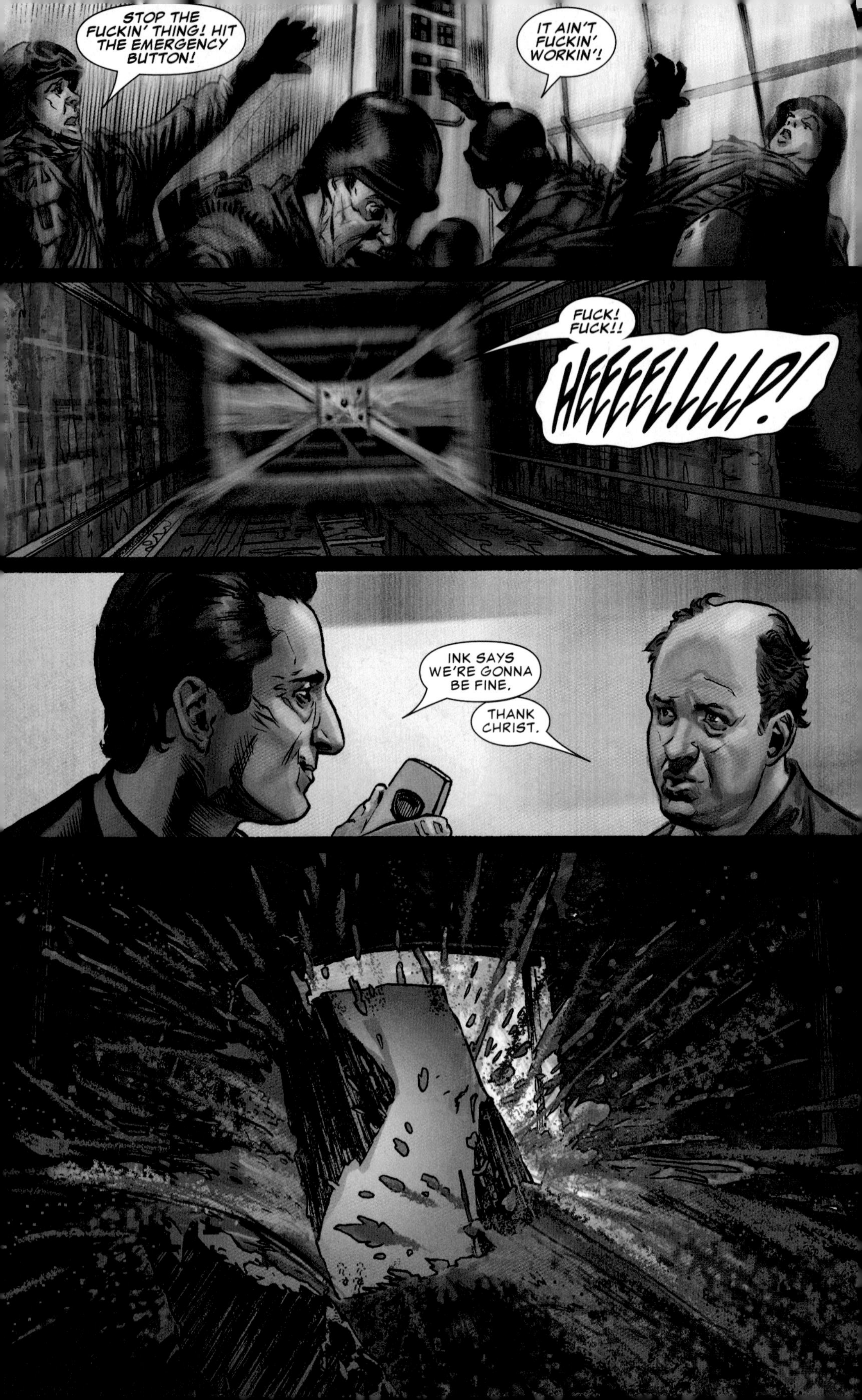
STOP THE FUCKIN' THING! HIT THE EMERGENCY BUTTON!
IT AIN'T FUCKIN' WORKIN'!
FUCK! FUCK!!
HEEEELLLP!
INK SAYS WE'RE GONNA BE FINE.
THANK CHRIST.

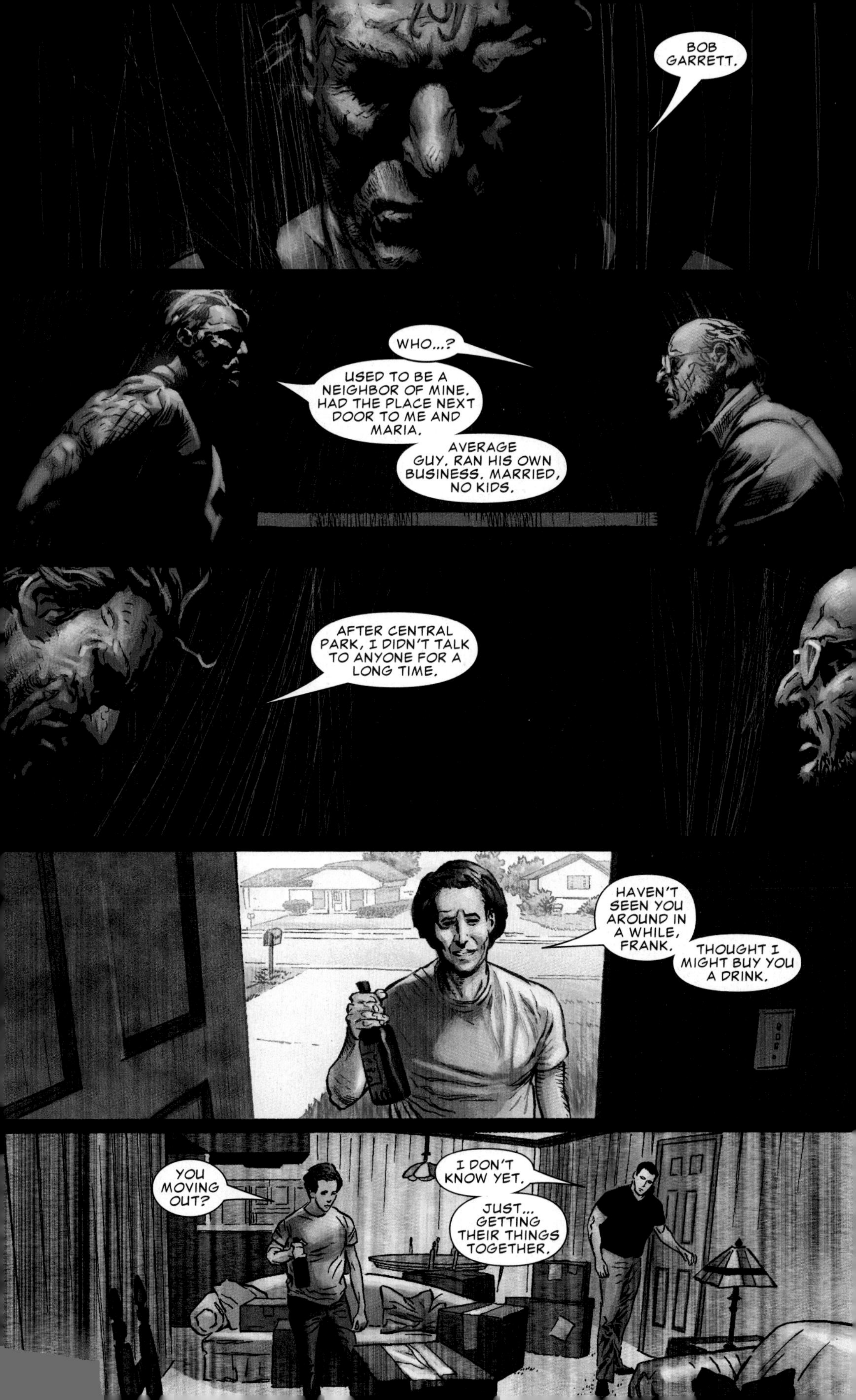
BOB GARRETT.
WHO...?
USED TO BE A NEIGHBOR OF MINE. HAD THE PLACE NEXT DOOR TO ME AND MARIA.
AVERAGE GUY. RAN HIS OWN BUSINESS. MARRIED, NO KIDS.
AFTER CENTRAL PARK, I DIDN'T TALK TO ANYONE FOR A LONG TIME.
HAVEN'T SEEN YOU AROUND IN A WHILE, FRANK.
THOUGHT I MIGHT BUY YOU A DRINK.
YOU MOVING OUT?
I DON'T KNOW YET.
JUST... GETTING THEIR THINGS TOGETHER.

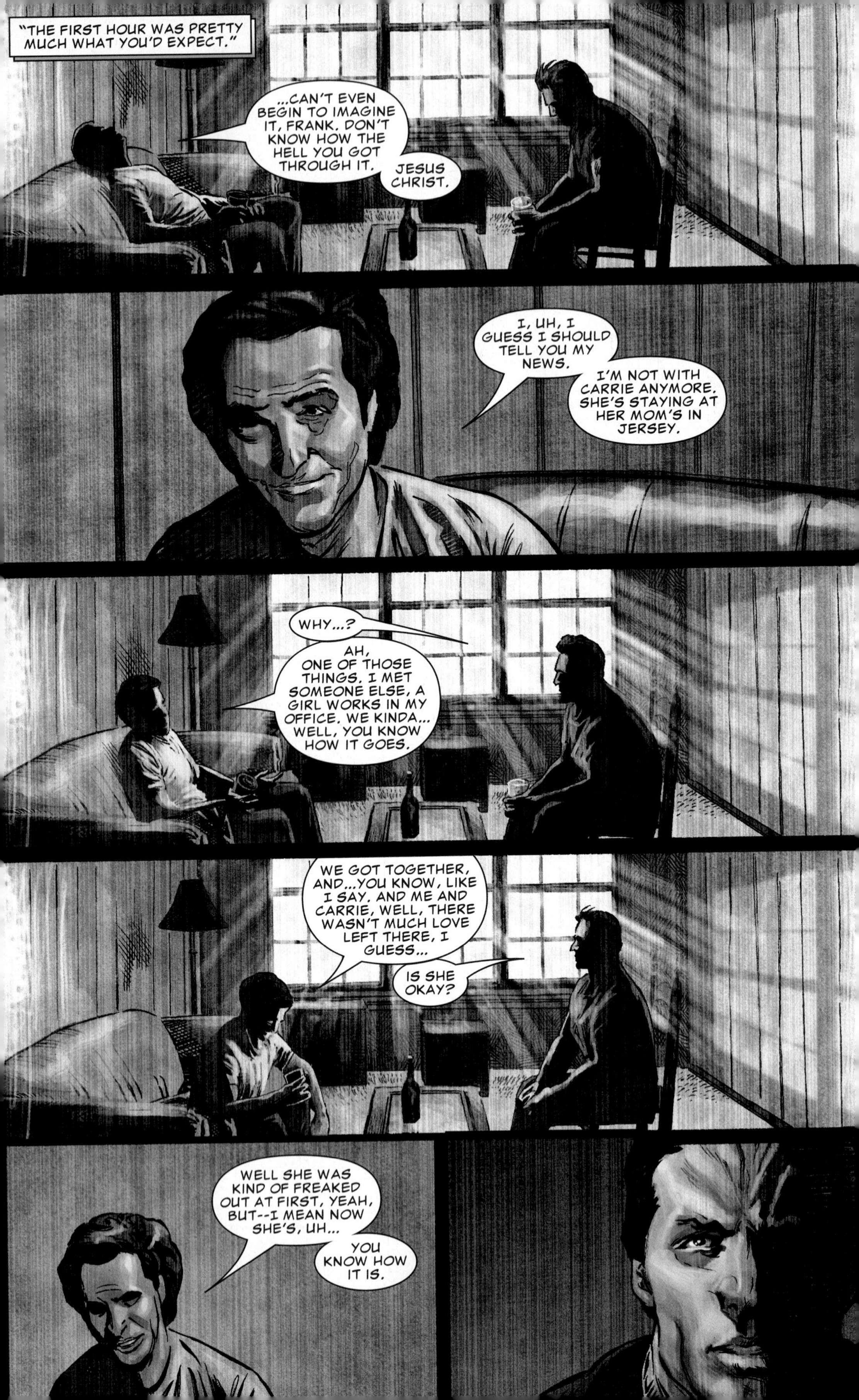
"THE FIRST HOUR WAS PRETTY MUCH WHAT YOU'D EXPECT."
...CAN'T EVEN BEGIN TO IMAGINE IT, FRANK. DON'T KNOW HOW THE HELL YOU GOT THROUGH IT.
JESUS CHRIST.
I, UH, I GUESS I SHOULD TELL YOU MY NEWS.
I'M NOT WITH CARRIE ANYMORE. SHE'S STAYING AT HER MOM'S IN JERSEY.
WHY...?
AH, ONE OF THOSE THINGS. I MET SOMEONE ELSE, A GIRL WORKS IN MY OFFICE. WE KINDA... WELL, YOU KNOW HOW IT GOES.
WE GOT TOGETHER, AND...YOU KNOW, LIKE I SAY. AND ME AND CARRIE, WELL, THERE WASN'T MUCH LOVE LEFT THERE, I GUESS...
IS SHE OKAY?
WELL SHE WAS KIND OF FREAKED OUT AT FIRST, YEAH, BUT--I MEAN NOW SHE'S, UH...
YOU KNOW HOW IT IS.

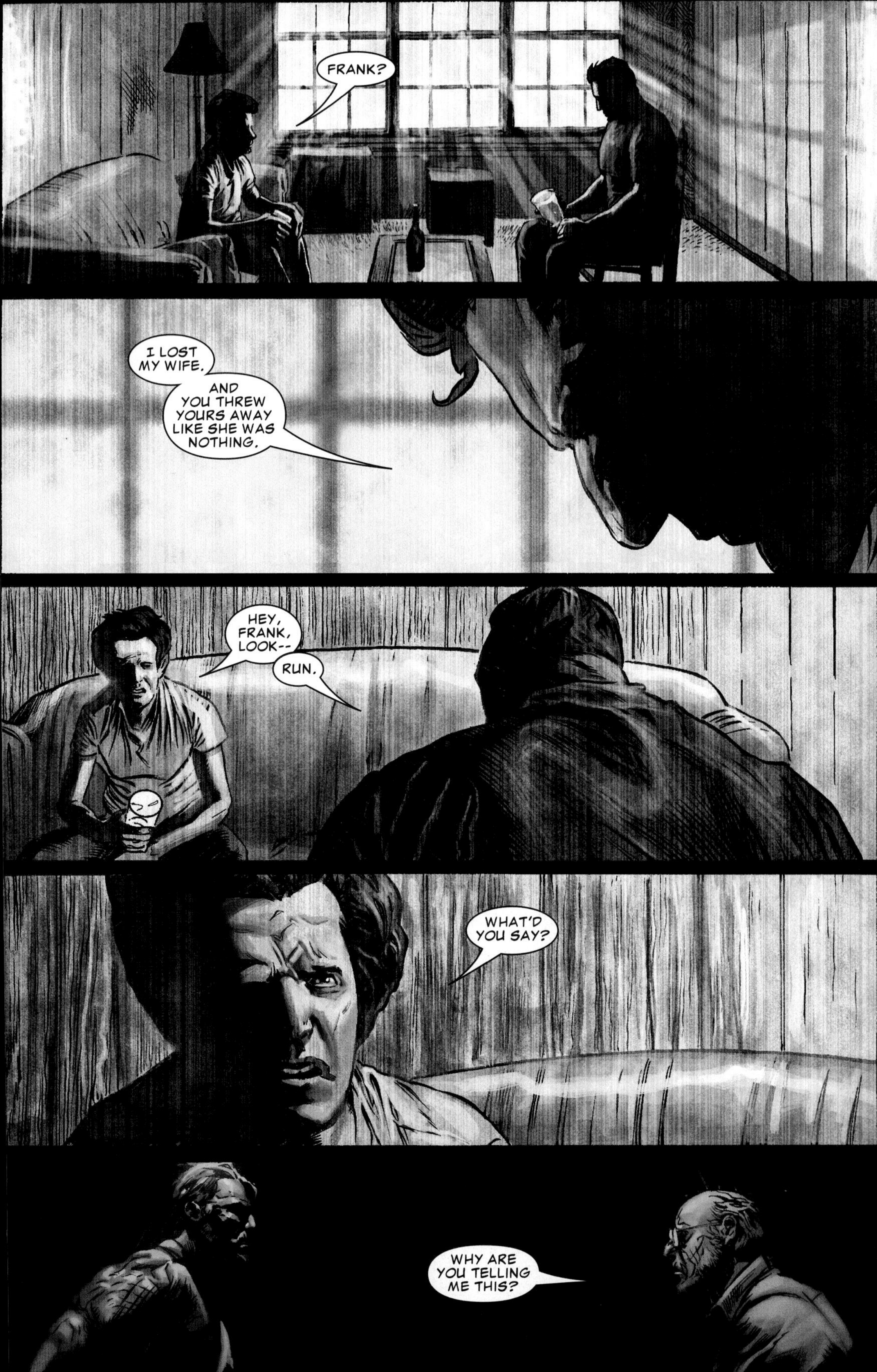
FRANK?
I LOST MY WIFE.
AND YOU THREW YOURS AWAY LIKE SHE WAS NOTHING.
HEY, FRANK, LOOK--
RUN.
WHAT'D YOU SAY?
WHY ARE YOU TELLING ME THIS?

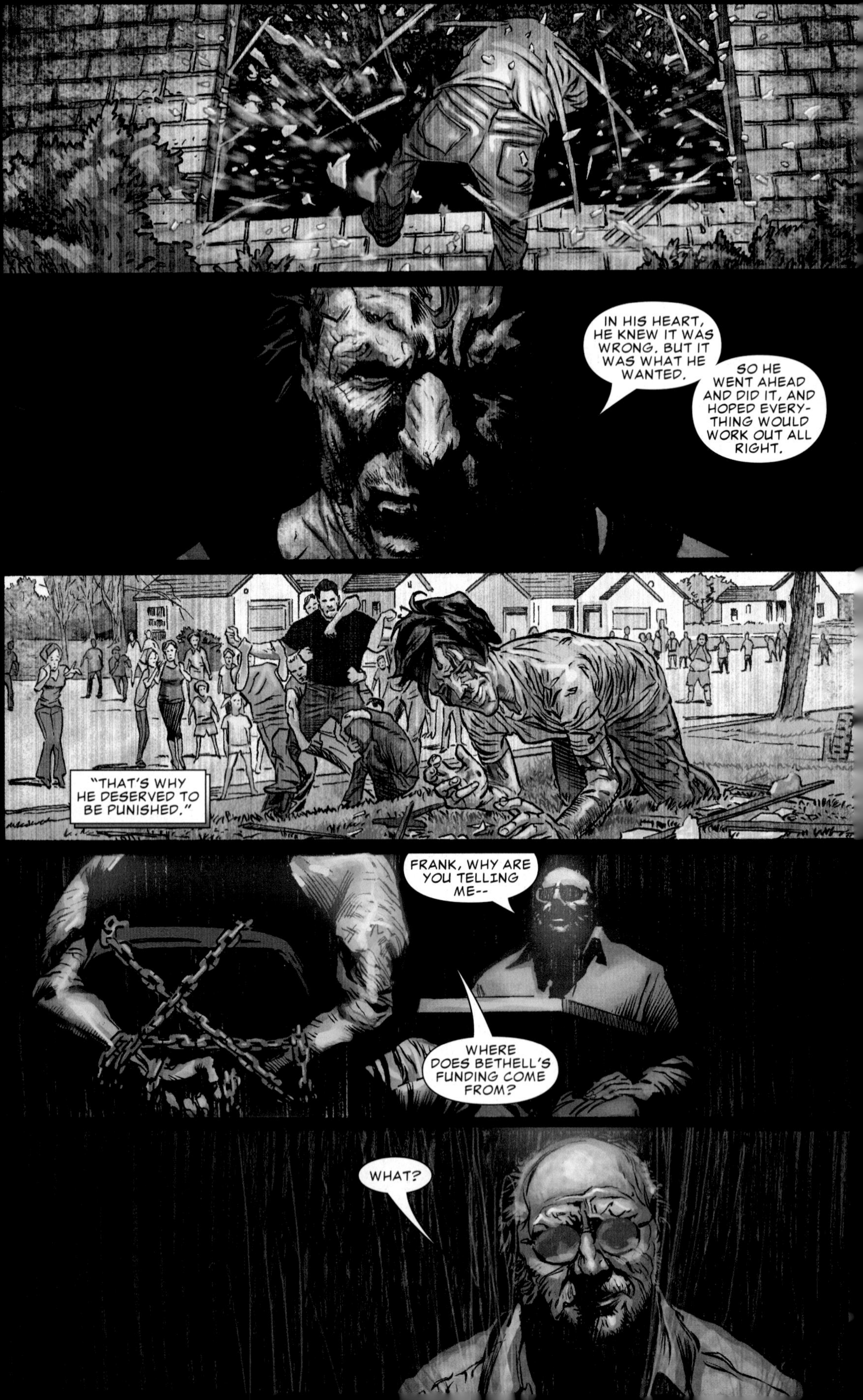
IN HIS HEART, HE KNEW IT WAS WRONG. BUT IT WAS WHAT HE WANTED.
SO HE WENT AHEAD AND DID IT, AND HOPED EVERY-THING WOULD WORK OUT ALL RIGHT.
"THAT'S WHY HE DESERVED TO BE PUNISHED."
FRANK, WHY ARE YOU TELLING ME--
WHERE DOES BETHELL'S FUNDING COME FROM?
WHAT?

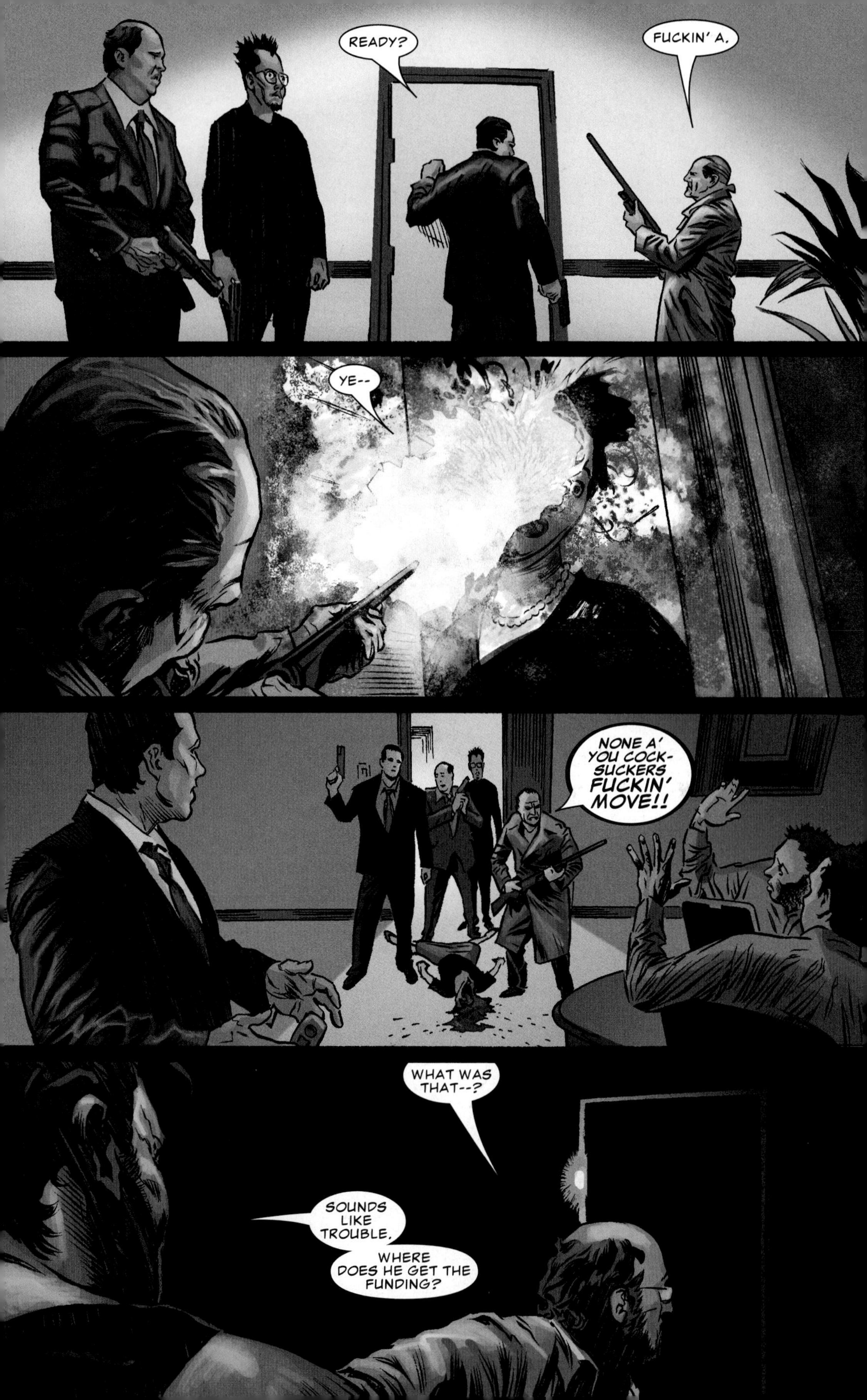
READY?
FUCKIN' A.
YE--
NONE A' YOU COCK-SUCKERS FUCKIN' MOVE!!
WHAT WAS THAT--?
SOUNDS LIKE TROUBLE.
WHERE DOES HE GET THE FUNDING?

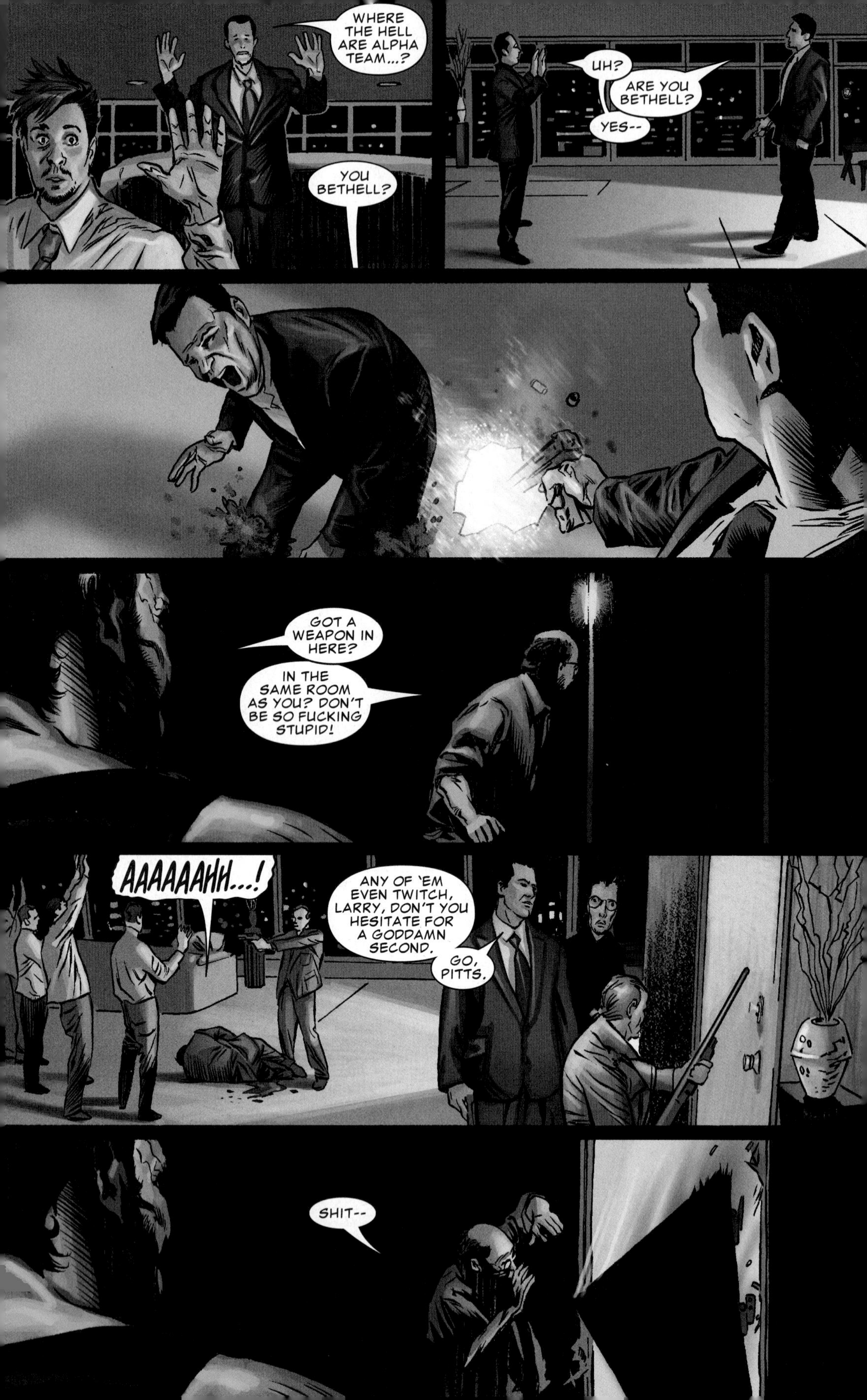
WHERE THE HELL ARE ALPHA TEAM...?
YOU BETHELL?
UH?
ARE YOU BETHELL?
YES--
GOT A WEAPON IN HERE?
IN THE SAME ROOM AS YOU? DON'T BE SO FUCKING STUPID!
AAAAAAHH...!
ANY OF 'EM EVEN TWITCH, LARRY, DON'T YOU HESITATE FOR A GODDAMN SECOND.
GO, PITTS.
SHIT--

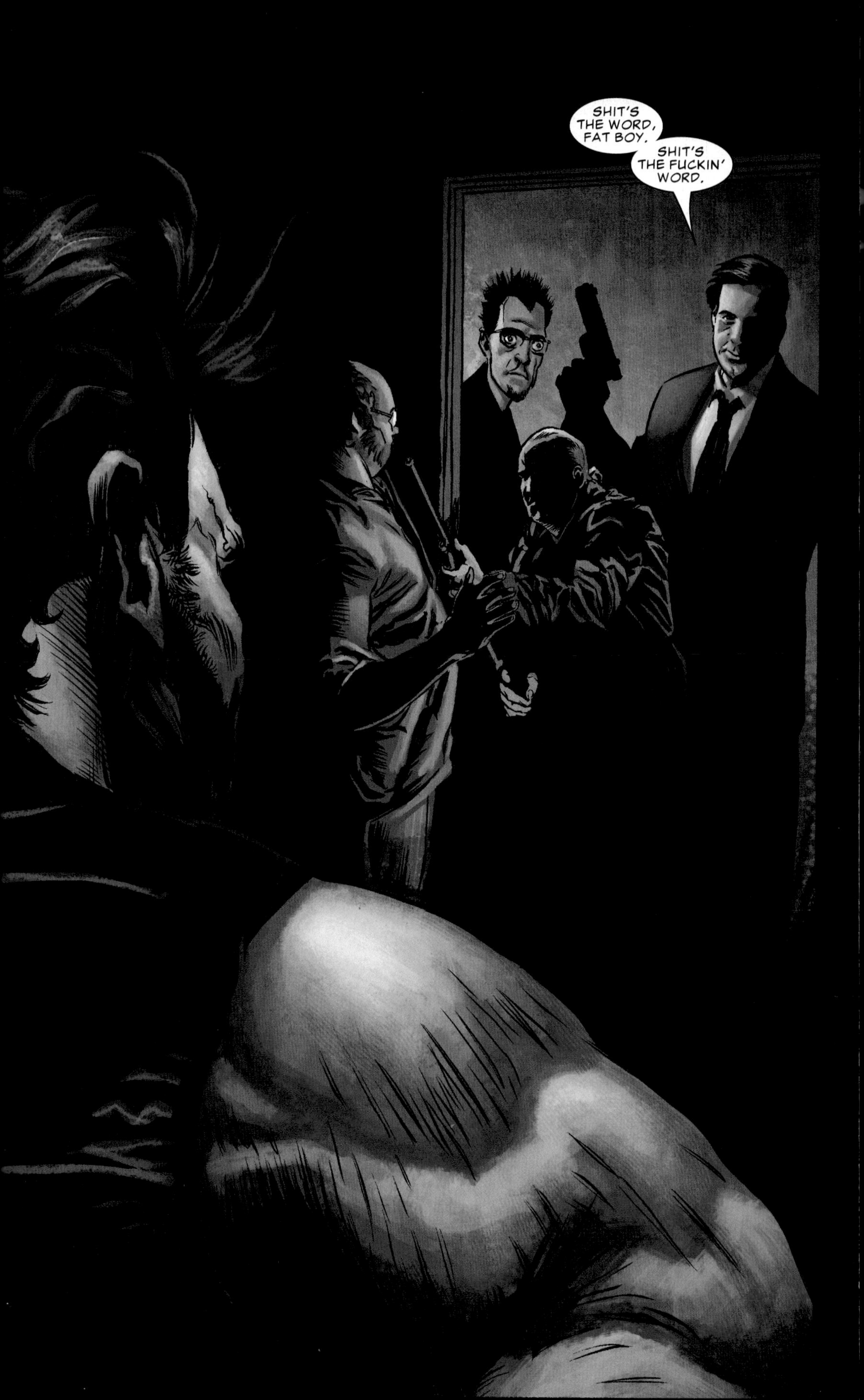
SHIT'S THE WORD, FAT BOY.
SHIT'S THE FUCKIN' WORD.

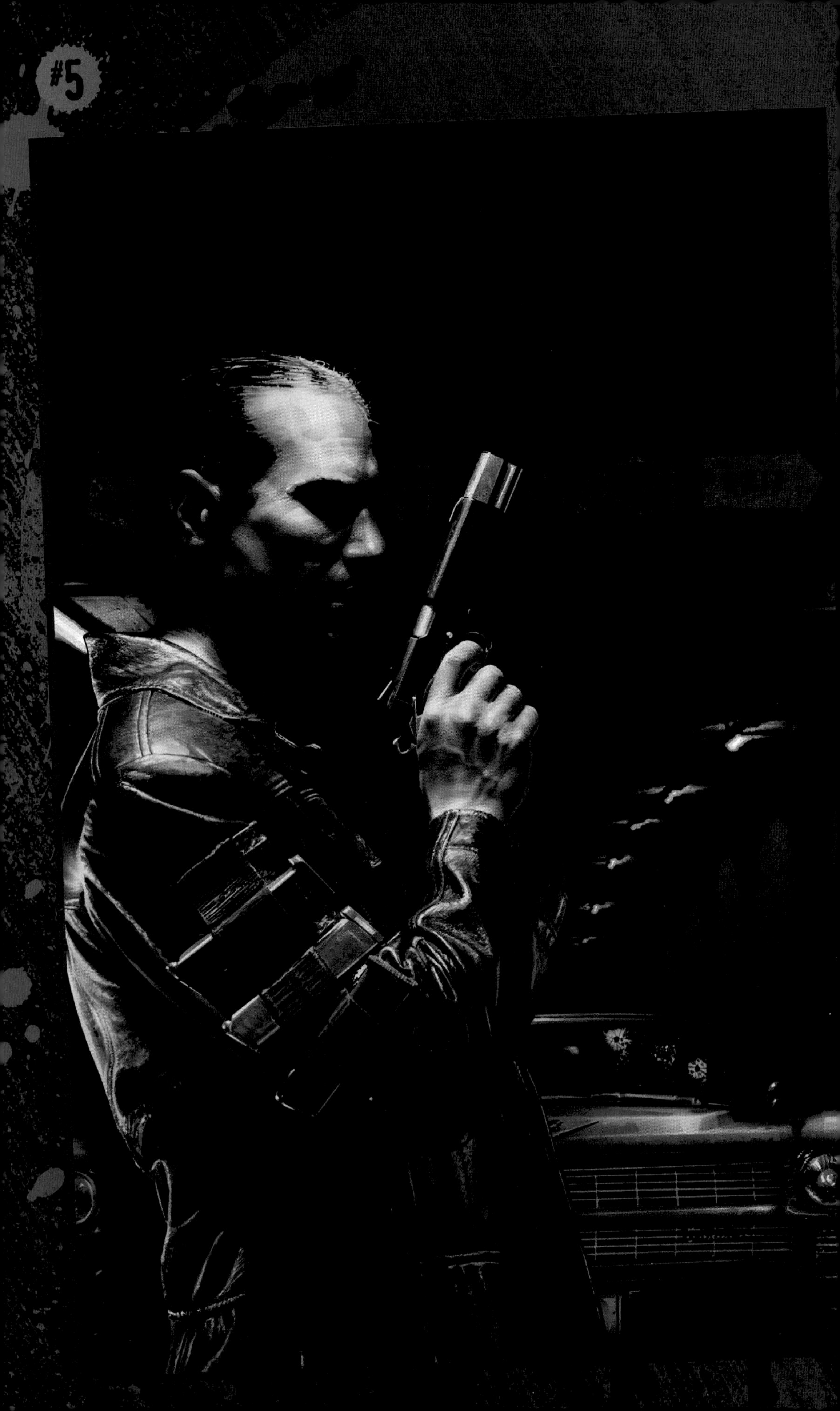
#5

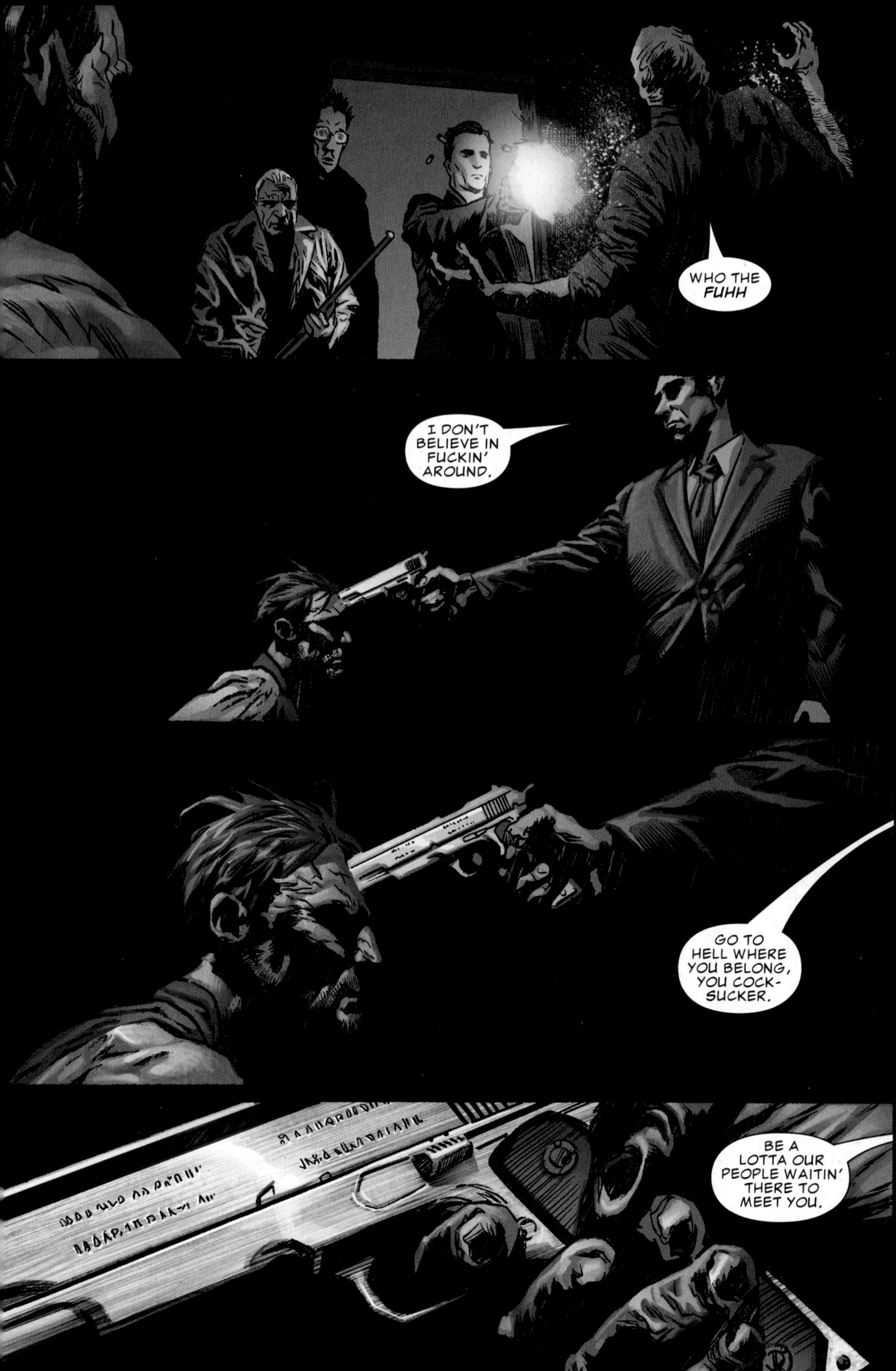
WHO THE FUHH
I DON'T BELIEVE IN FUCKIN' AROUND.
GO TO HELL WHERE YOU BELONG, YOU COCK-SUCKER.
BE A LOTTA OUR PEOPLE WAITIN' THERE TO MEET YOU.

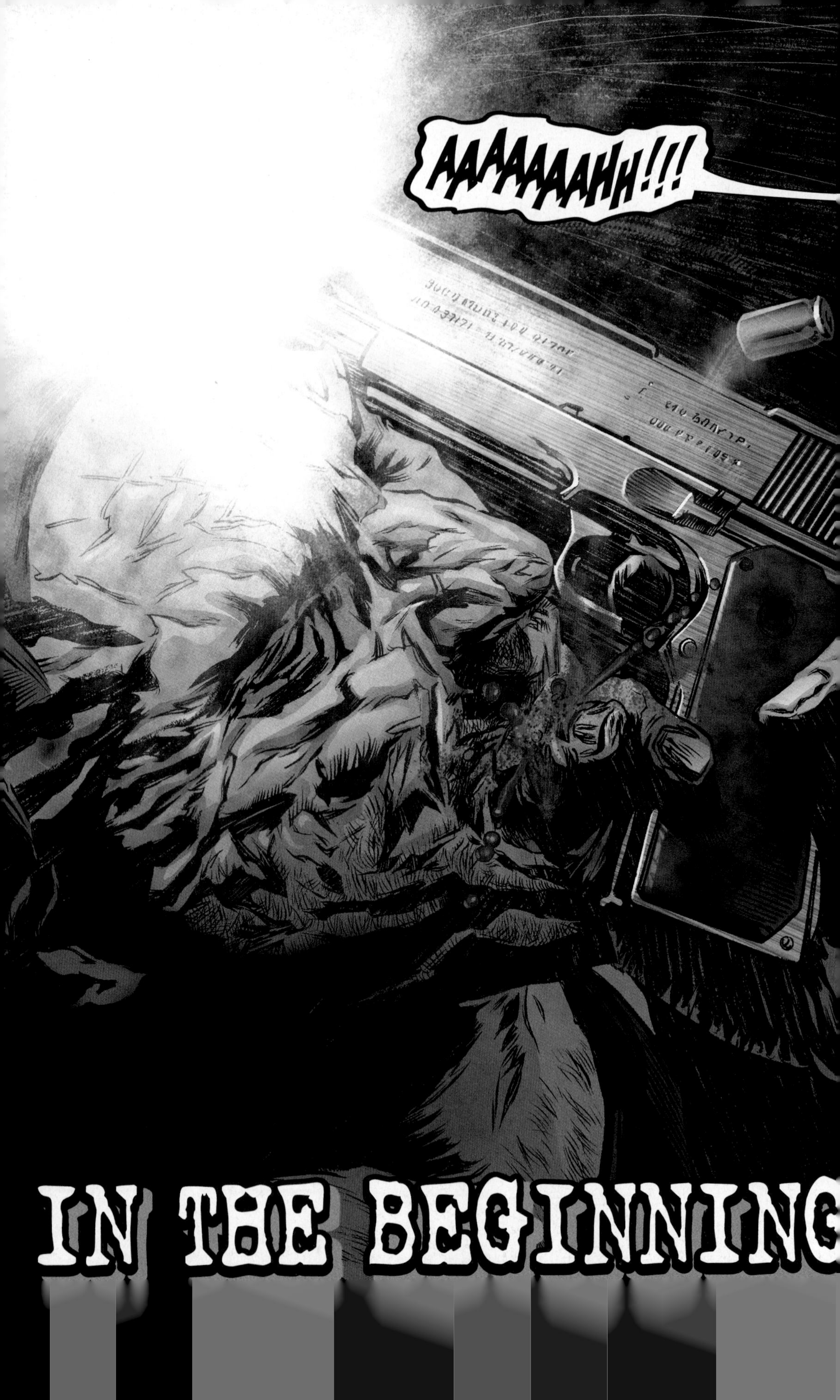
AAAAAAAHH!!!
IN THE BEGINNING

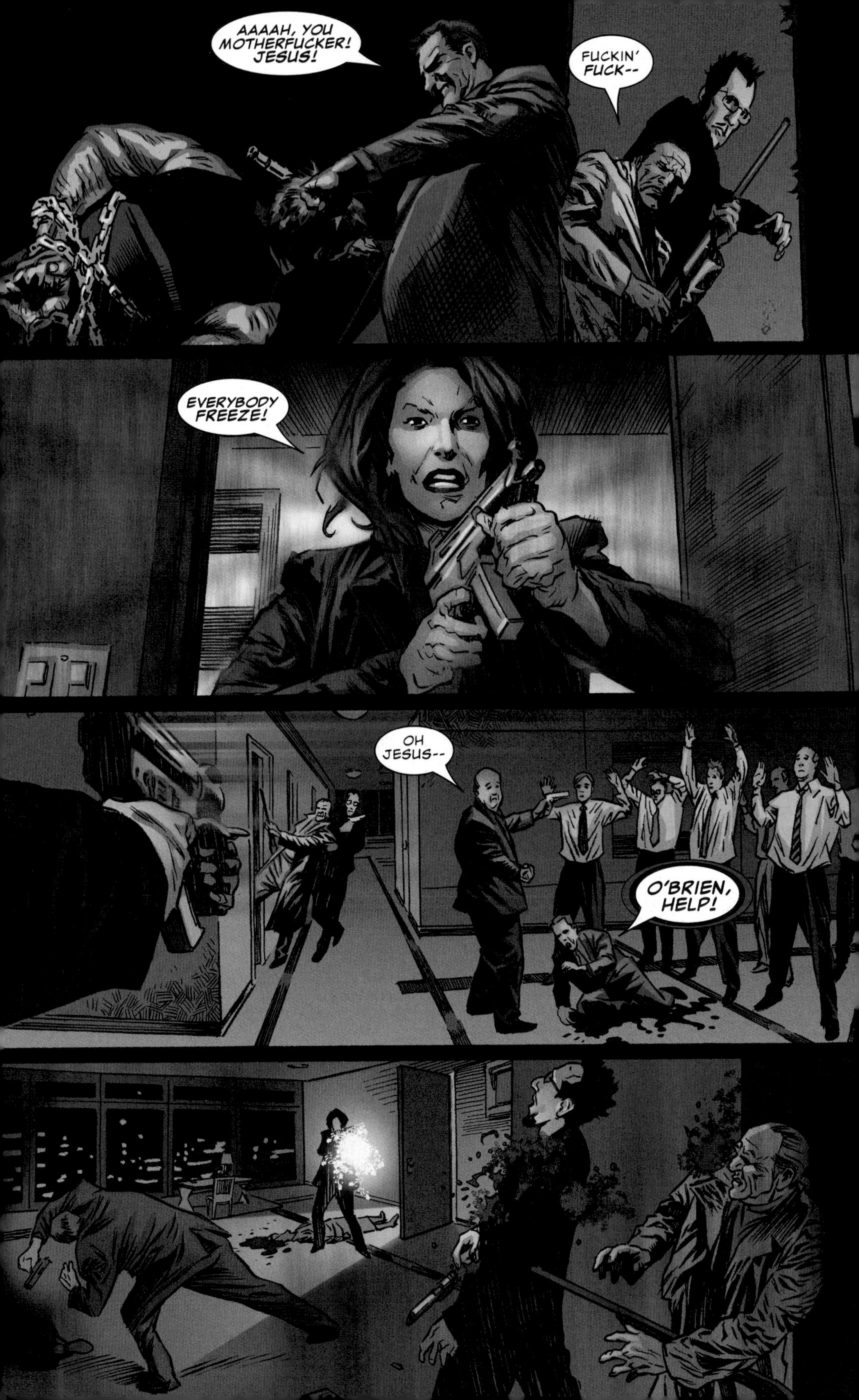
AAAAH, YOU MOTHERFUCKER! JESUS!
FUCKIN' FUCK--
EVERYBODY FREEZE!
OH JESUS--
O'BRIEN, HELP!

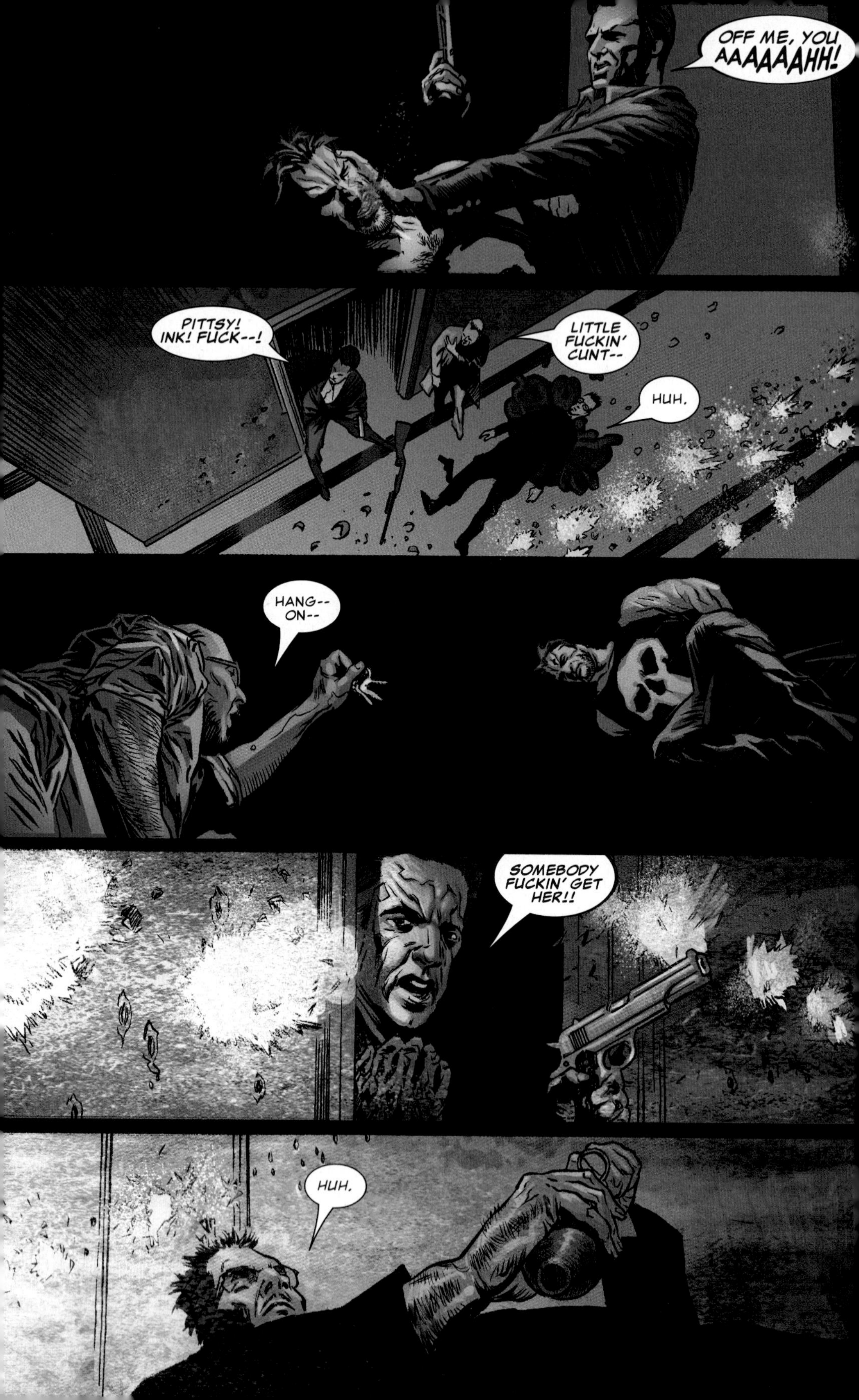
OFF ME, YOU AAAAAAHH!
PITTSY! INK! FUCK--!
LITTLE FUCKIN' CUNT--
HUH.
HANG-- ON--
SOMEBODY FUCKIN' GET HER!!
HUH.

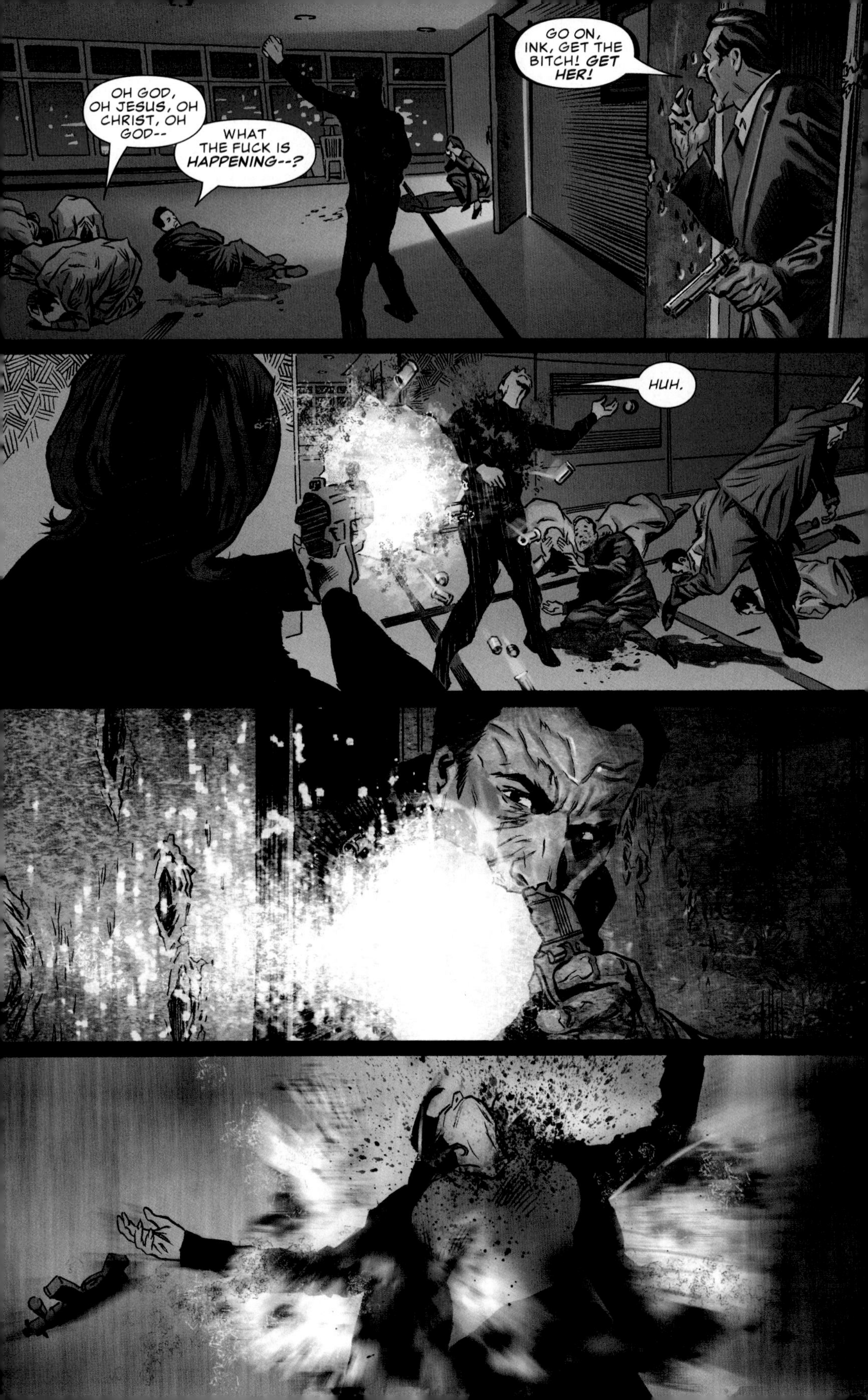
OH GOD, OH JESUS, OH CHRIST, OH GOD--
WHAT THE FUCK IS HAPPENING--?
GO ON, INK, GET THE BITCH! GET HER!
HUH.

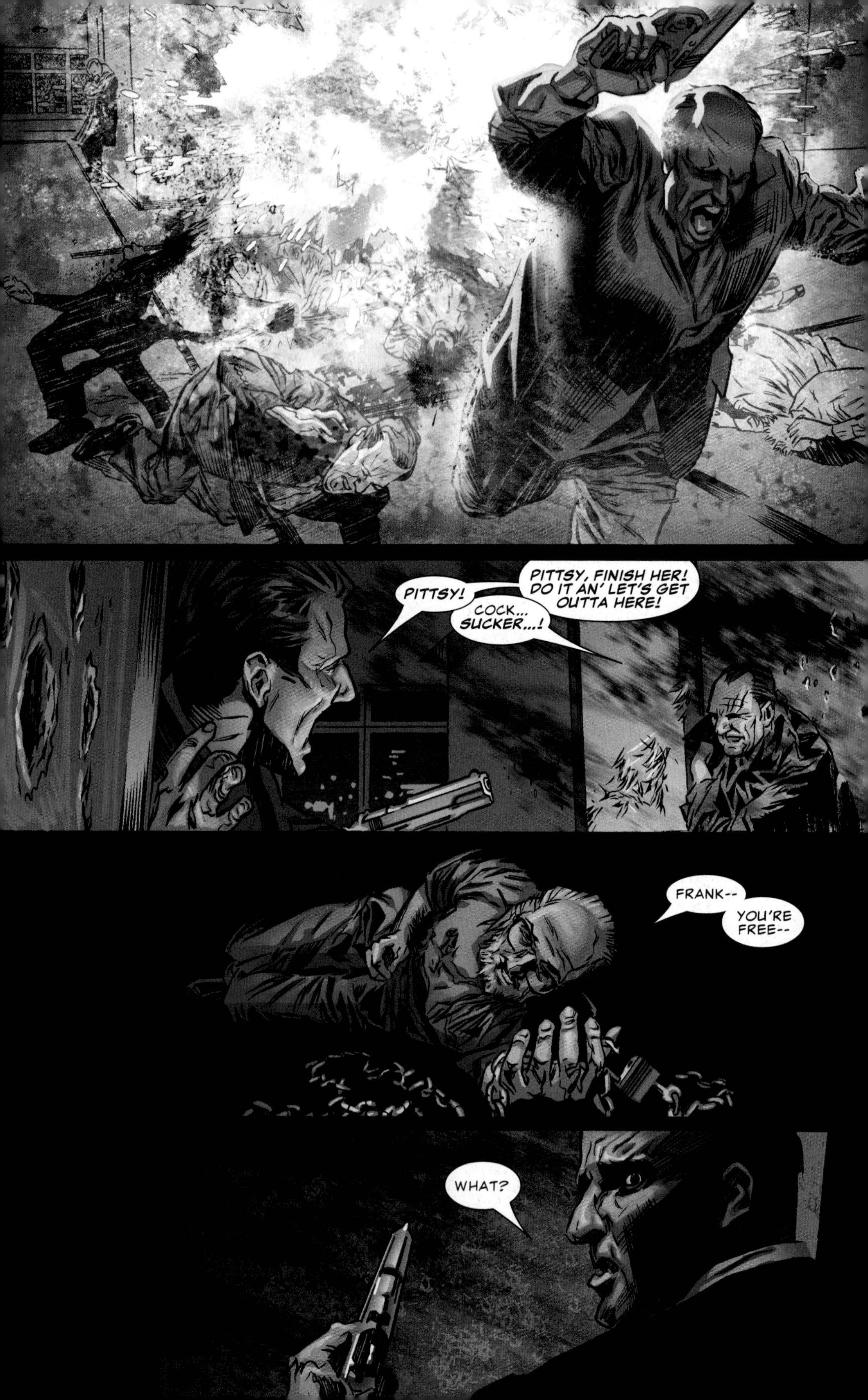
PITTSY!
PITTSY, FINISH HER! DO IT AN' LET'S GET OUTTA HERE!
COCK... SUCKER...!
FRANK--
YOU'RE FREE--
WHAT?

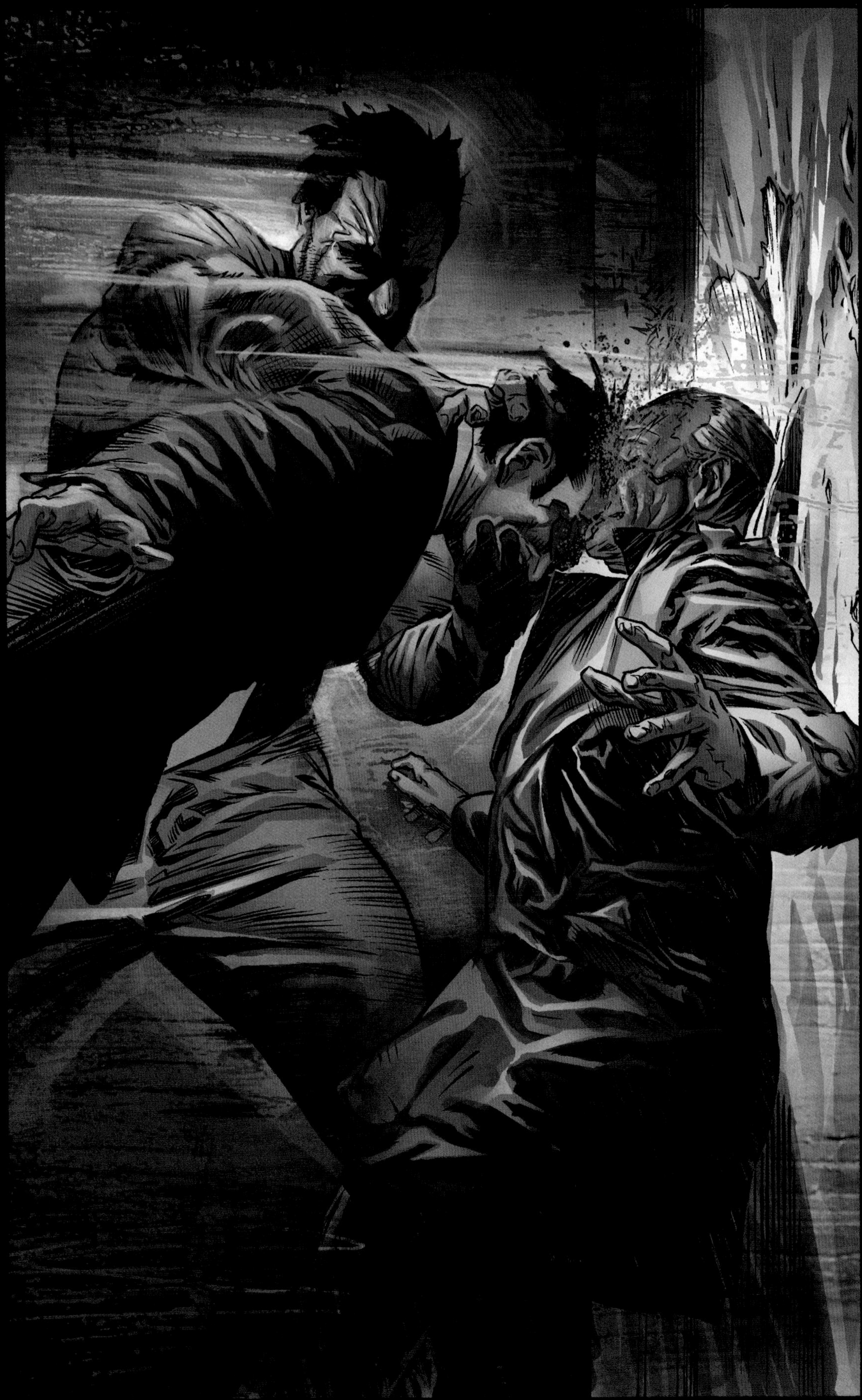

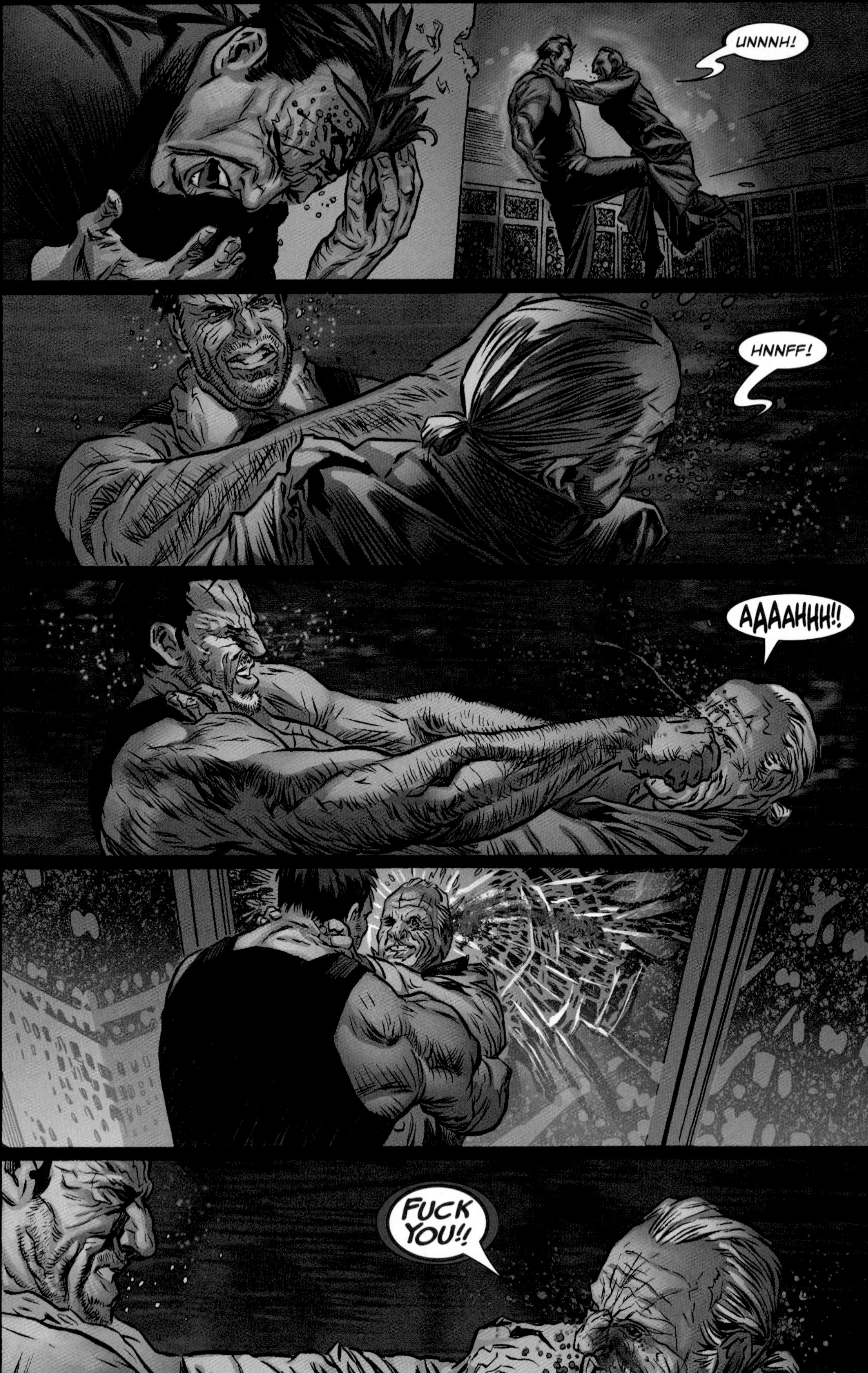

UNNNH!
HNNFF!
AAAAHHH!!
FUCK YOU!!

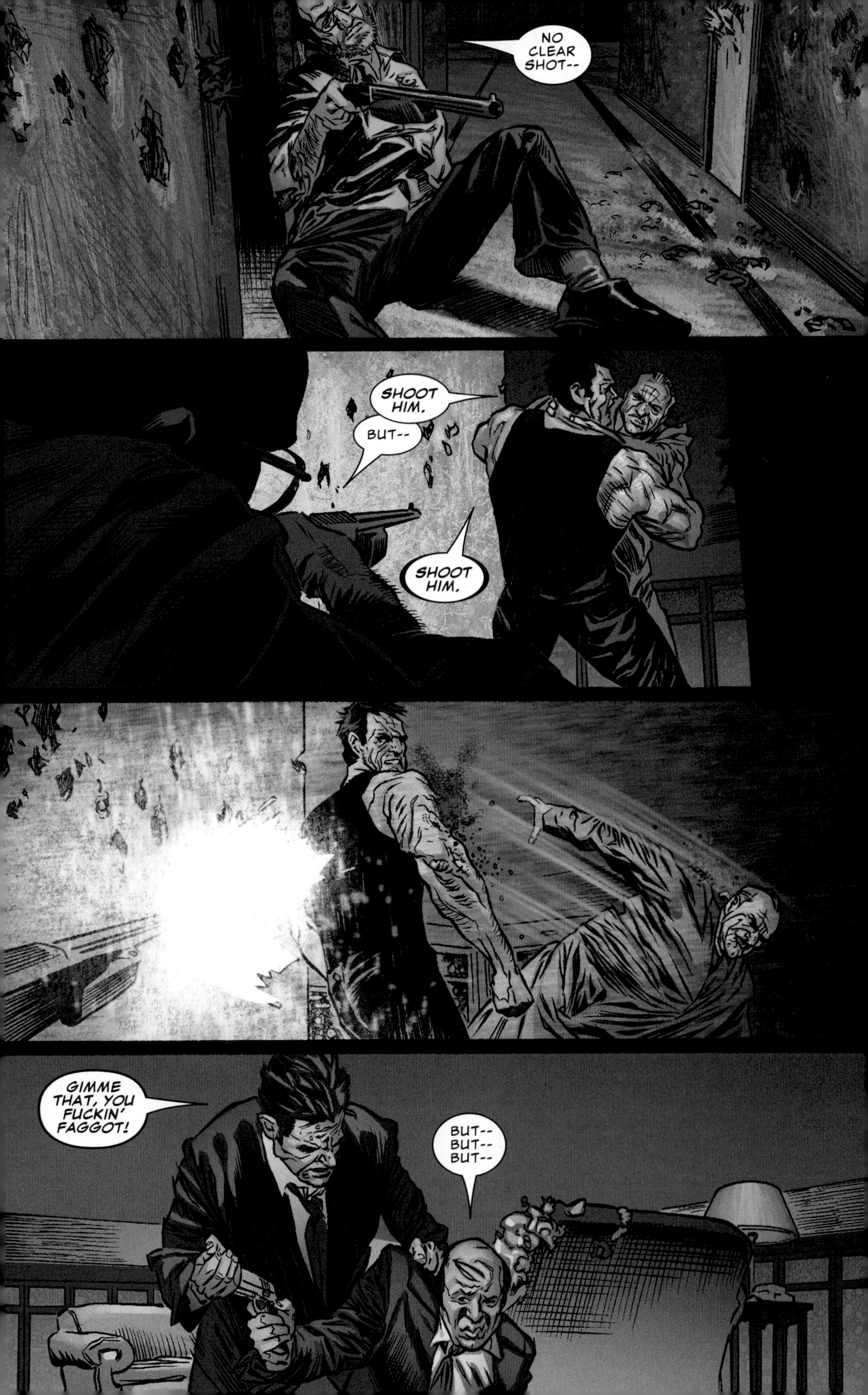
NO CLEAR SHOT--
SHOOT HIM.
BUT--
SHOOT HIM.
GIMME THAT, YOU FUCKIN' FAGGOT!
BUT-- BUT-- BUT--

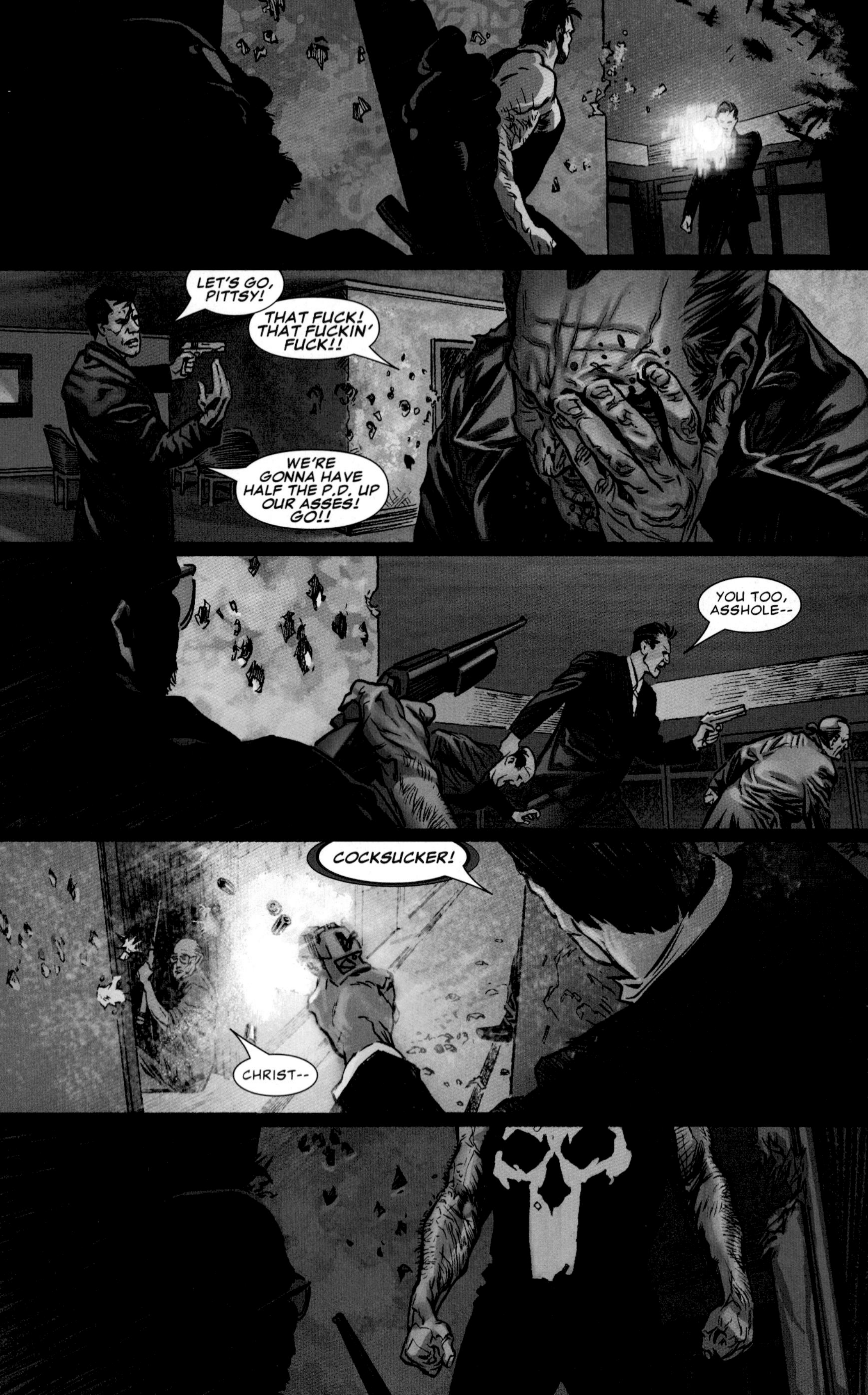
LET'S GO, PITTSY!
THAT FUCK! THAT FUCKIN' FUCK!!
WE'RE GONNA HAVE HALF THE P.D. UP OUR ASSES! GO!!
YOU TOO, ASSHOLE--
COCKSUCKER!
CHRIST--

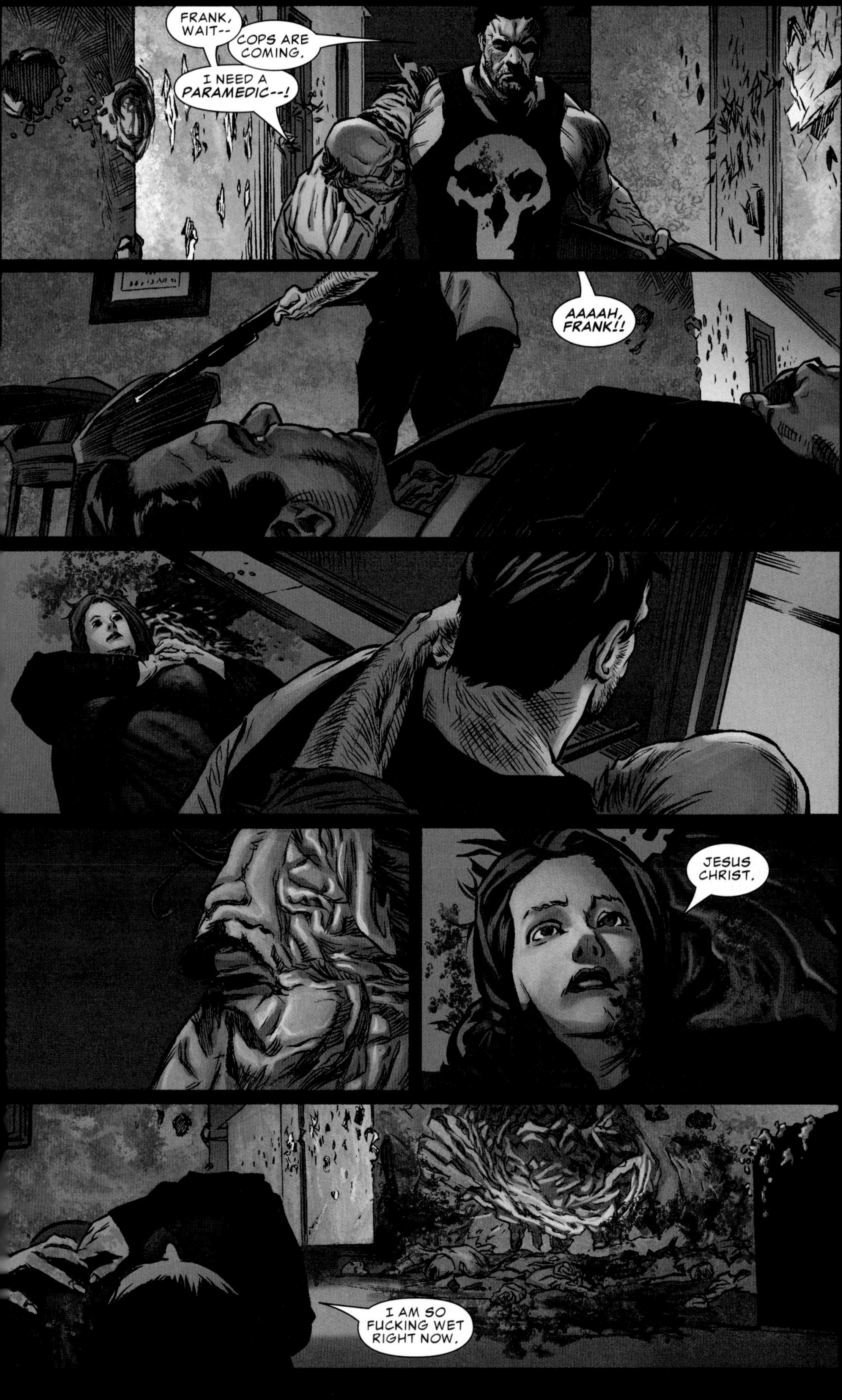
FRANK, WAIT--
COPS ARE COMING.
I NEED A PARAMEDIC--!
AAAAH, FRANK!!
JESUS CHRIST.
I AM SO FUCKING WET RIGHT NOW.

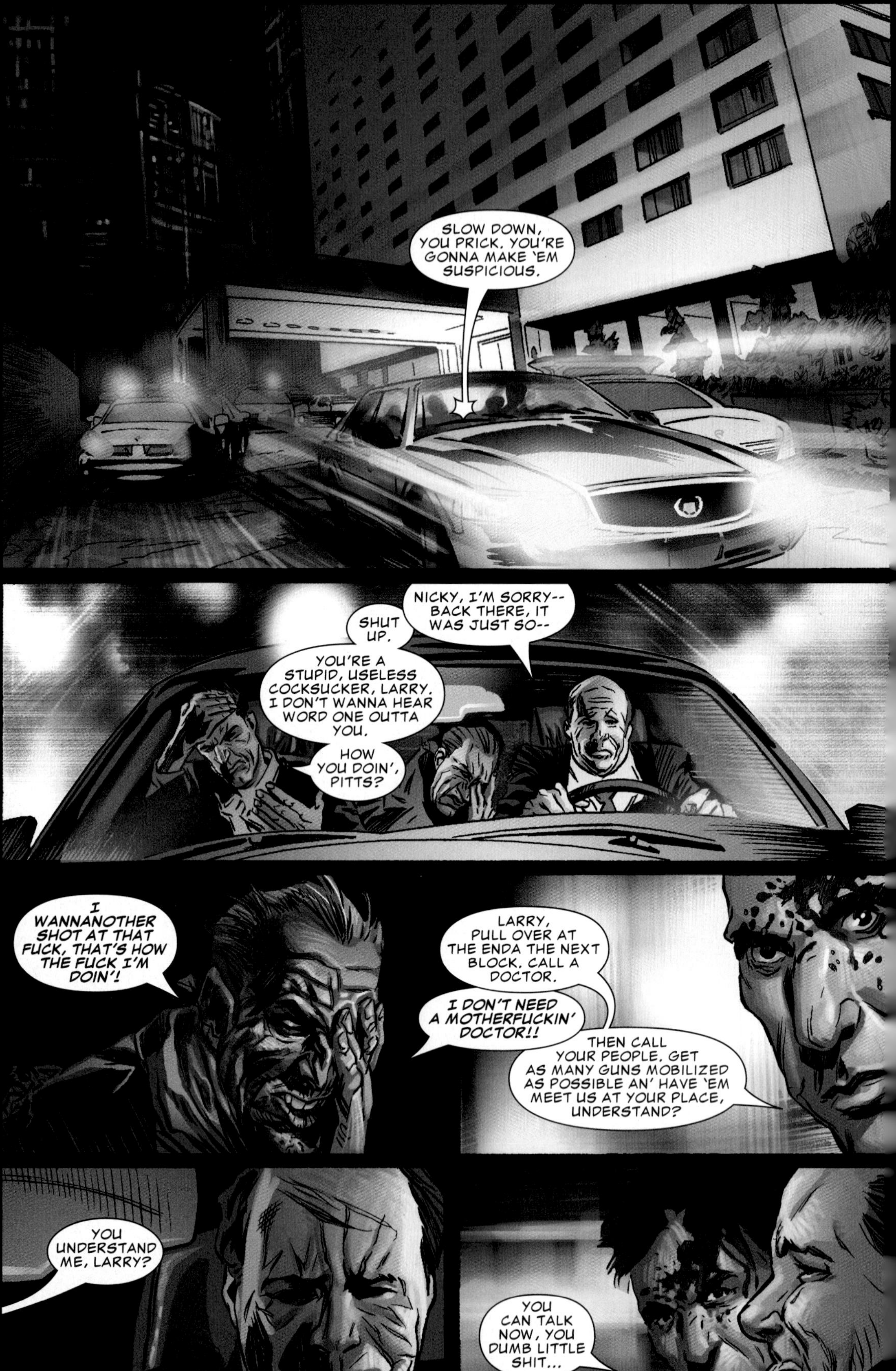
SLOW DOWN, YOU PRICK. YOU'RE GONNA MAKE 'EM SUSPICIOUS.
NICKY, I'M SORRY-- BACK THERE, IT WAS JUST SO--
SHUT UP.
YOU'RE A STUPID, USELESS COCKSUCKER, LARRY. I DON'T WANNA HEAR WORD ONE OUTTA YOU.
HOW YOU DOIN', PITTS?
I WANNANOTHER SHOT AT THAT FUCK, THAT'S HOW THE FUCK I'M DOIN'!
LARRY, PULL OVER AT THE ENDA THE NEXT BLOCK. CALL A DOCTOR.
I DON'T NEED A MOTHERFUCKIN' DOCTOR!!
THEN CALL YOUR PEOPLE. GET AS MANY GUNS MOBILIZED AS POSSIBLE AN' HAVE 'EM MEET US AT YOUR PLACE, UNDERSTAND?
YOU UNDERSTAND ME, LARRY?
YOU CAN TALK NOW, YOU DUMB LITTLE SHIT...

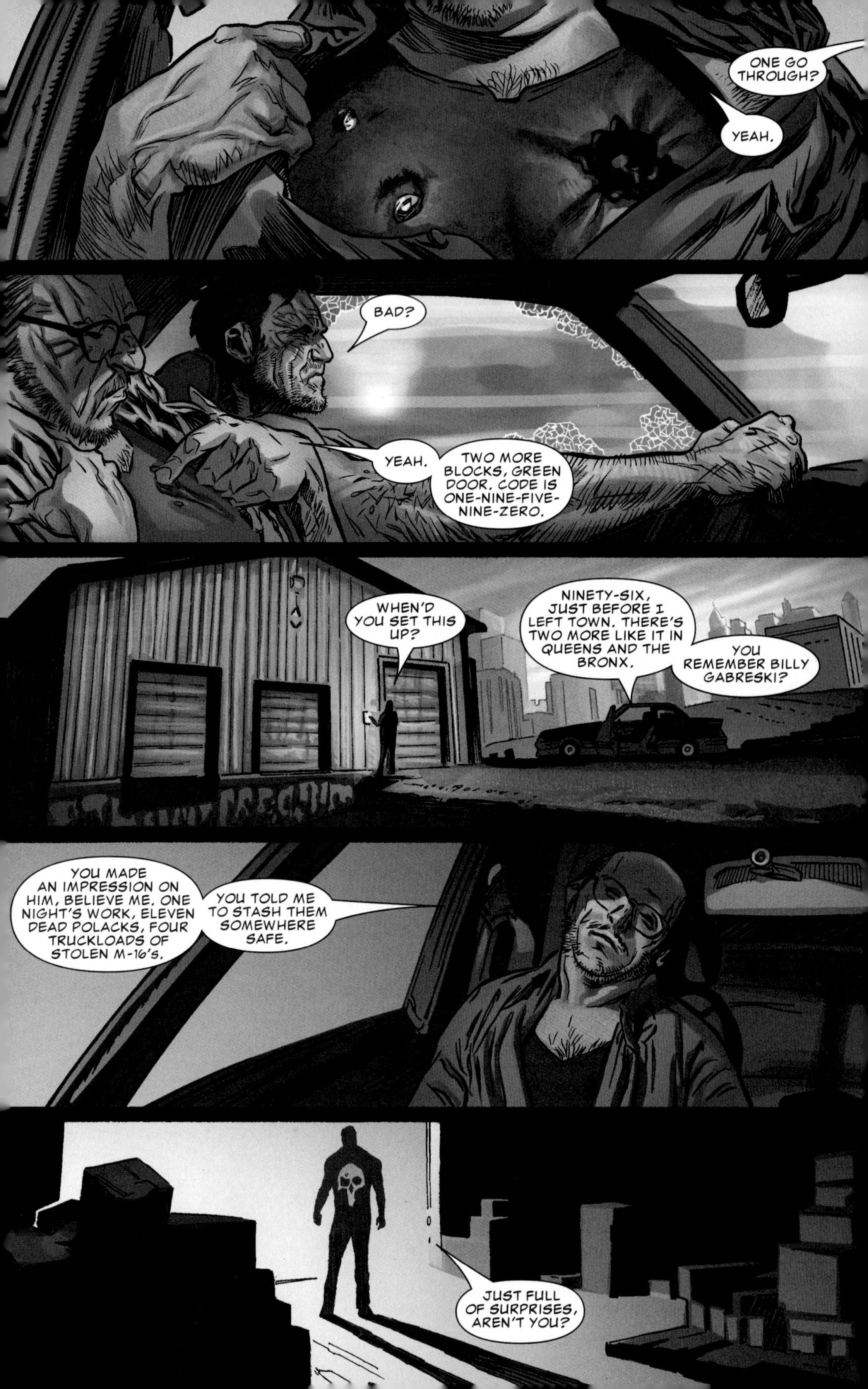
ONE GO THROUGH?
YEAH.
BAD?
YEAH.
TWO MORE BLOCKS, GREEN DOOR. CODE IS ONE-NINE-FIVE-NINE-ZERO.
WHEN'D YOU SET THIS UP?
NINETY-SIX, JUST BEFORE I LEFT TOWN. THERE'S TWO MORE LIKE IT IN QUEENS AND THE BRONX.
YOU REMEMBER BILLY GABRESKI?
YOU MADE AN IMPRESSION ON HIM, BELIEVE ME. ONE NIGHT'S WORK, ELEVEN DEAD POLACKS, FOUR TRUCKLOADS OF STOLEN M-16's.
YOU TOLD ME TO STASH THEM SOMEWHERE SAFE.
JUST FULL OF SURPRISES, AREN'T YOU?

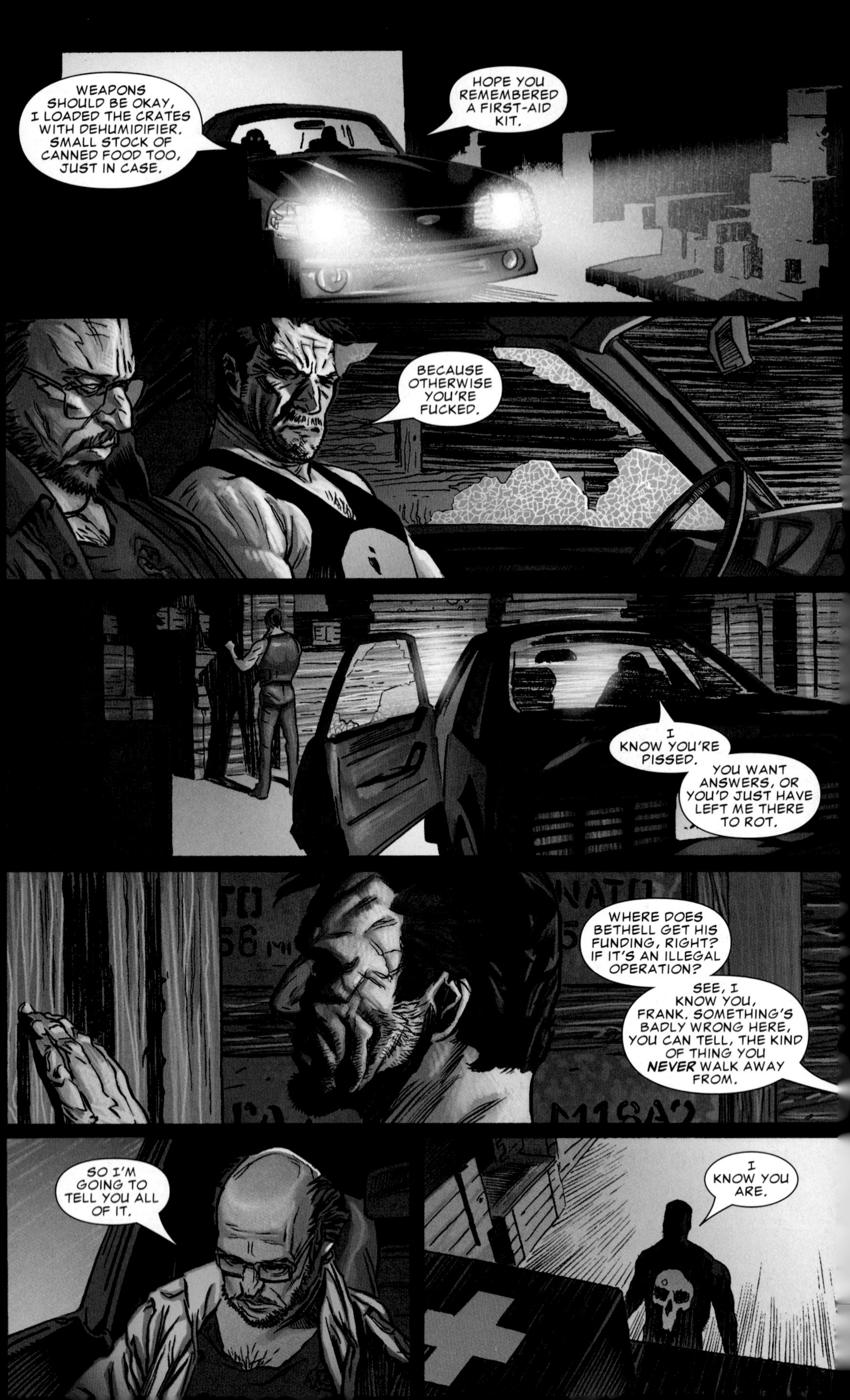
WEAPONS SHOULD BE OKAY, I LOADED THE CRATES WITH DEHUMIDIFIER. SMALL STOCK OF CANNED FOOD TOO, JUST IN CASE.
HOPE YOU REMEMBERED A FIRST-AID KIT.
BECAUSE OTHERWISE YOU'RE FUCKED.
I KNOW YOU'RE PISSED.
YOU WANT ANSWERS, OR YOU'D JUST HAVE LEFT ME THERE TO ROT.
WHERE DOES BETHELL GET HIS FUNDING, RIGHT? IF IT'S AN ILLEGAL OPERATION?
SEE, I KNOW YOU, FRANK. SOMETHING'S BADLY WRONG HERE, YOU CAN TELL, THE KIND OF THING YOU NEVER WALK AWAY FROM.
SO I'M GOING TO TELL YOU ALL OF IT.
I KNOW YOU ARE.

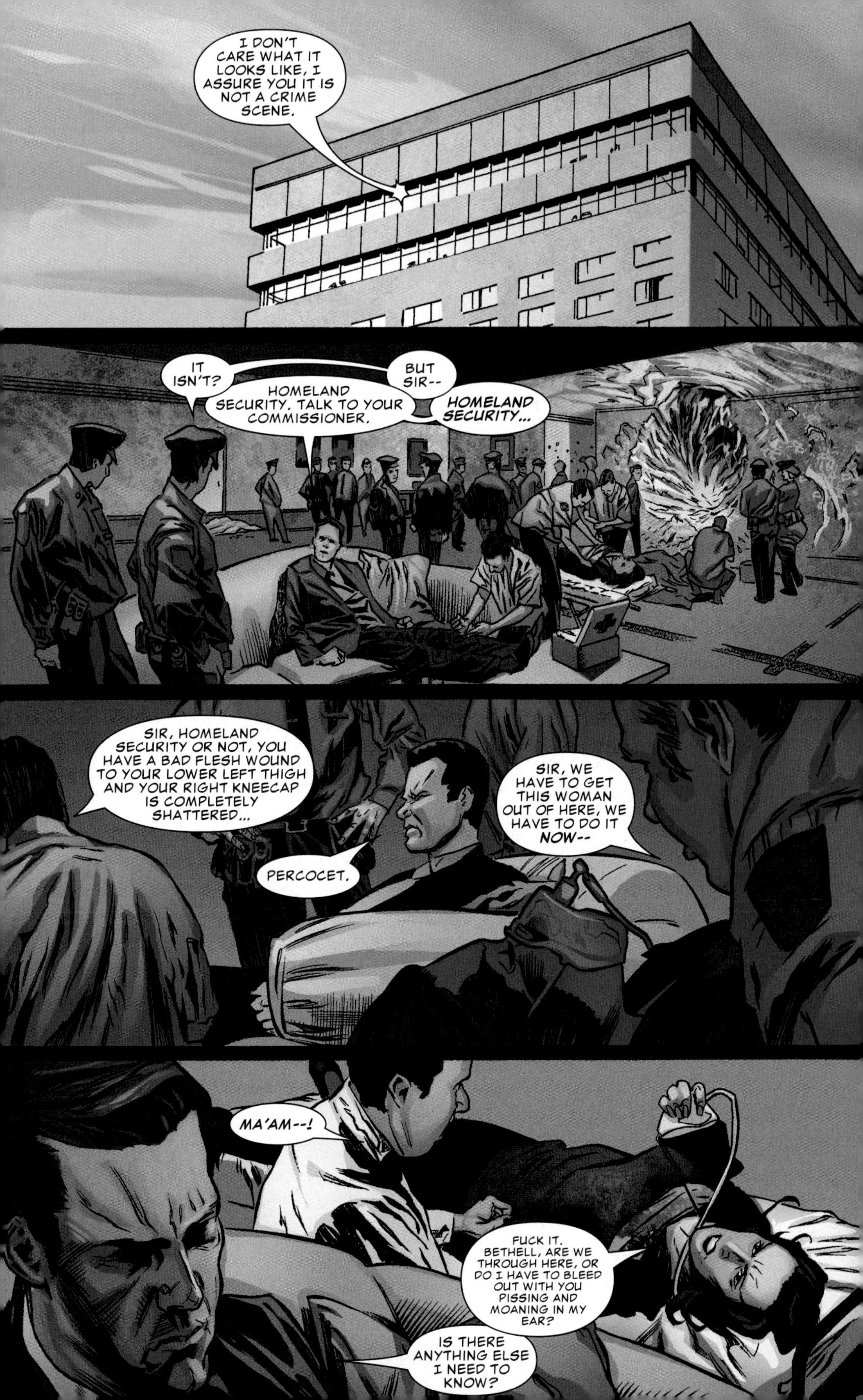
I DON'T CARE WHAT IT LOOKS LIKE, I ASSURE YOU IT IS NOT A CRIME SCENE.
IT ISN'T?
HOMELAND SECURITY. TALK TO YOUR COMMISSIONER.
BUT SIR--
HOMELAND SECURITY...
SIR, HOMELAND SECURITY OR NOT, YOU HAVE A BAD FLESH WOUND TO YOUR LOWER LEFT THIGH AND YOUR RIGHT KNEECAP IS COMPLETELY SHATTERED...
PERCOCET.
SIR, WE HAVE TO GET THIS WOMAN OUT OF HERE, WE HAVE TO DO IT NOW--
MA'AM--!
FUCK IT. BETHELL, ARE WE THROUGH HERE, OR DO I HAVE TO BLEED OUT WITH YOU PISSING AND MOANING IN MY EAR?
IS THERE ANYTHING ELSE I NEED TO KNOW?

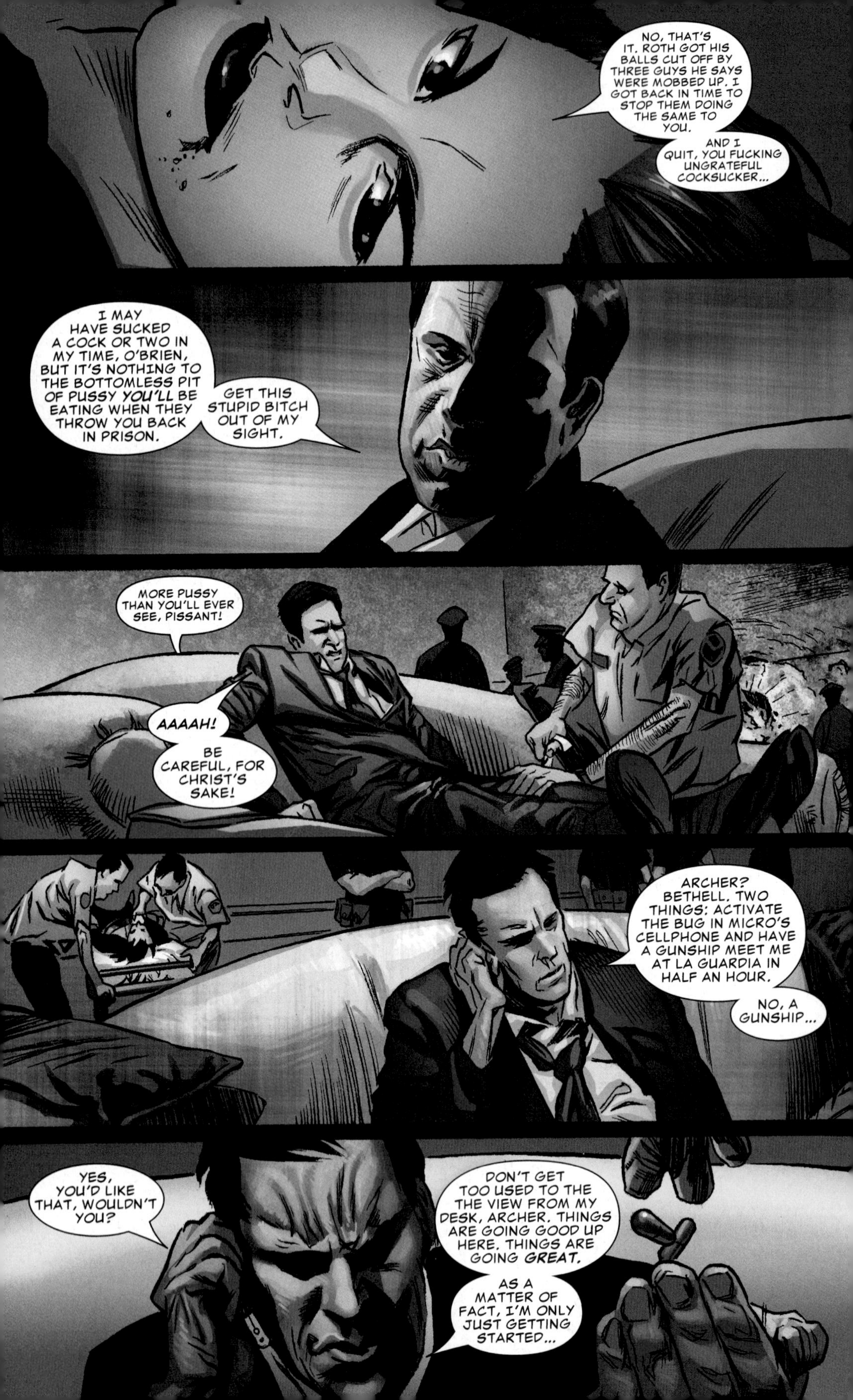
NO, THAT'S IT. ROTH GOT HIS BALLS CUT OFF BY THREE GUYS HE SAYS WERE MOBBED UP. I GOT BACK IN TIME TO STOP THEM DOING THE SAME TO YOU.
AND I QUIT, YOU FUCKING UNGRATEFUL COCKSUCKER...
I MAY HAVE SUCKED A COCK OR TWO IN MY TIME, O'BRIEN, BUT IT'S NOTHING TO THE BOTTOMLESS PIT OF PUSSY YOU'LL BE EATING WHEN THEY THROW YOU BACK IN PRISON.
GET THIS STUPID BITCH OUT OF MY SIGHT.
MORE PUSSY THAN YOU'LL EVER SEE, PISSANT!
AAAAH!
BE CAREFUL, FOR CHRIST'S SAKE!
ARCHER? BETHELL. TWO THINGS: ACTIVATE THE BUG IN MICRO'S CELLPHONE AND HAVE A GUNSHIP MEET ME AT LA GUARDIA IN HALF AN HOUR.
NO, A GUNSHIP...
YES, YOU'D LIKE THAT, WOULDN'T YOU?
DON'T GET TOO USED TO THE THE VIEW FROM MY DESK, ARCHER. THINGS ARE GOING GOOD UP HERE. THINGS ARE GOING GREAT.
AS A MATTER OF FACT, I'M ONLY JUST GETTING STARTED...

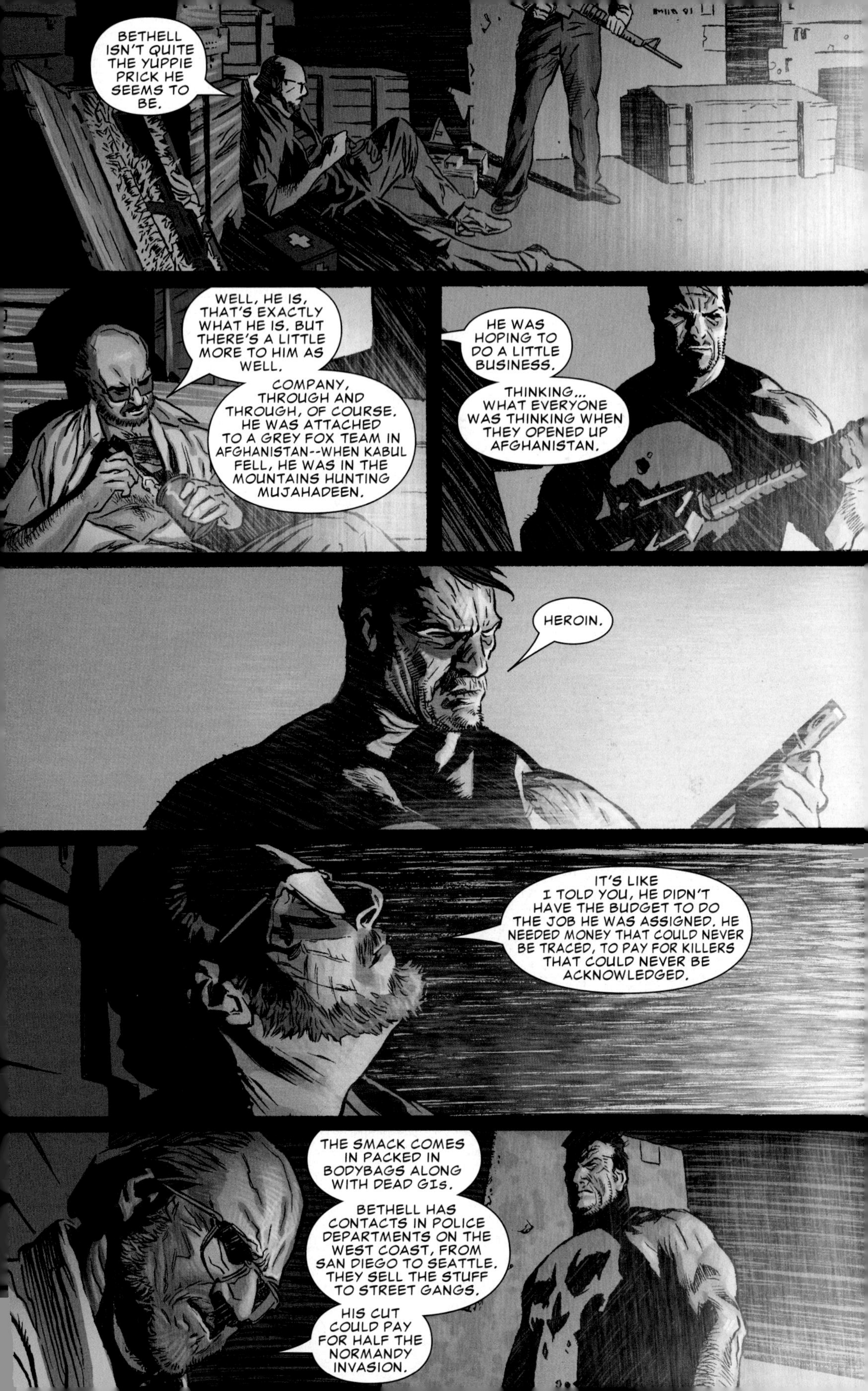
BETHELL ISN'T QUITE THE YUPPIE PRICK HE SEEMS TO BE.
WELL, HE IS, THAT'S EXACTLY WHAT HE IS. BUT THERE'S A LITTLE MORE TO HIM AS WELL.
COMPANY, THROUGH AND THROUGH, OF COURSE. HE WAS ATTACHED TO A GREY FOX TEAM IN AFGHANISTAN--WHEN KABUL FELL, HE WAS IN THE MOUNTAINS HUNTING MUJAHADEEN.
HE WAS HOPING TO DO A LITTLE BUSINESS.
THINKING... WHAT EVERYONE WAS THINKING WHEN THEY OPENED UP AFGHANISTAN.
HEROIN.
IT'S LIKE I TOLD YOU, HE DIDN'T HAVE THE BUDGET TO DO THE JOB HE WAS ASSIGNED. HE NEEDED MONEY THAT COULD NEVER BE TRACED, TO PAY FOR KILLERS THAT COULD NEVER BE ACKNOWLEDGED.
THE SMACK COMES IN PACKED IN BODYBAGS ALONG WITH DEAD GIS.
BETHELL HAS CONTACTS IN POLICE DEPARTMENTS ON THE WEST COAST, FROM SAN DIEGO TO SEATTLE. THEY SELL THE STUFF TO STREET GANGS.
HIS CUT COULD PAY FOR HALF THE NORMANDY INVASION.

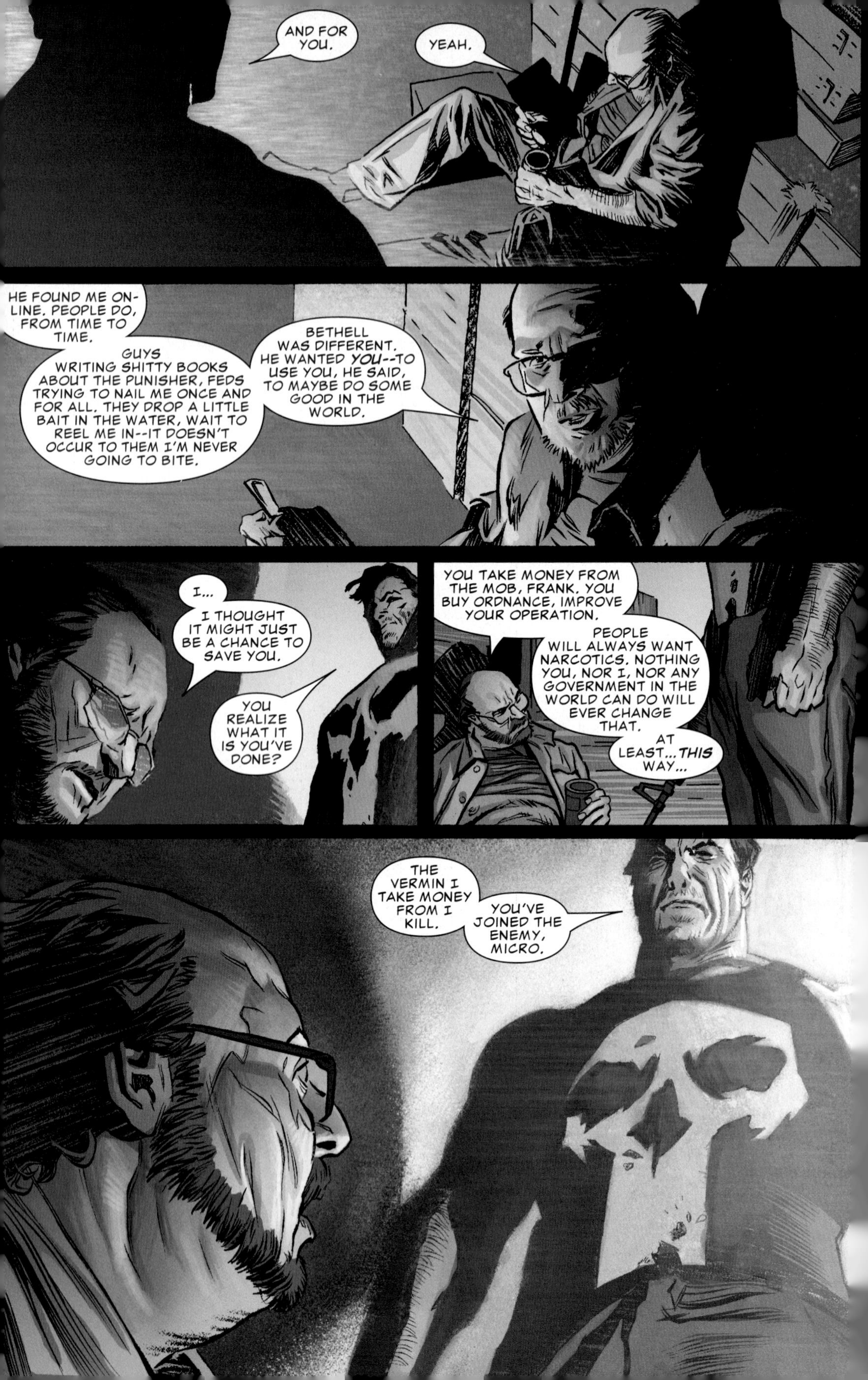
AND FOR YOU.
YEAH.
HE FOUND ME ON-LINE. PEOPLE DO, FROM TIME TO TIME.
GUYS WRITING SHITTY BOOKS ABOUT THE PUNISHER, FEDS TRYING TO NAIL ME ONCE AND FOR ALL. THEY DROP A LITTLE BAIT IN THE WATER, WAIT TO REEL ME IN--IT DOESN'T OCCUR TO THEM I'M NEVER GOING TO BITE.
BETHELL WAS DIFFERENT. HE WANTED *YOU*--TO USE YOU, HE SAID, TO MAYBE DO SOME GOOD IN THE WORLD.
I...
I THOUGHT IT MIGHT JUST BE A CHANCE TO SAVE YOU.
YOU REALIZE WHAT IT IS YOU'VE DONE?
YOU TAKE MONEY FROM THE MOB, FRANK. YOU BUY ORDNANCE, IMPROVE YOUR OPERATION.
PEOPLE WILL ALWAYS WANT NARCOTICS. NOTHING YOU, NOR I, NOR ANY GOVERNMENT IN THE WORLD CAN DO WILL EVER CHANGE THAT.
AT LEAST...*THIS* WAY...
THE VERMIN I TAKE MONEY FROM I KILL.
YOU'VE JOINED THE ENEMY, MICRO.

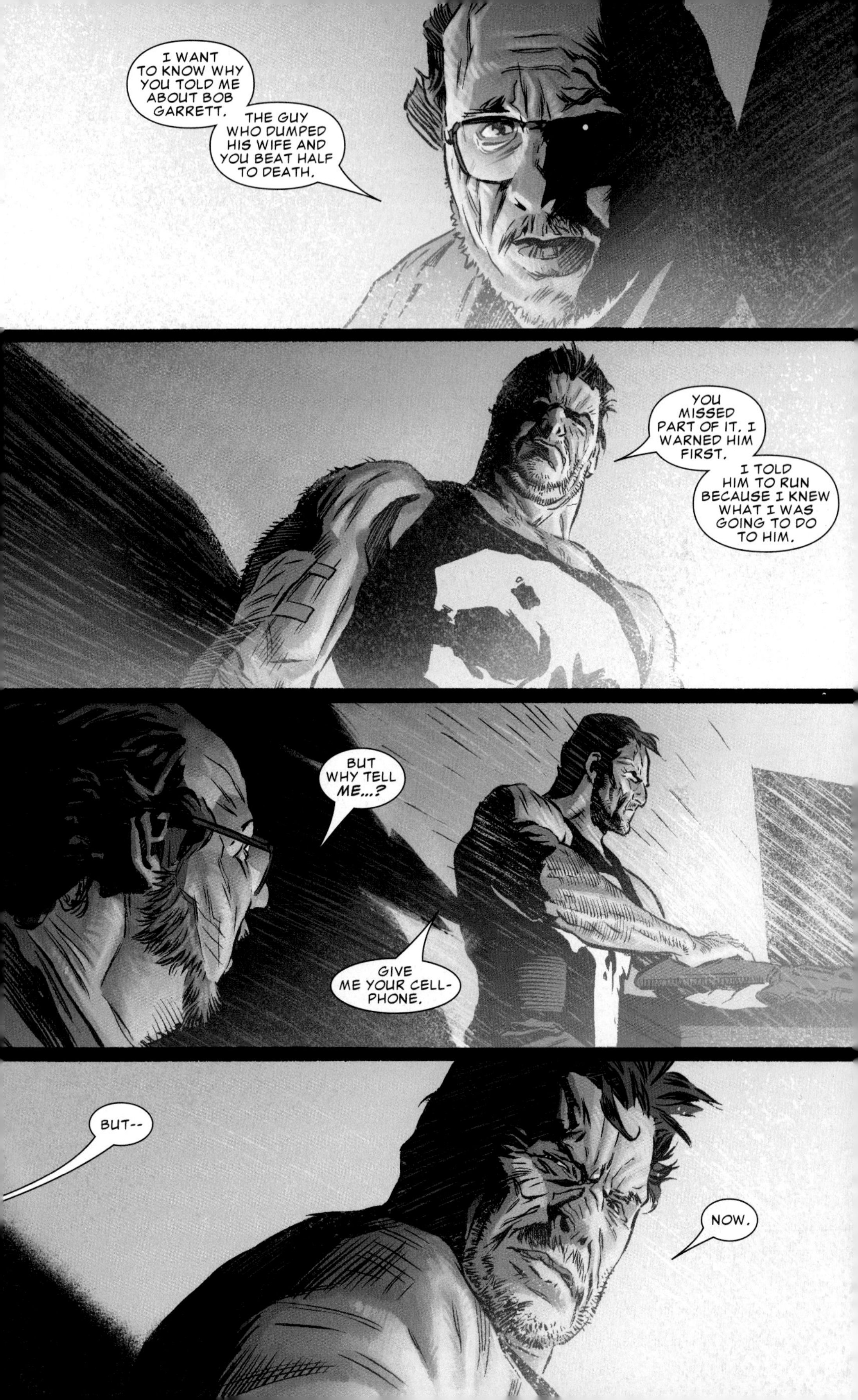
I WANT TO KNOW WHY YOU TOLD ME ABOUT BOB GARRETT.
THE GUY WHO DUMPED HIS WIFE AND YOU BEAT HALF TO DEATH.
YOU MISSED PART OF IT. I WARNED HIM FIRST.
I TOLD HIM TO RUN BECAUSE I KNEW WHAT I WAS GOING TO DO TO HIM.
BUT WHY TELL ME...?
GIVE ME YOUR CELL-PHONE.
BUT--
NOW.

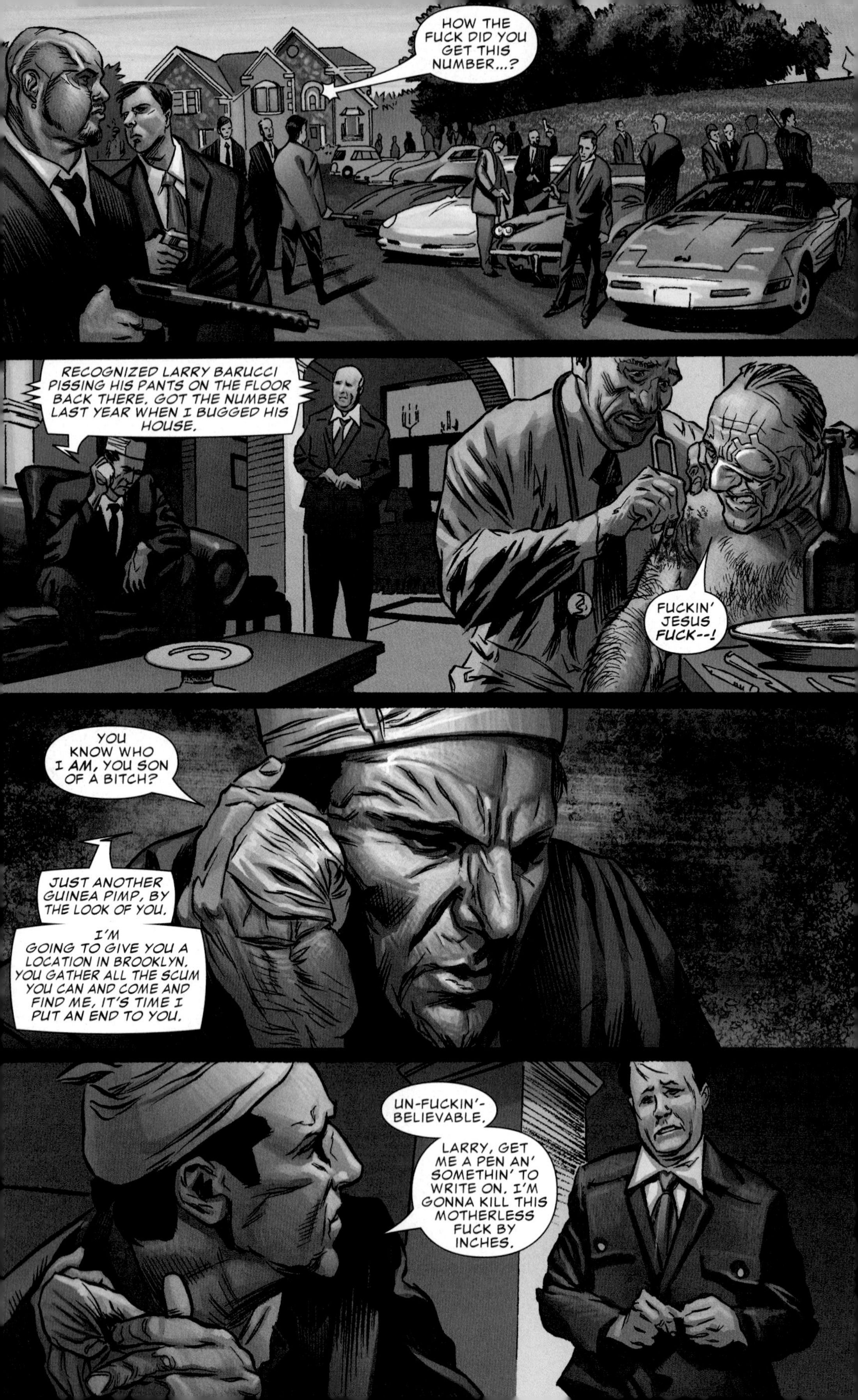
HOW THE FUCK DID YOU GET THIS NUMBER...?
RECOGNIZED LARRY BARUCCI PISSING HIS PANTS ON THE FLOOR BACK THERE. GOT THE NUMBER LAST YEAR WHEN I BUGGED HIS HOUSE.
FUCKIN' JESUS FUCK--!
YOU KNOW WHO I AM, YOU SON OF A BITCH?
JUST ANOTHER GUINEA PIMP, BY THE LOOK OF YOU.
I'M GOING TO GIVE YOU A LOCATION IN BROOKLYN. YOU GATHER ALL THE SCUM YOU CAN AND COME AND FIND ME. IT'S TIME I PUT AN END TO YOU.
UN-FUCKIN'-BELIEVABLE.
LARRY, GET ME A PEN AN' SOMETHIN' TO WRITE ON. I'M GONNA KILL THIS MOTHERLESS FUCK BY INCHES.

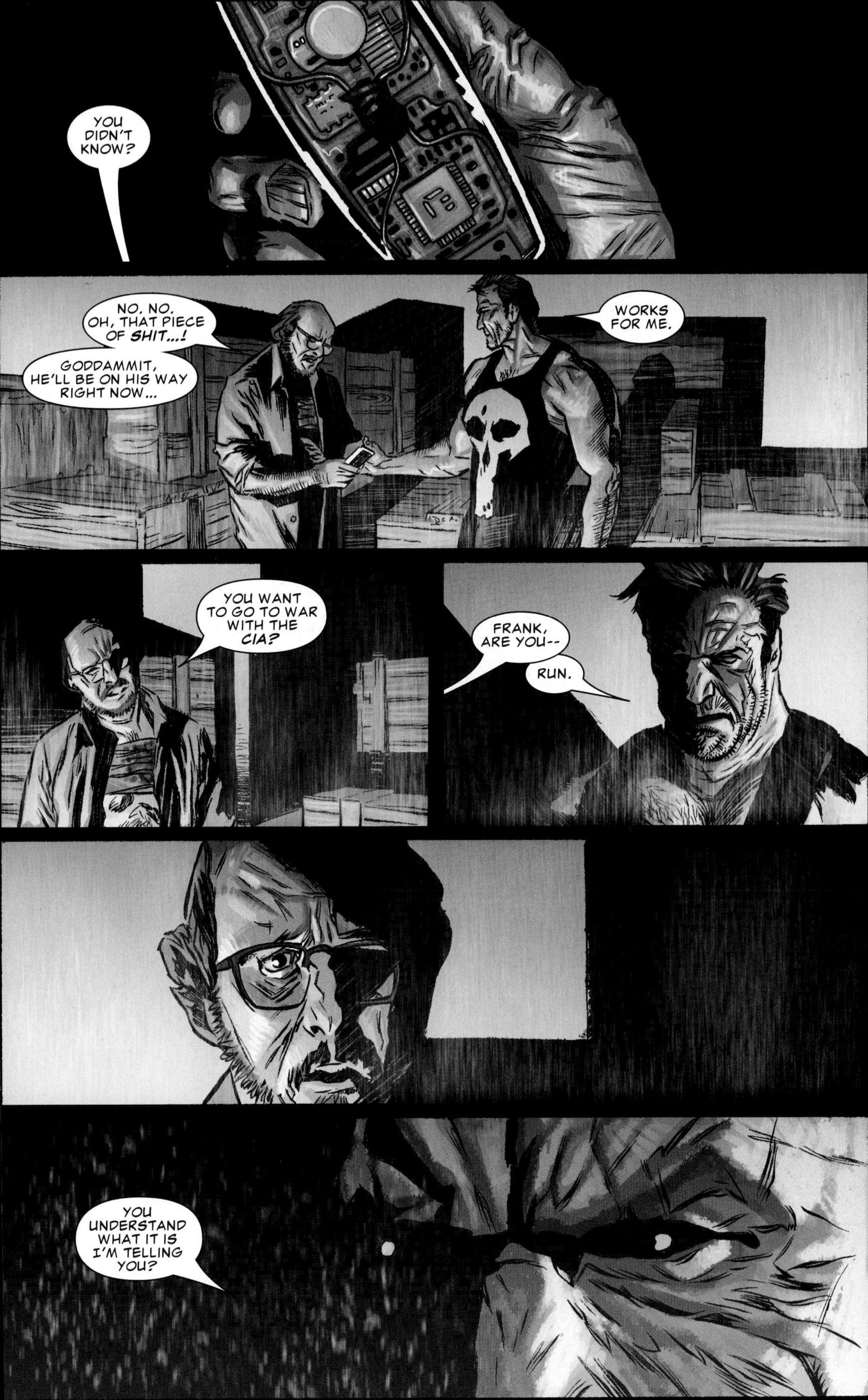
YOU DIDN'T KNOW?
NO. NO. OH, THAT PIECE OF ***SHIT...!***
GODDAMMIT, HE'LL BE ON HIS WAY RIGHT NOW...
WORKS FOR ME.
YOU WANT TO GO TO WAR WITH THE ***CIA?***
FRANK, ARE YOU--
RUN.
YOU UNDERSTAND WHAT IT IS I'M TELLING YOU?

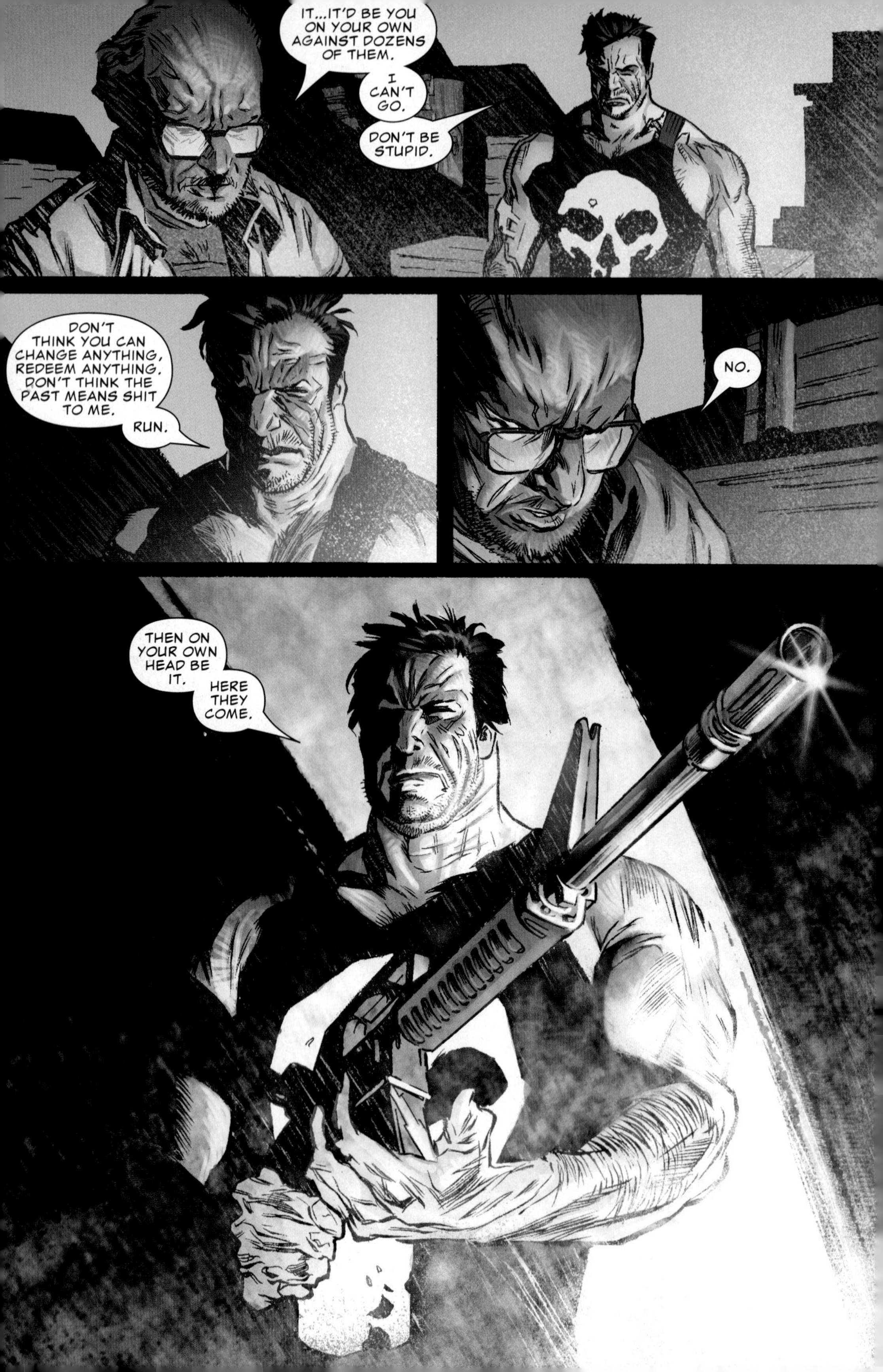
IT...IT'D BE YOU ON YOUR OWN AGAINST DOZENS OF THEM.
I CAN'T GO.
DON'T BE STUPID.
DON'T THINK YOU CAN CHANGE ANYTHING, REDEEM ANYTHING. DON'T THINK THE PAST MEANS SHIT TO ME.
RUN.
NO.
THEN ON YOUR OWN HEAD BE IT.
HERE THEY COME.

#6

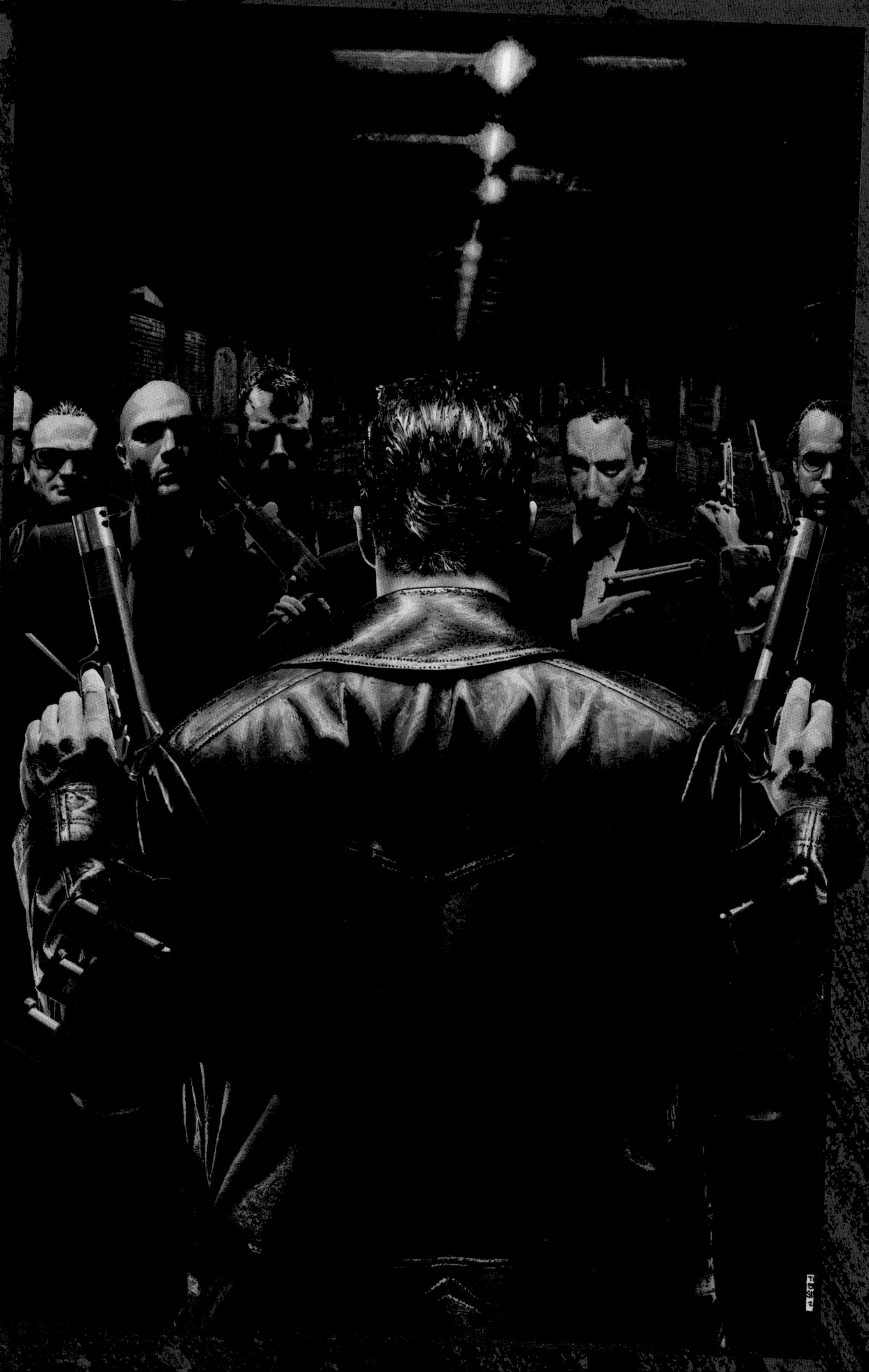

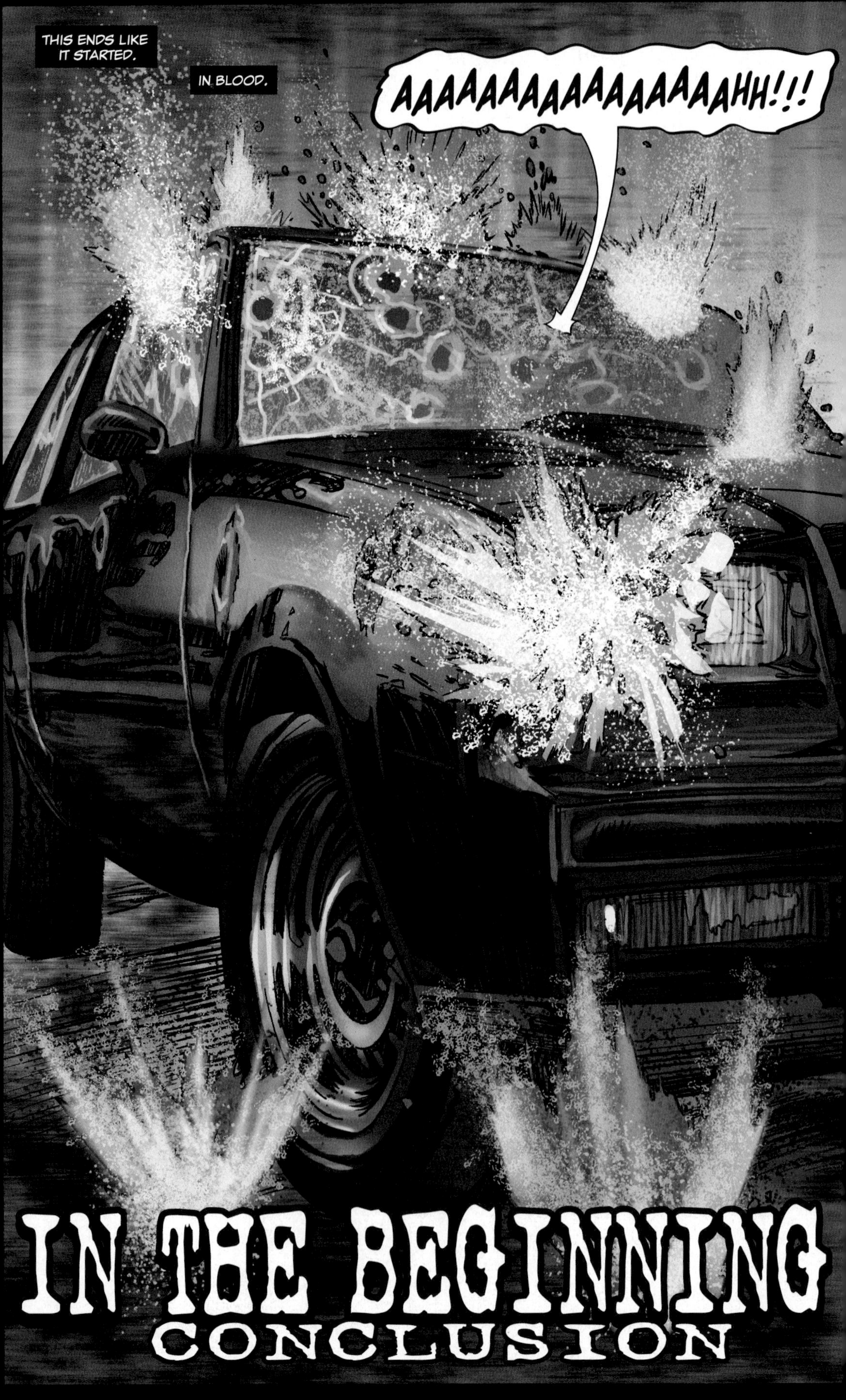
THIS ENDS LIKE IT STARTED.
IN BLOOD.
AAAAAAAAAAAAAAAAAHH!!!
IN THE BEGINNING
CONCLUSION

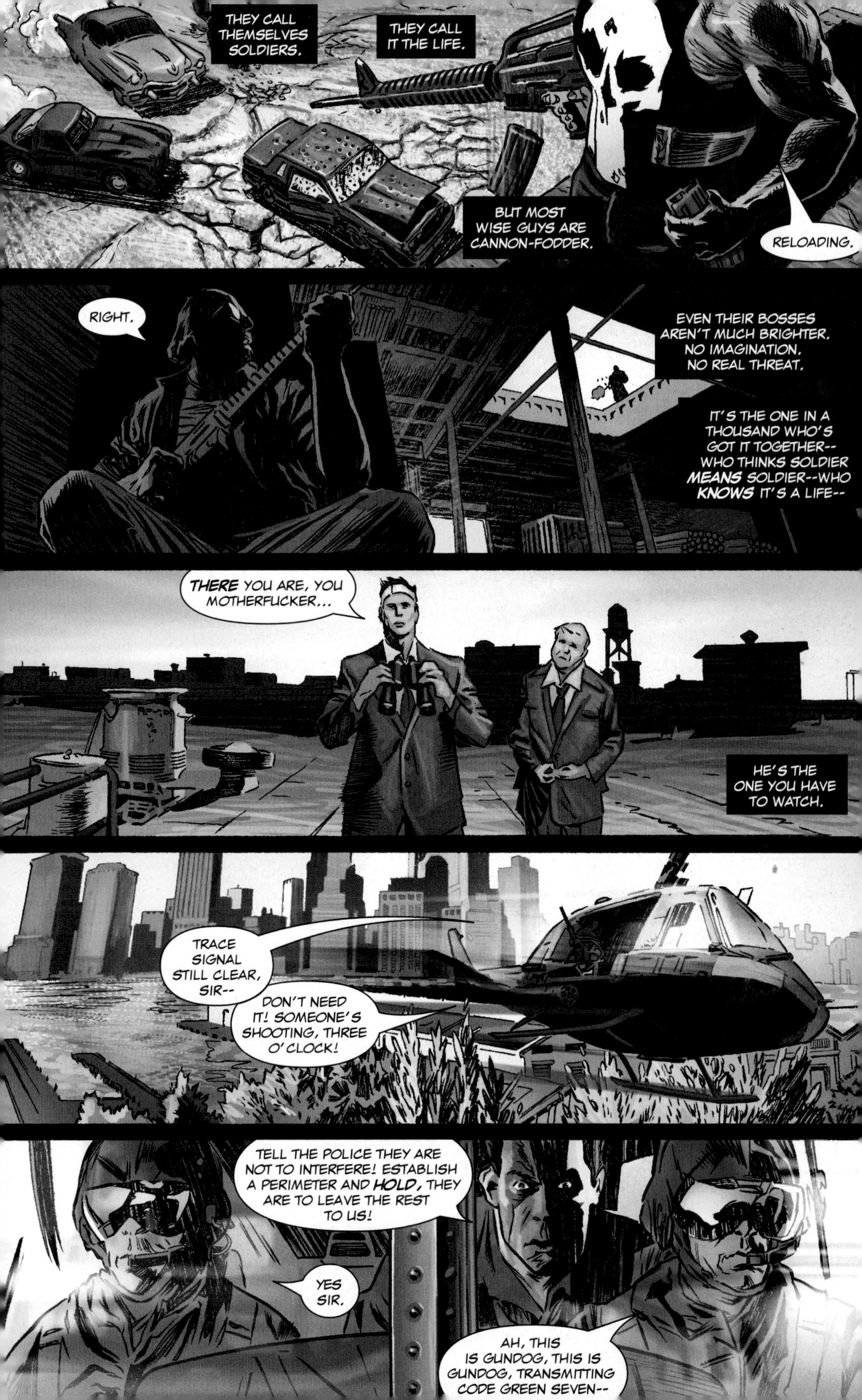

THEY CALL THEMSELVES SOLDIERS.
THEY CALL IT THE LIFE.
BUT MOST WISE GUYS ARE CANNON-FODDER.
RELOADING.
RIGHT.
EVEN THEIR BOSSES AREN'T MUCH BRIGHTER. NO IMAGINATION. NO REAL THREAT.
IT'S THE ONE IN A THOUSAND WHO'S GOT IT TOGETHER-- WHO THINKS SOLDIER MEANS SOLDIER--WHO KNOWS IT'S A LIFE--
THERE YOU ARE, YOU MOTHERFUCKER...
HE'S THE ONE YOU HAVE TO WATCH.
TRACE SIGNAL STILL CLEAR, SIR--
DON'T NEED IT! SOMEONE'S SHOOTING, THREE O' CLOCK!
TELL THE POLICE THEY ARE NOT TO INTERFERE! ESTABLISH A PERIMETER AND HOLD. THEY ARE TO LEAVE THE REST TO US!
YES SIR.
AH, THIS IS GUNDOG, THIS IS GUNDOG, TRANSMITTING CODE GREEN SEVEN--

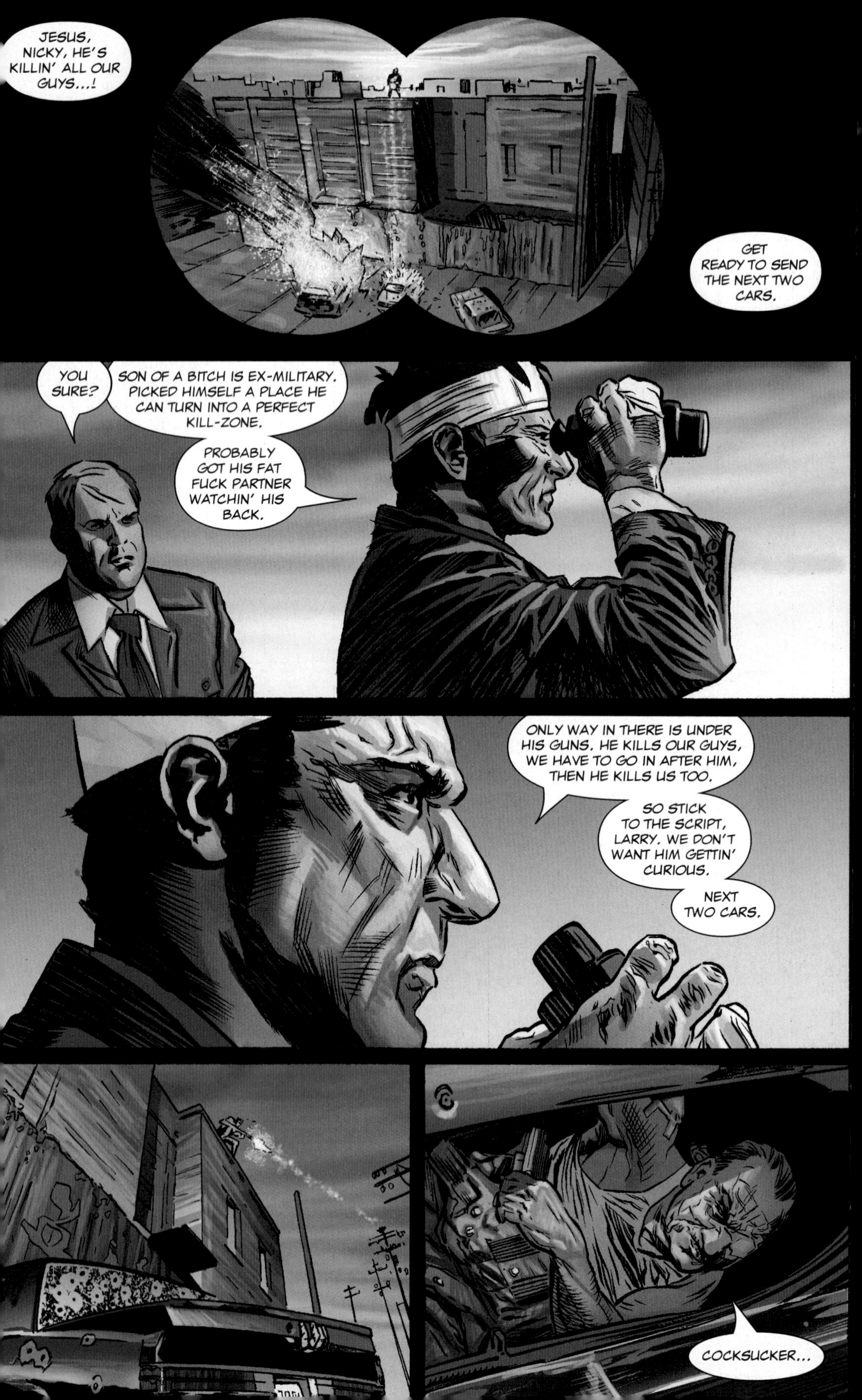
JESUS, NICKY, HE'S KILLIN' ALL OUR GUYS...!
GET READY TO SEND THE NEXT TWO CARS.
YOU SURE?
SON OF A BITCH IS EX-MILITARY. PICKED HIMSELF A PLACE HE CAN TURN INTO A PERFECT KILL-ZONE.
PROBABLY GOT HIS FAT FUCK PARTNER WATCHIN' HIS BACK.
ONLY WAY IN THERE IS UNDER HIS GUNS. HE KILLS OUR GUYS, WE HAVE TO GO IN AFTER HIM, THEN HE KILLS US TOO.
SO STICK TO THE SCRIPT, LARRY. WE DON'T WANT HIM GETTIN' CURIOUS.
NEXT TWO CARS.
COCKSUCKER...

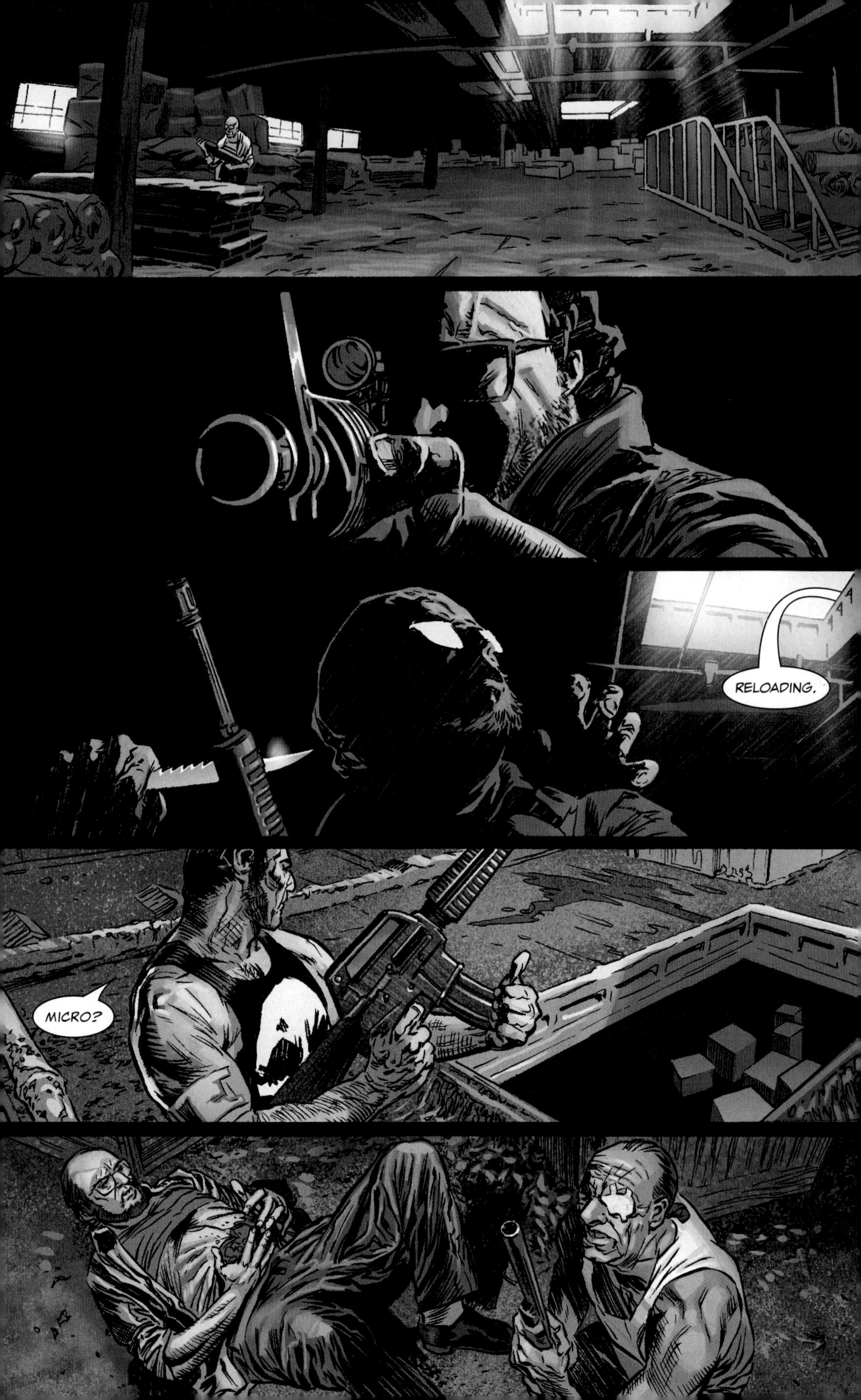
RELOADING.
MICRO?

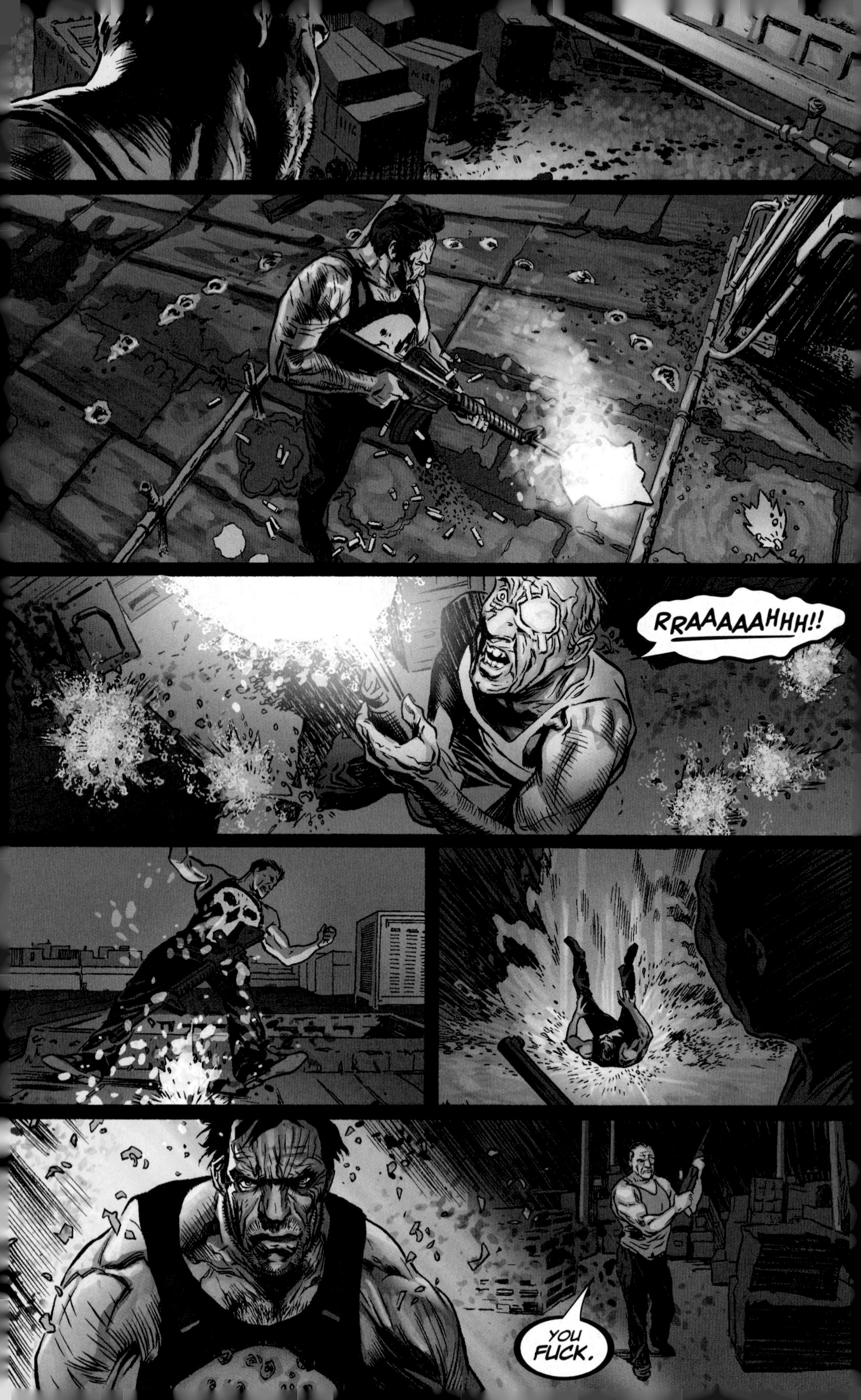
RRAAAAAHHH!!
YOU FUCK.

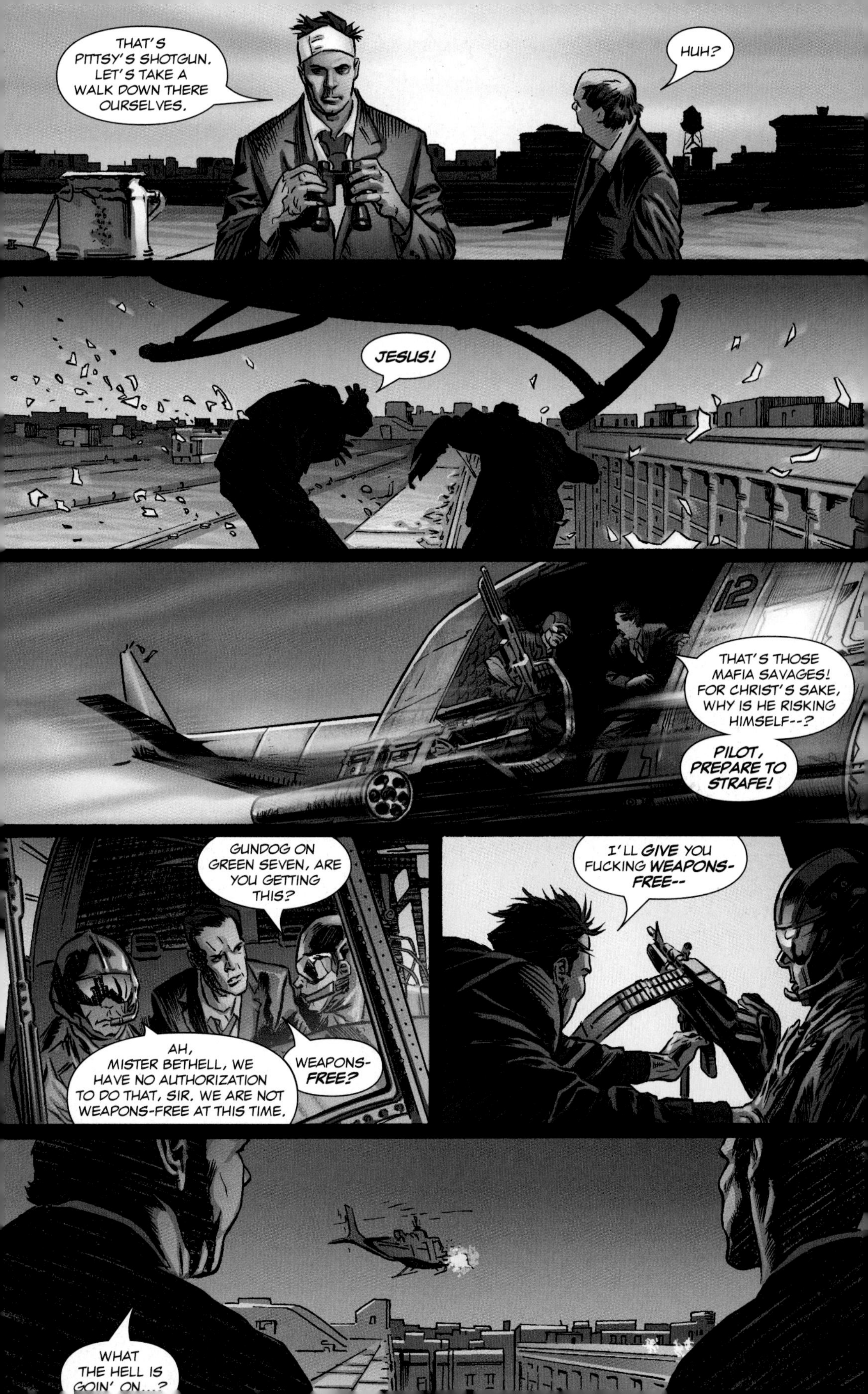
THAT'S PITTSY'S SHOTGUN. LET'S TAKE A WALK DOWN THERE OURSELVES.
HUH?
JESUS!
THAT'S THOSE MAFIA SAVAGES! FOR CHRIST'S SAKE, WHY IS HE RISKING HIMSELF--?
PILOT, PREPARE TO STRAFE!
GUNDOG ON GREEN SEVEN, ARE YOU GETTING THIS?
AH, MISTER BETHELL, WE HAVE NO AUTHORIZATION TO DO THAT, SIR. WE ARE NOT WEAPONS-FREE AT THIS TIME.
WEAPONS-FREE?
I'LL GIVE YOU FUCKING WEAPONS-FREE--
WHAT THE HELL IS GOIN' ON...?

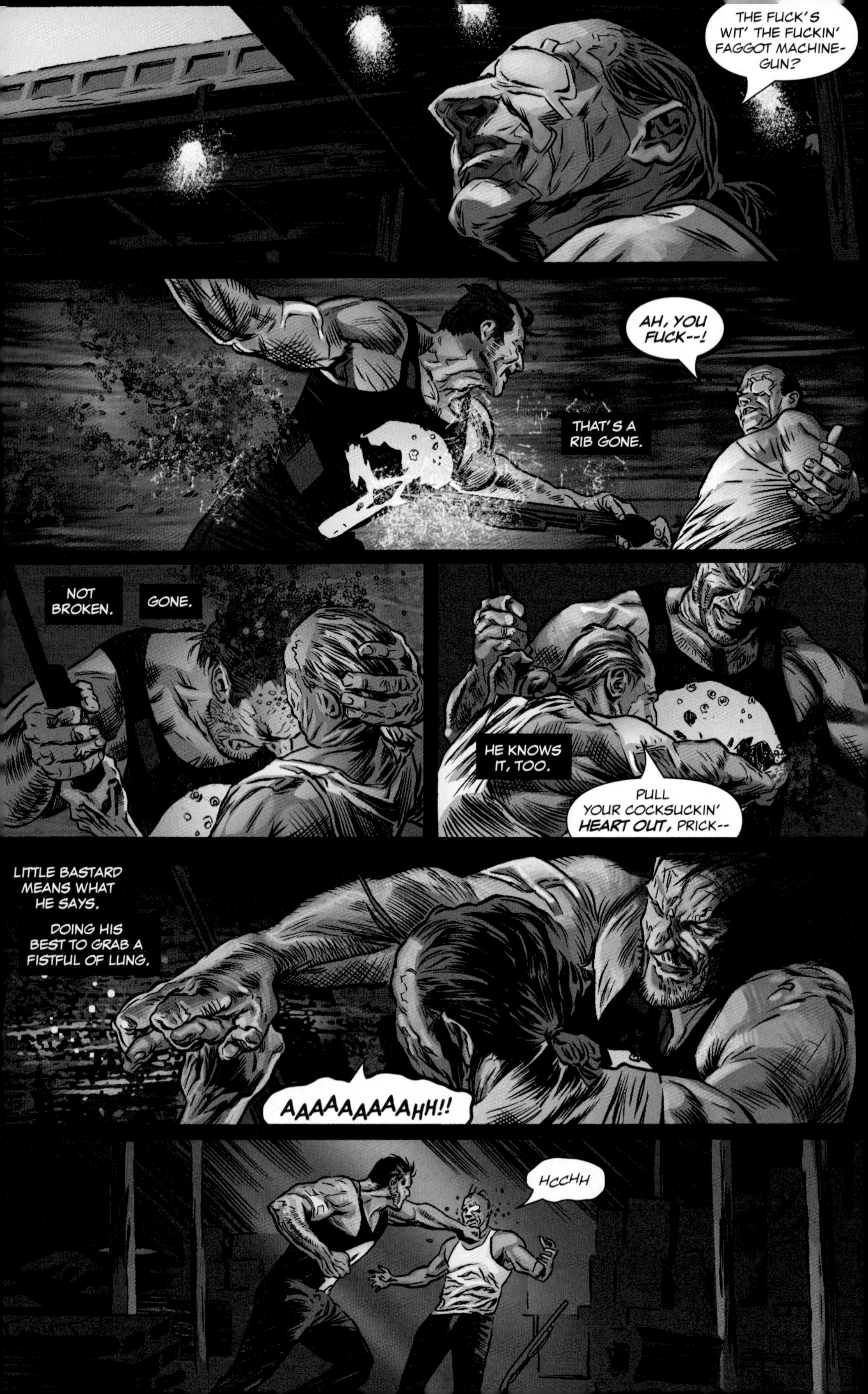
THE FUCK'S WIT' THE FUCKIN' FAGGOT MACHINE-GUN?
AH, YOU FUCK--!
THAT'S A RIB GONE.
NOT BROKEN.
GONE.
HE KNOWS IT, TOO.
PULL YOUR COCKSUCKIN' HEART OUT, PRICK--
LITTLE BASTARD MEANS WHAT HE SAYS.
DOING HIS BEST TO GRAB A FISTFUL OF LUNG.
AAAAAAAAAHH!!
HCCHH

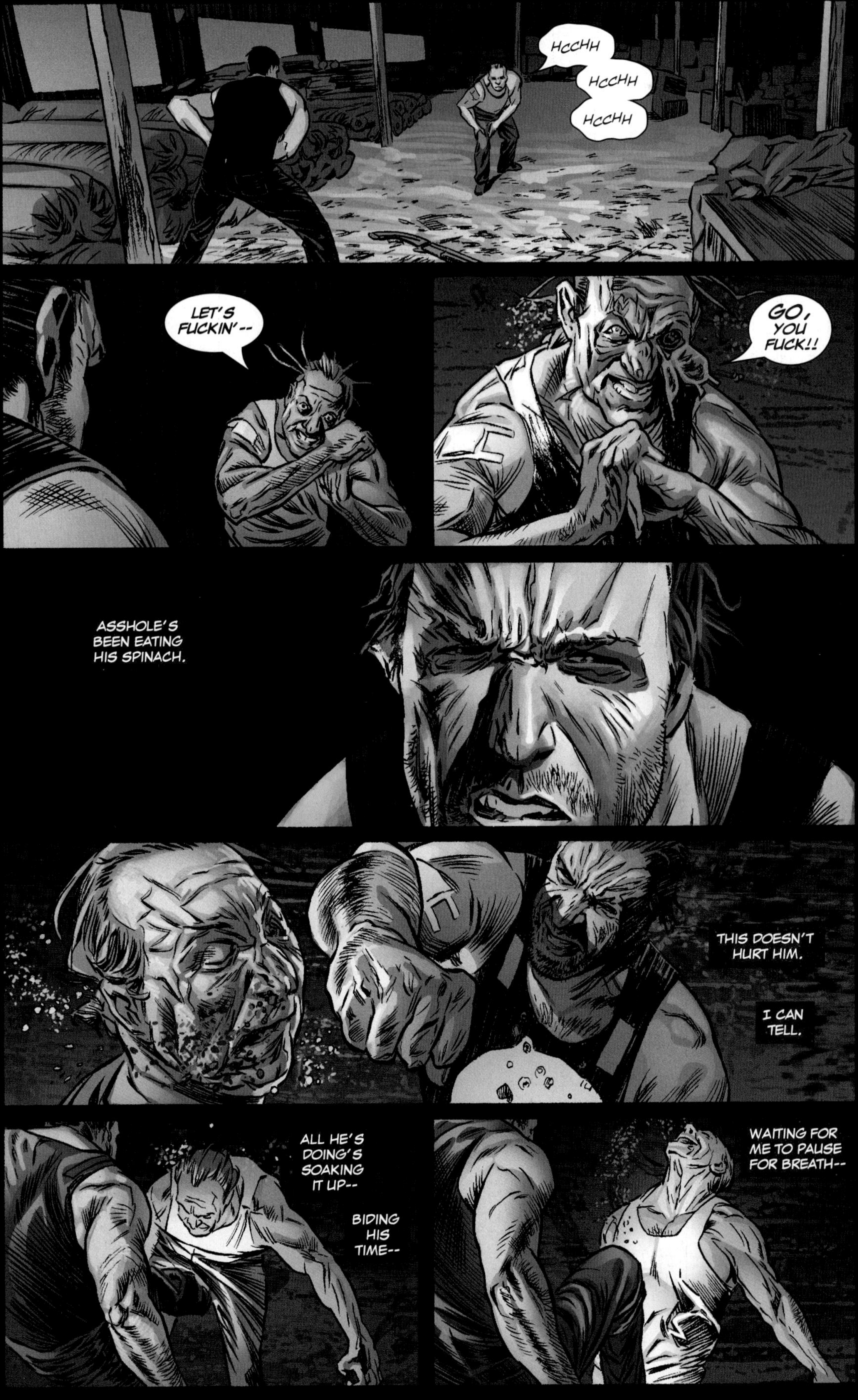
HCCHH
HCCHH
HCCHH
LET'S FUCKIN'--
GO, YOU FUCK!!
ASSHOLE'S BEEN EATING HIS SPINACH.
THIS DOESN'T HURT HIM.
I CAN TELL.
ALL HE'S DOING'S SOAKING IT UP--
BIDING HIS TIME--
WAITING FOR ME TO PAUSE FOR BREATH--

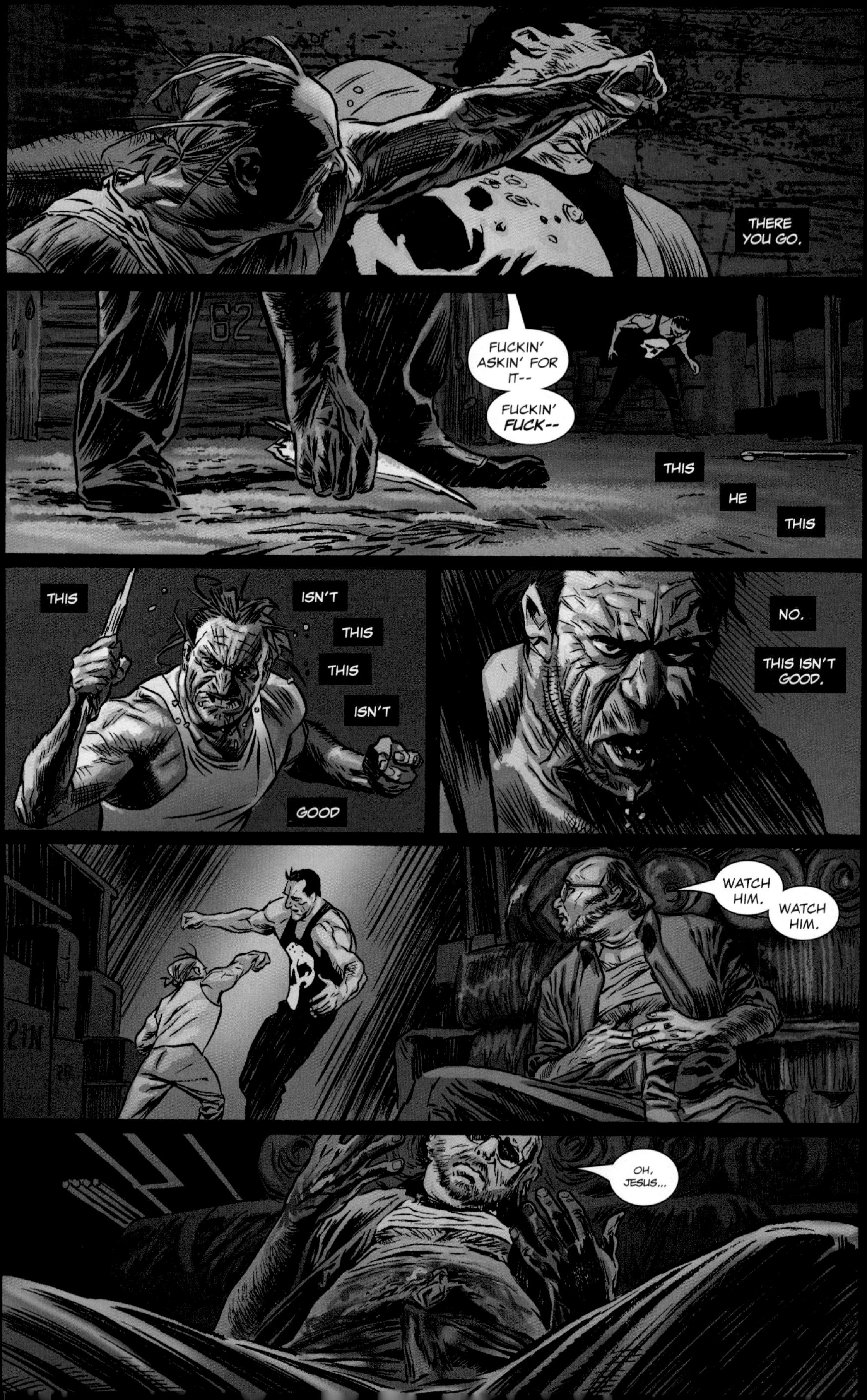
THERE YOU GO.
FUCKIN' ASKIN' FOR IT--
FUCKIN' FUCK--
THIS
HE
THIS
THIS
ISN'T
THIS
THIS
ISN'T
GOOD
NO.
THIS ISN'T GOOD.
WATCH HIM.
WATCH HIM.
OH, JESUS...

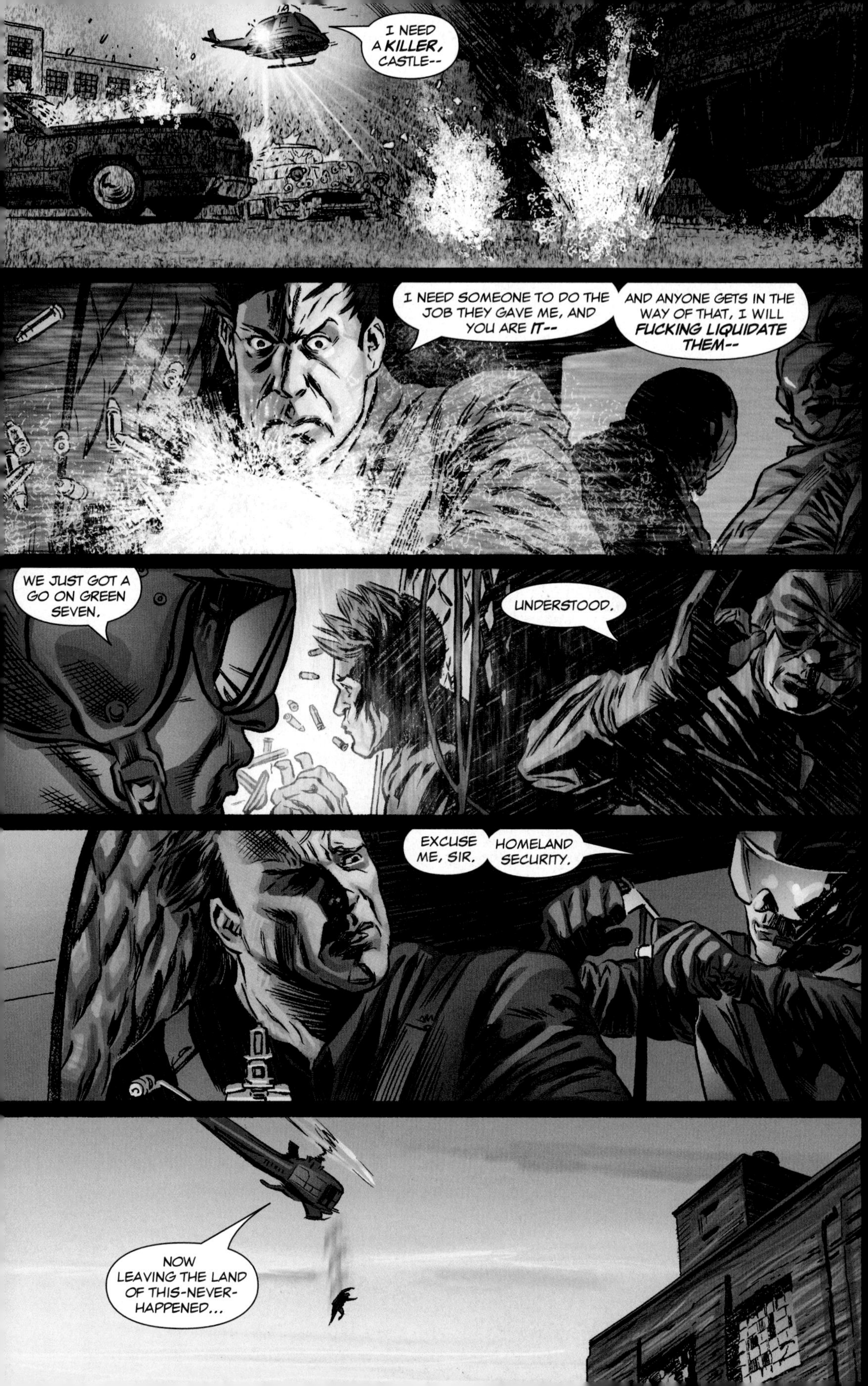
I NEED A KILLER, CASTLE--
I NEED SOMEONE TO DO THE JOB THEY GAVE ME, AND YOU ARE IT--
AND ANYONE GETS IN THE WAY OF THAT, I WILL FUCKING LIQUIDATE THEM--
WE JUST GOT A GO ON GREEN SEVEN.
UNDERSTOOD.
EXCUSE ME, SIR.
HOMELAND SECURITY.
NOW LEAVING THE LAND OF THIS-NEVER-HAPPENED...

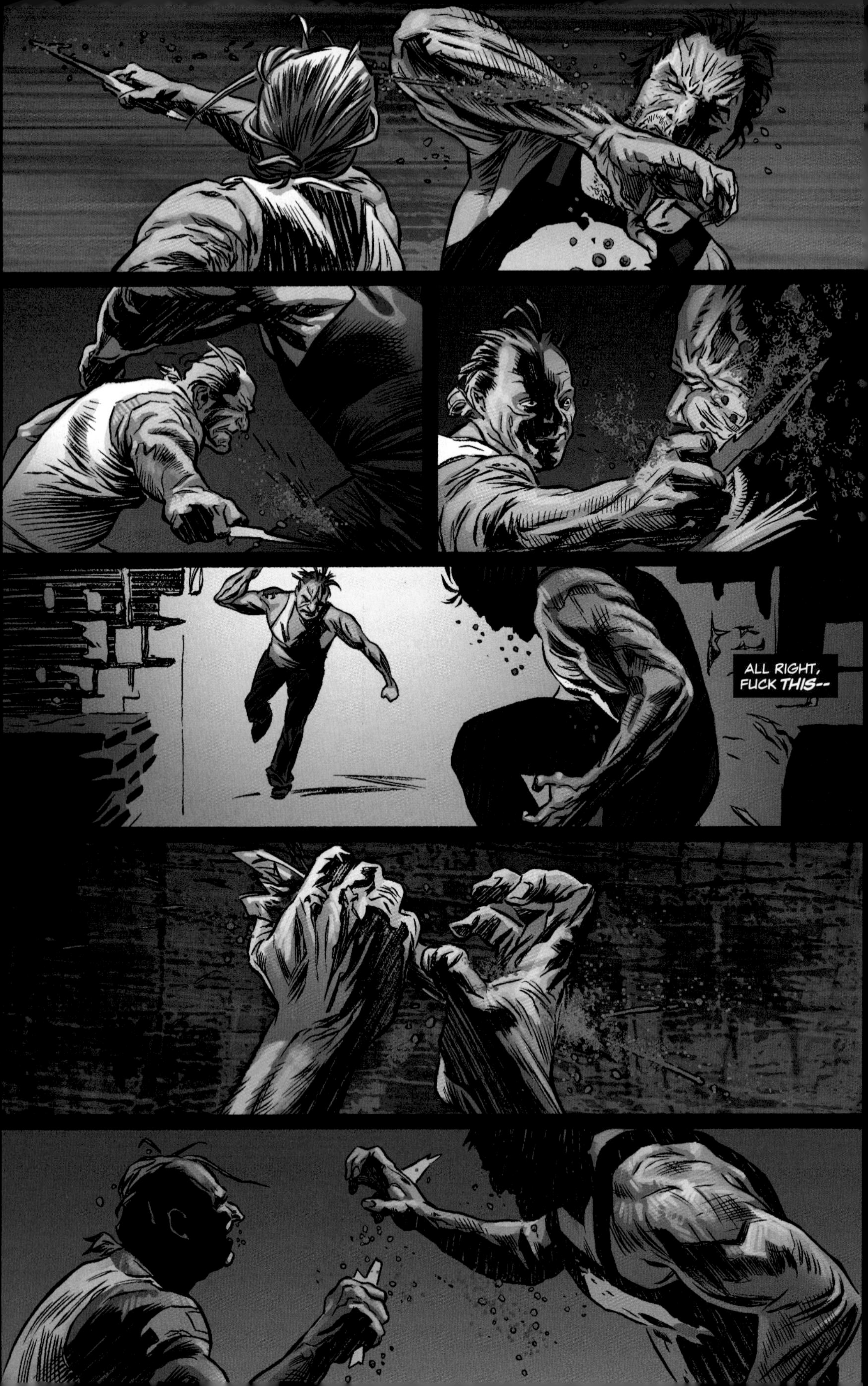
ALL RIGHT, FUCK THIS--

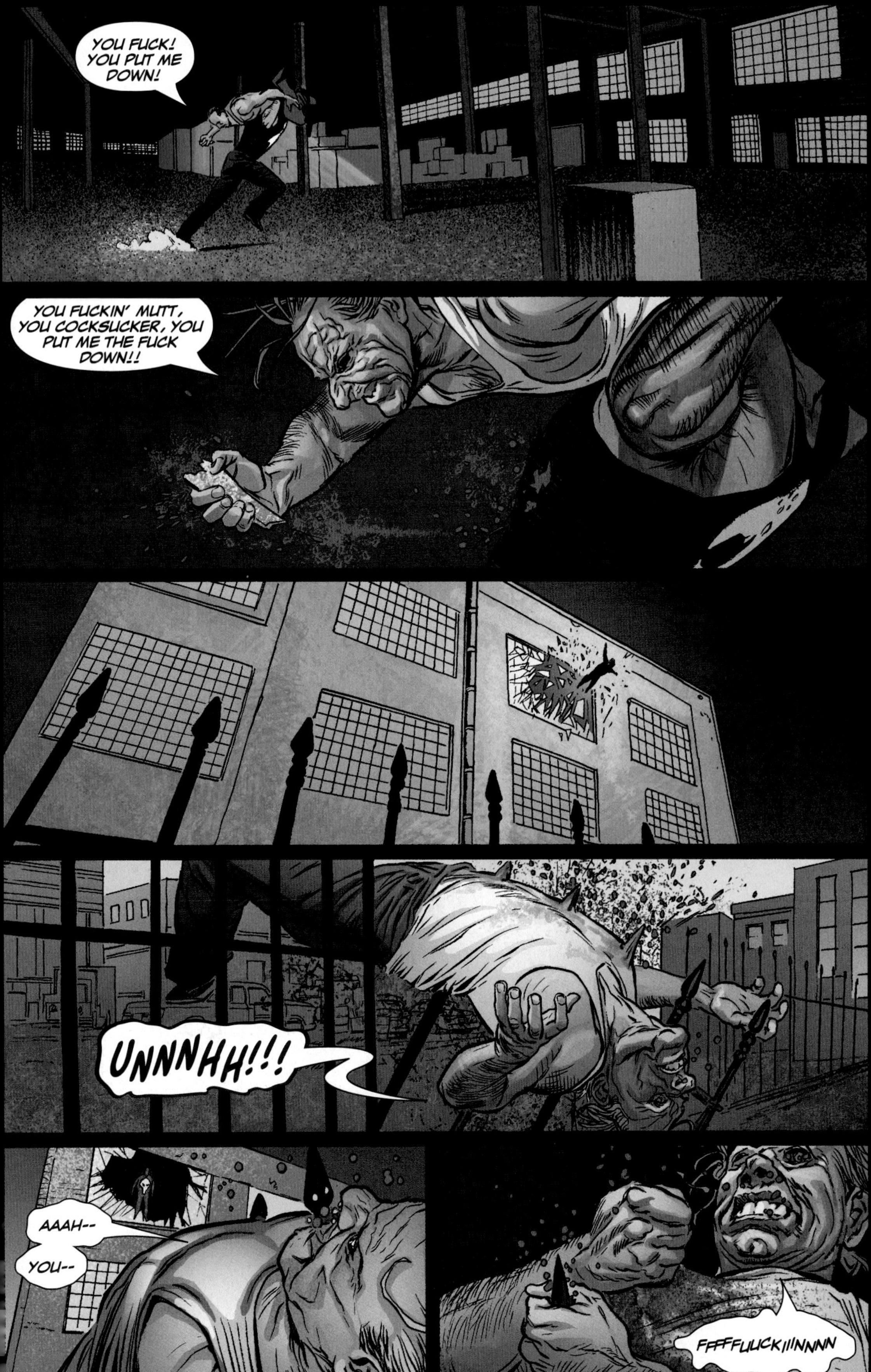
YOU FUCK! YOU PUT ME DOWN!
YOU FUCKIN' MUTT, YOU COCKSUCKER, YOU PUT ME THE FUCK DOWN!!
UNNNHH!!!
AAAH--
YOU--
FFFFFUUCKIIINNNNN

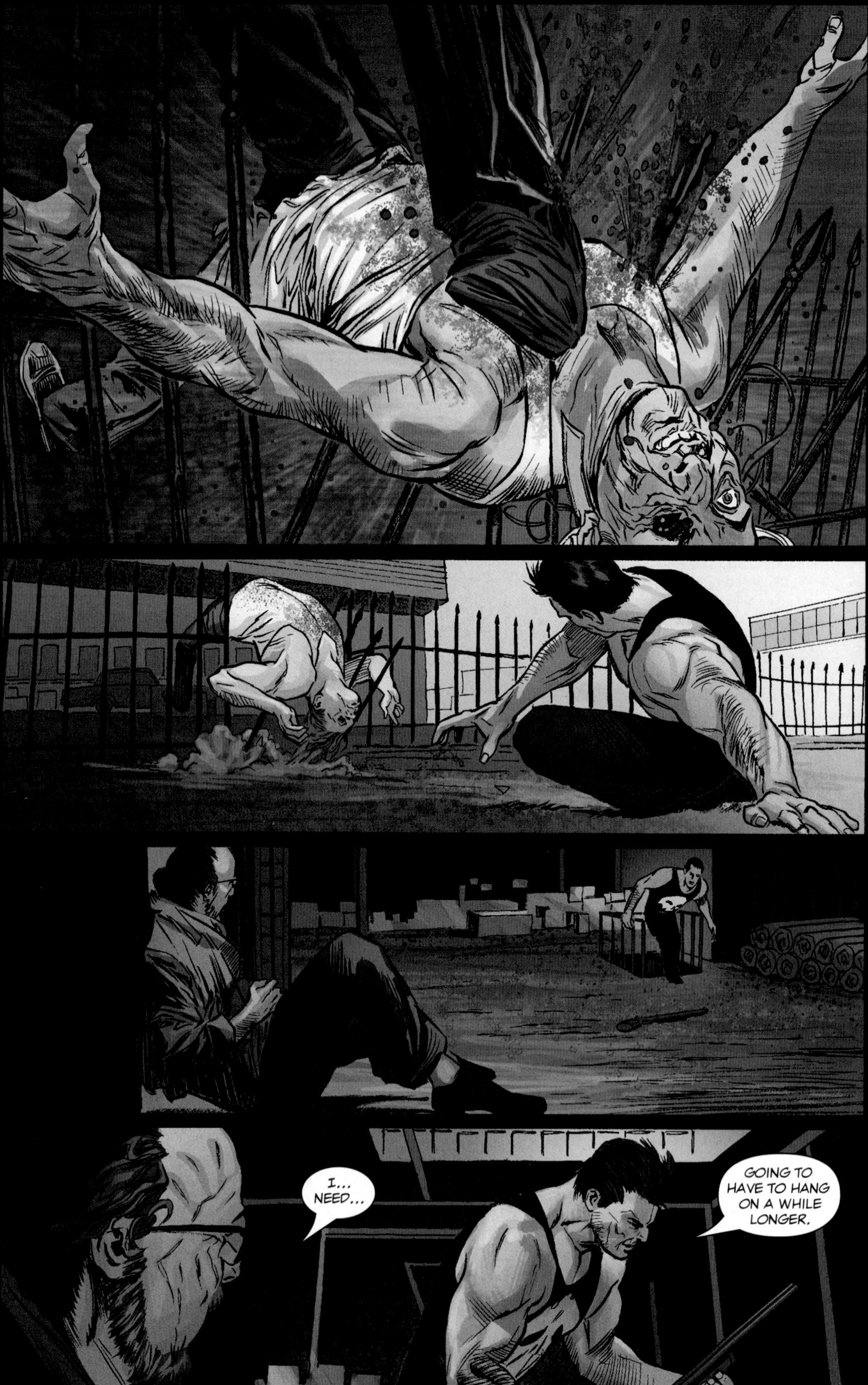
I... NEED...
GOING TO HAVE TO HANG ON A WHILE LONGER.

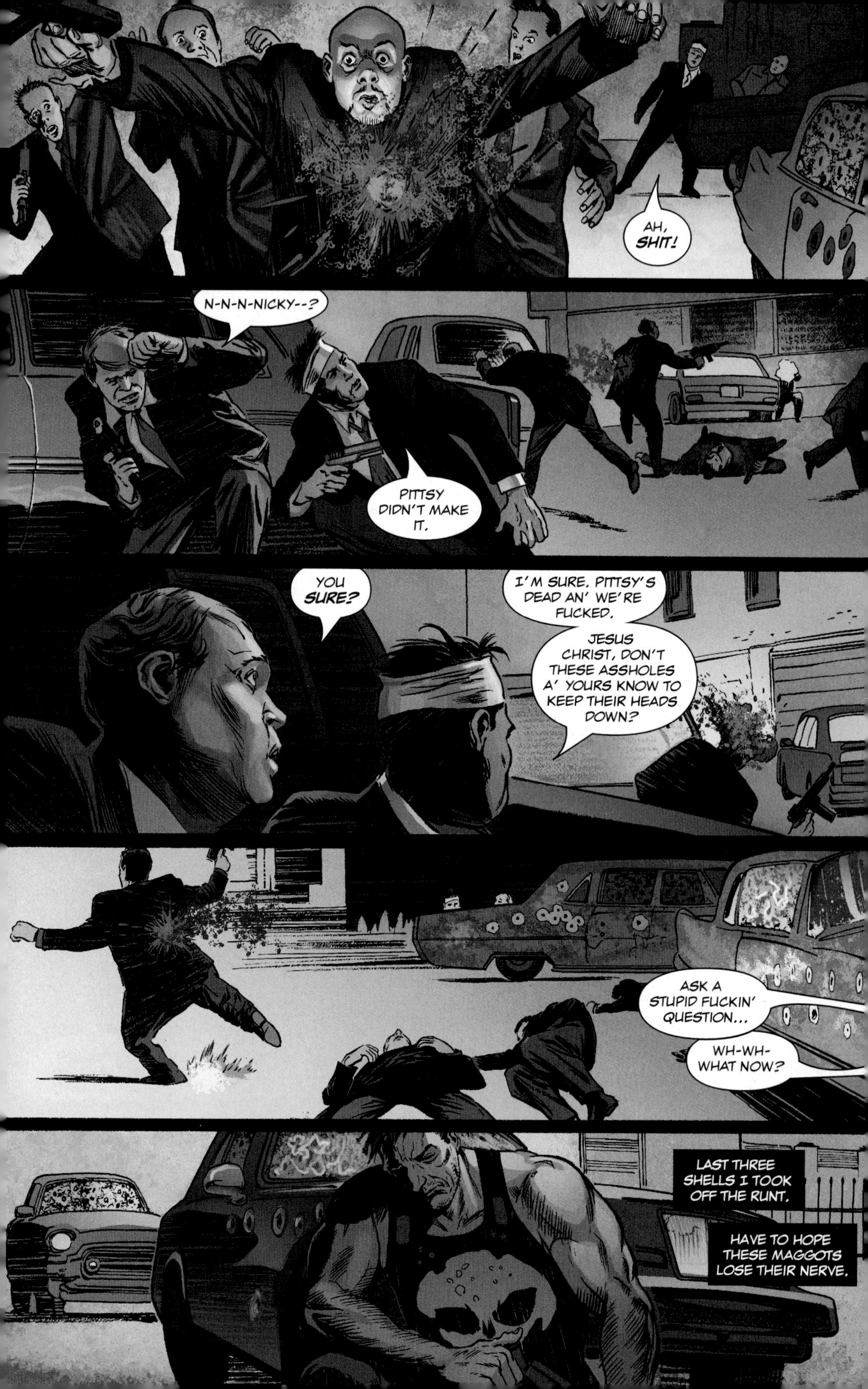
AH, SHIT!
N-N-N-NICKY--?
PITTSY DIDN'T MAKE IT.
YOU SURE?
I'M SURE. PITTSY'S DEAD AN' WE'RE FUCKED.
JESUS CHRIST, DON'T THESE ASSHOLES A' YOURS KNOW TO KEEP THEIR HEADS DOWN?
ASK A STUPID FUCKIN' QUESTION...
WH-WH-WHAT NOW?
LAST THREE SHELLS I TOOK OFF THE RUNT.
HAVE TO HOPE THESE MAGGOTS LOSE THEIR NERVE.

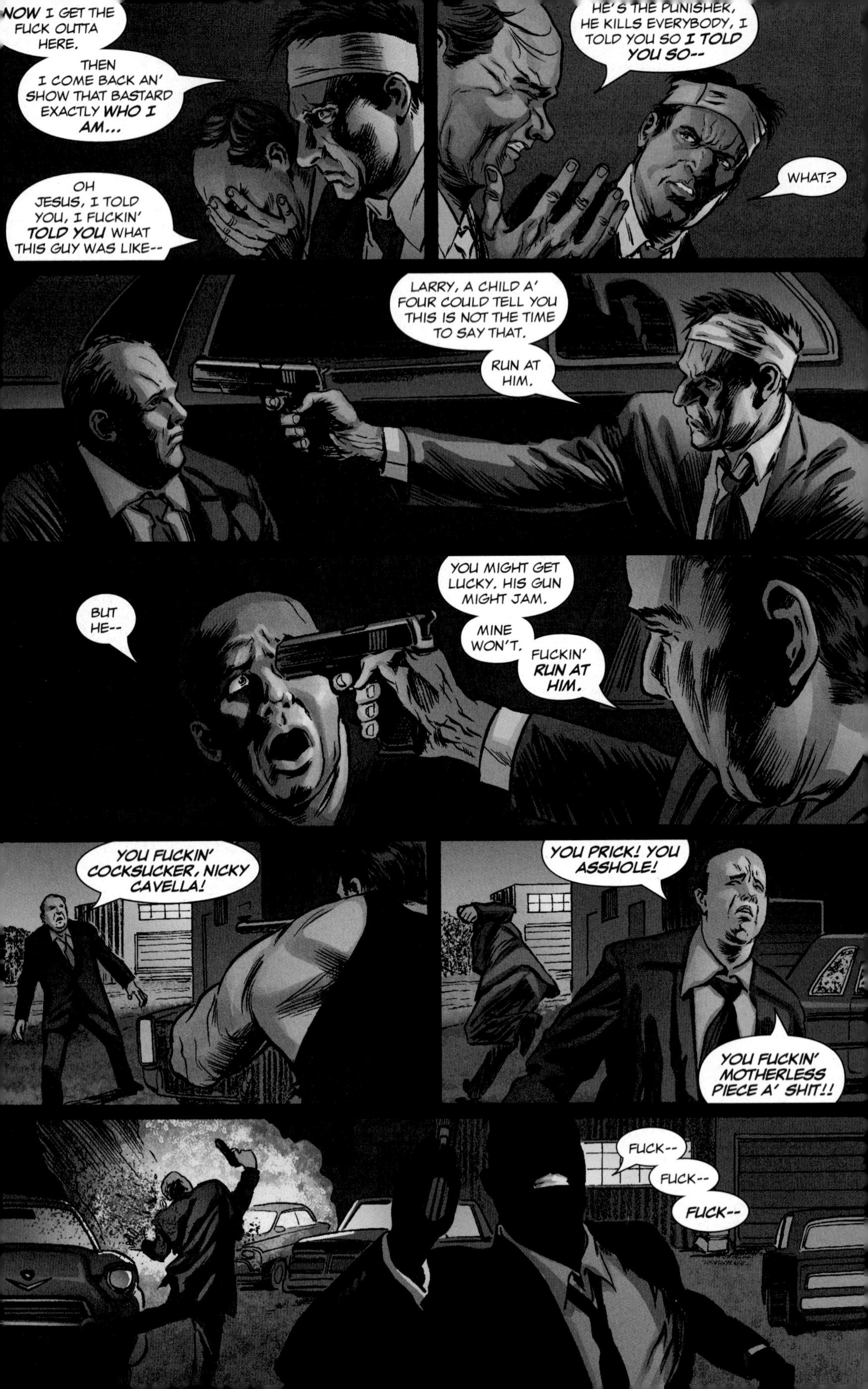
NOW I GET THE FUCK OUTTA HERE.
THEN I COME BACK AN' SHOW THAT BASTARD EXACTLY WHO I AM...
OH JESUS, I TOLD YOU, I FUCKIN' TOLD YOU WHAT THIS GUY WAS LIKE--
HE'S THE PUNISHER, HE KILLS EVERYBODY, I TOLD YOU SO I TOLD YOU SO--
WHAT?
LARRY, A CHILD A' FOUR COULD TELL YOU THIS IS NOT THE TIME TO SAY THAT.
RUN AT HIM.
BUT HE--
YOU MIGHT GET LUCKY. HIS GUN MIGHT JAM.
MINE WON'T.
FUCKIN' RUN AT HIM.
YOU FUCKIN' COCKSUCKER, NICKY CAVELLA!
YOU PRICK! YOU ASSHOLE!
YOU FUCKIN' MOTHERLESS PIECE A' SHIT!!
FUCK--
FUCK--
FUCK--

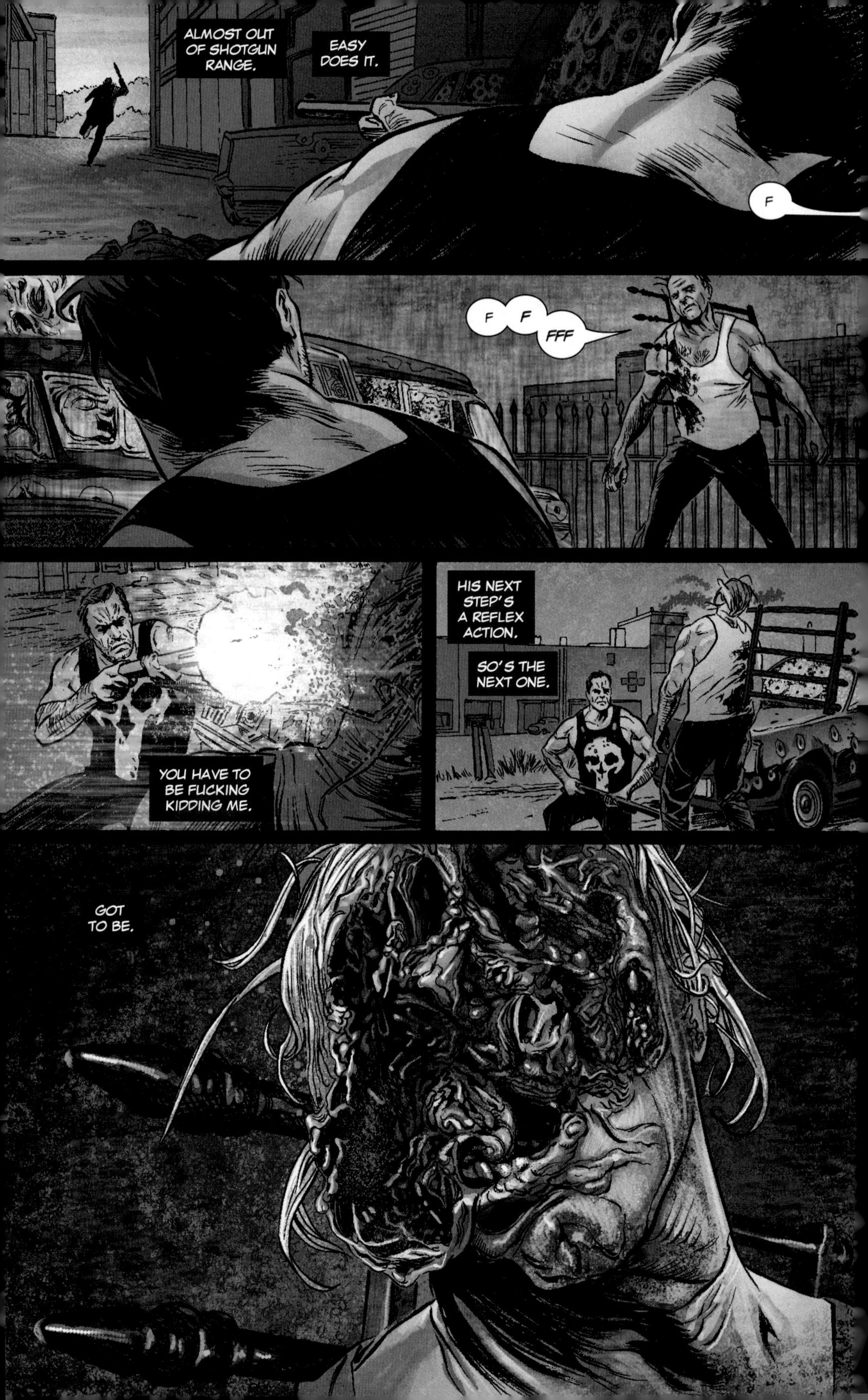

ALMOST OUT OF SHOTGUN RANGE.
EASY DOES IT.
F
F F FFF
YOU HAVE TO BE FUCKING KIDDING ME.
HIS NEXT STEP'S A REFLEX ACTION.
SO'S THE NEXT ONE.
GOT TO BE.

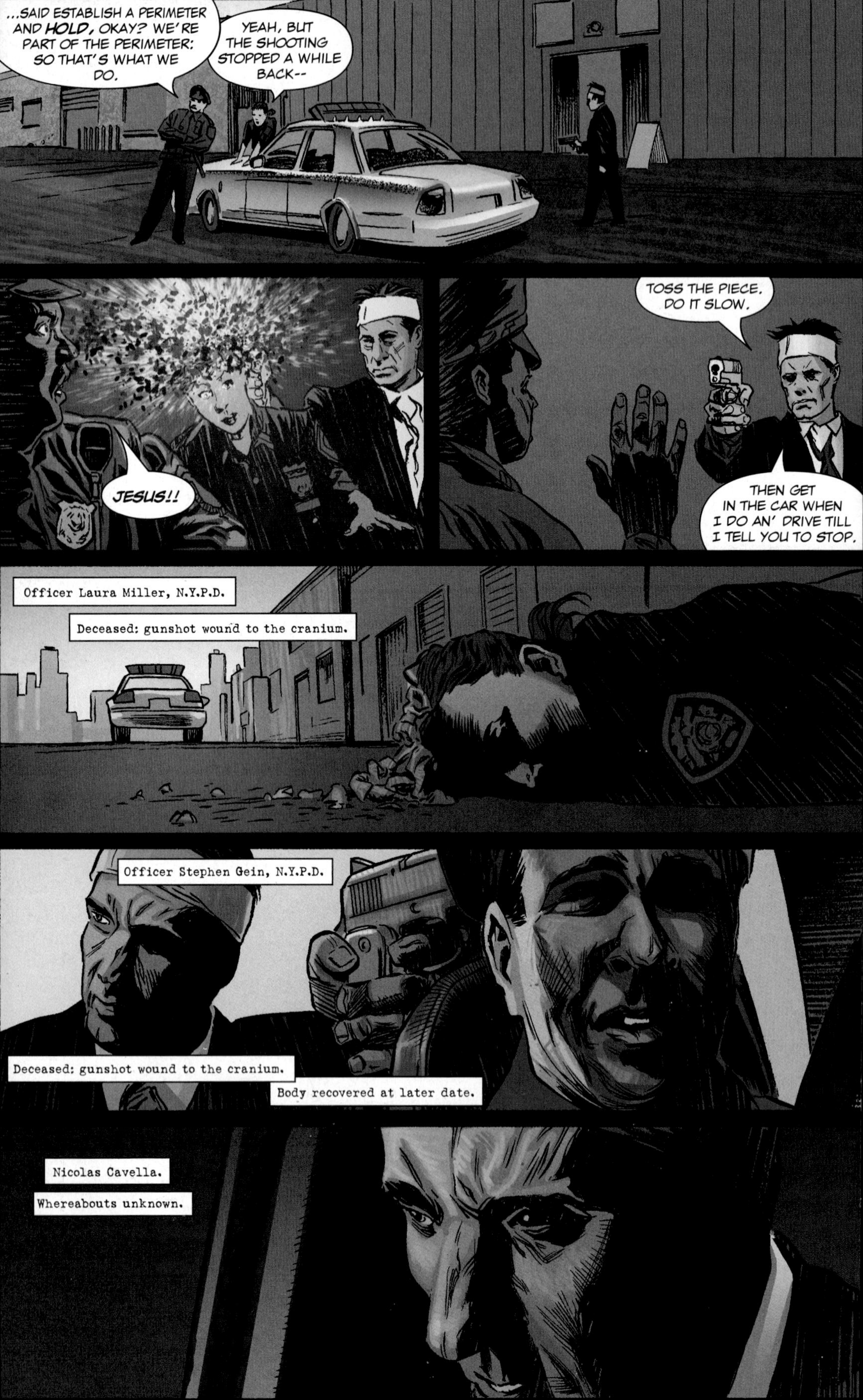
...SAID ESTABLISH A PERIMETER AND HOLD, OKAY? WE'RE PART OF THE PERIMETER: SO THAT'S WHAT WE DO.
YEAH, BUT THE SHOOTING STOPPED A WHILE BACK--
JESUS!!
TOSS THE PIECE. DO IT SLOW.
THEN GET IN THE CAR WHEN I DO AN' DRIVE TILL I TELL YOU TO STOP.
Officer Laura Miller, N.Y.P.D.
Deceased: gunshot wound to the cranium.
Officer Stephen Gein, N.Y.P.D.
Deceased: gunshot wound to the cranium.
Body recovered at later date.
Nicolas Cavella.
Whereabouts unknown.

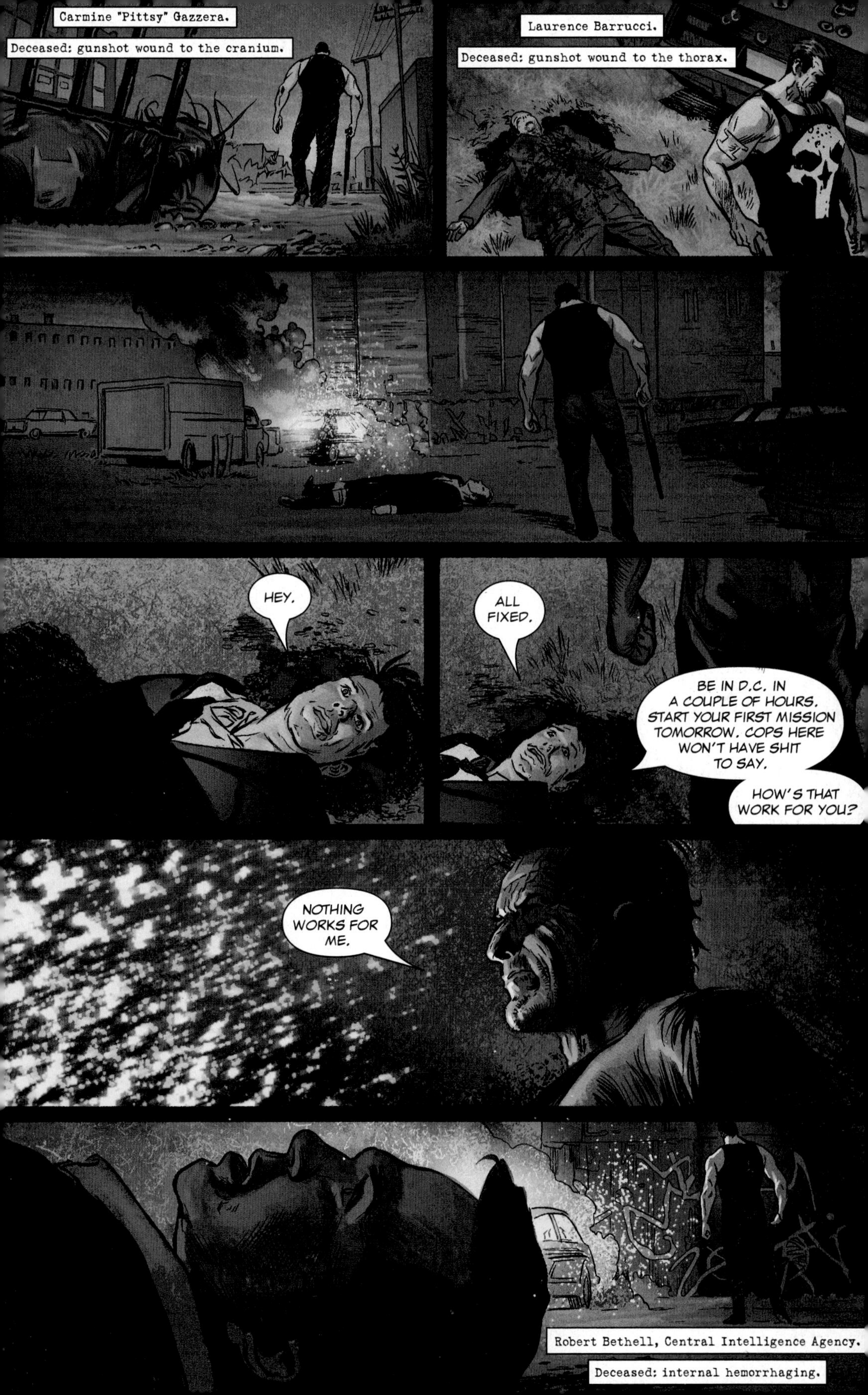
Carmine "Pittsy" Gazzera.
Deceased: gunshot wound to the cranium.
Laurence Barrucci.
Deceased: gunshot wound to the thorax.
HEY.
ALL FIXED.
BE IN D.C. IN A COUPLE OF HOURS. START YOUR FIRST MISSION TOMORROW. COPS HERE WON'T HAVE SHIT TO SAY.
HOW'S THAT WORK FOR YOU?
NOTHING WORKS FOR ME.
Robert Bethell, Central Intelligence Agency.
Deceased: internal hemorrhaging.

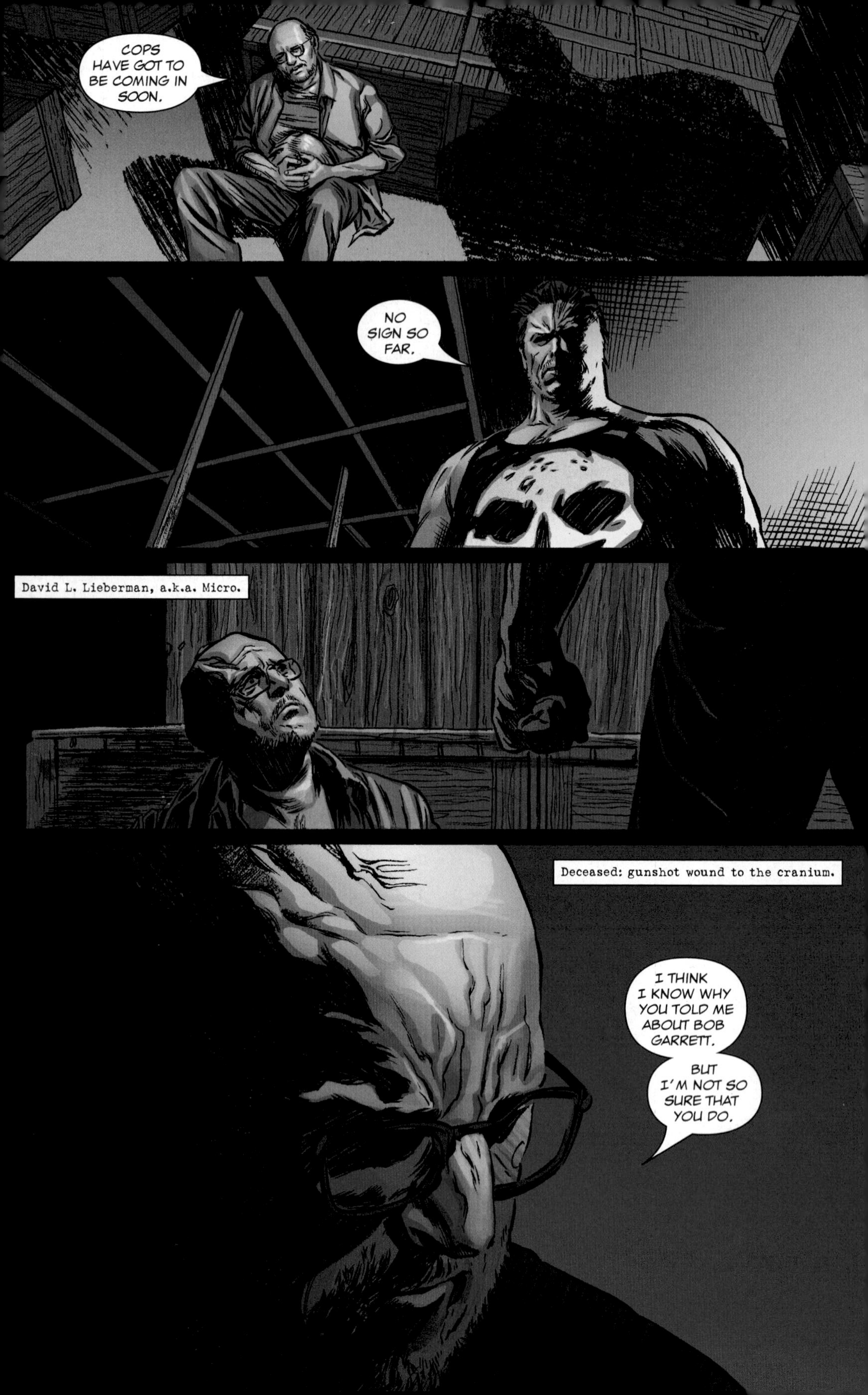
COPS HAVE GOT TO BE COMING IN SOON.
NO SIGN SO FAR.
David L. Lieberman, a.k.a. Micro.
Deceased: gunshot wound to the cranium.
I THINK I KNOW WHY YOU TOLD ME ABOUT BOB GARRETT.
BUT I'M NOT SO SURE THAT YOU DO.

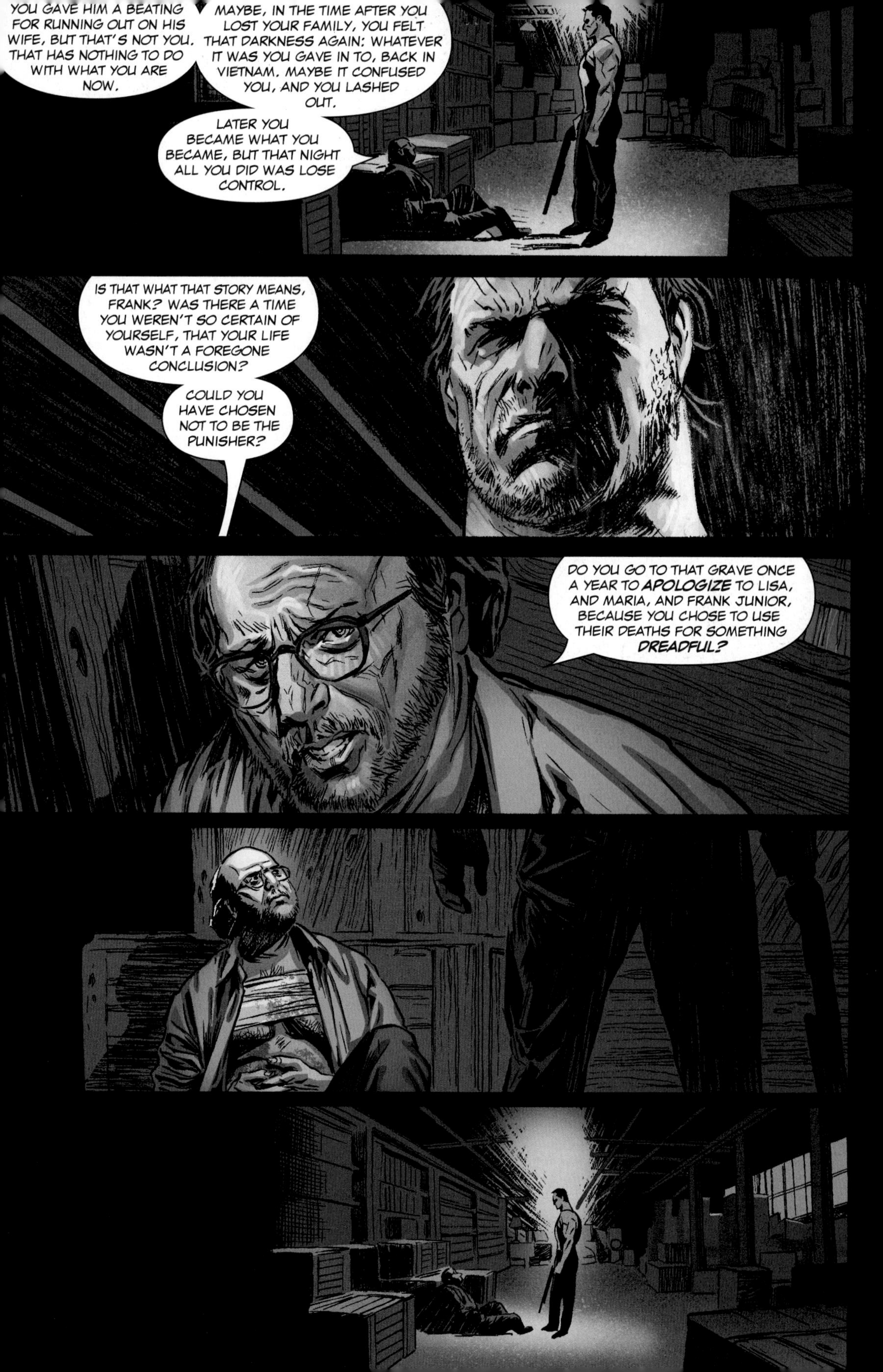
YOU GAVE HIM A BEATING FOR RUNNING OUT ON HIS WIFE, BUT THAT'S NOT YOU. THAT HAS NOTHING TO DO WITH WHAT YOU ARE NOW.
MAYBE, IN THE TIME AFTER YOU LOST YOUR FAMILY, YOU FELT THAT DARKNESS AGAIN: WHATEVER IT WAS YOU GAVE IN TO, BACK IN VIETNAM. MAYBE IT CONFUSED YOU, AND YOU LASHED OUT.
LATER YOU BECAME WHAT YOU BECAME, BUT THAT NIGHT ALL YOU DID WAS LOSE CONTROL.
IS THAT WHAT THAT STORY MEANS, FRANK? WAS THERE A TIME YOU WEREN'T SO CERTAIN OF YOURSELF, THAT YOUR LIFE WASN'T A FOREGONE CONCLUSION?
COULD YOU HAVE CHOSEN NOT TO BE THE PUNISHER?
DO YOU GO TO THAT GRAVE ONCE A YEAR TO ***APOLOGIZE*** TO LISA, AND MARIA, AND FRANK JUNIOR, BECAUSE YOU CHOSE TO USE THEIR DEATHS FOR SOMETHING ***DREADFUL?***

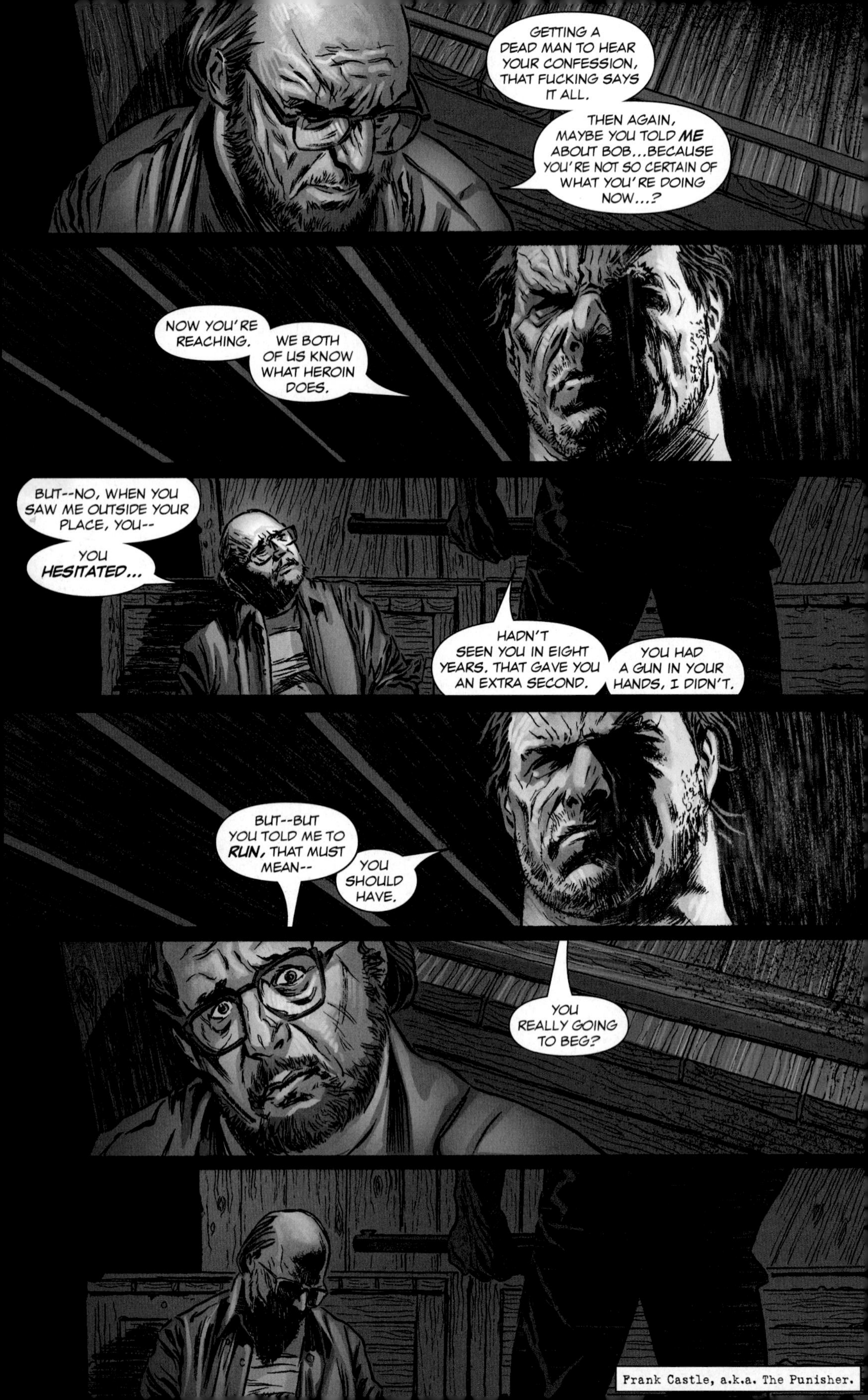
GETTING A DEAD MAN TO HEAR YOUR CONFESSION, THAT FUCKING SAYS IT ALL.
THEN AGAIN, MAYBE YOU TOLD ME ABOUT BOB...BECAUSE YOU'RE NOT SO CERTAIN OF WHAT YOU'RE DOING NOW...?
NOW YOU'RE REACHING.
WE BOTH OF US KNOW WHAT HEROIN DOES.
BUT--NO, WHEN YOU SAW ME OUTSIDE YOUR PLACE, YOU--
YOU HESITATED...
HADN'T SEEN YOU IN EIGHT YEARS. THAT GAVE YOU AN EXTRA SECOND.
YOU HAD A GUN IN YOUR HANDS, I DIDN'T.
BUT--BUT YOU TOLD ME TO RUN, THAT MUST MEAN--
YOU SHOULD HAVE.
YOU REALLY GOING TO BEG?
Frank Castle, a.k.a. The Punisher.

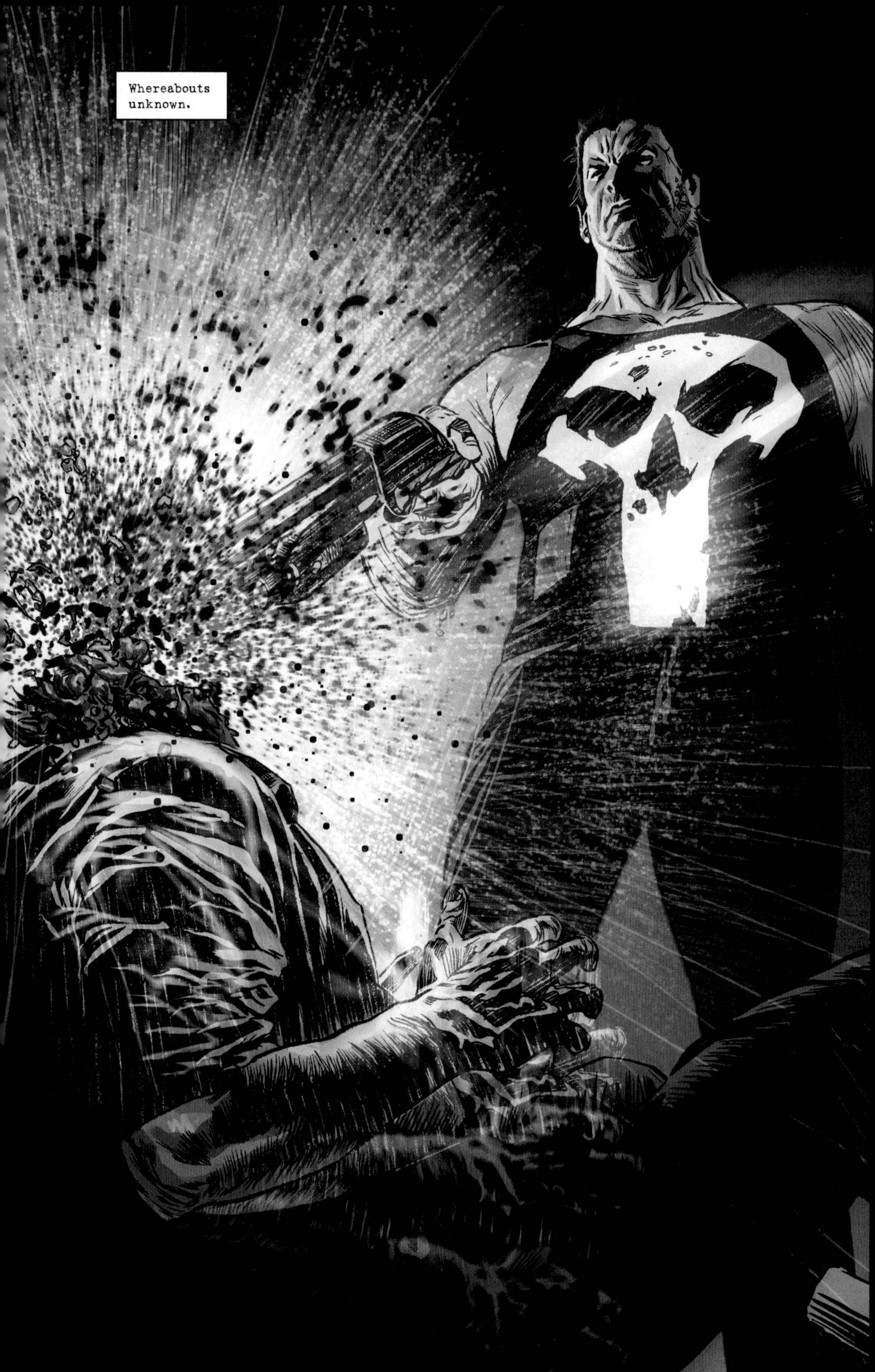
Whereabouts unknown.

Next: Kitchen Irish

PUNISHER DESIGN BY LEWIS LAROSA

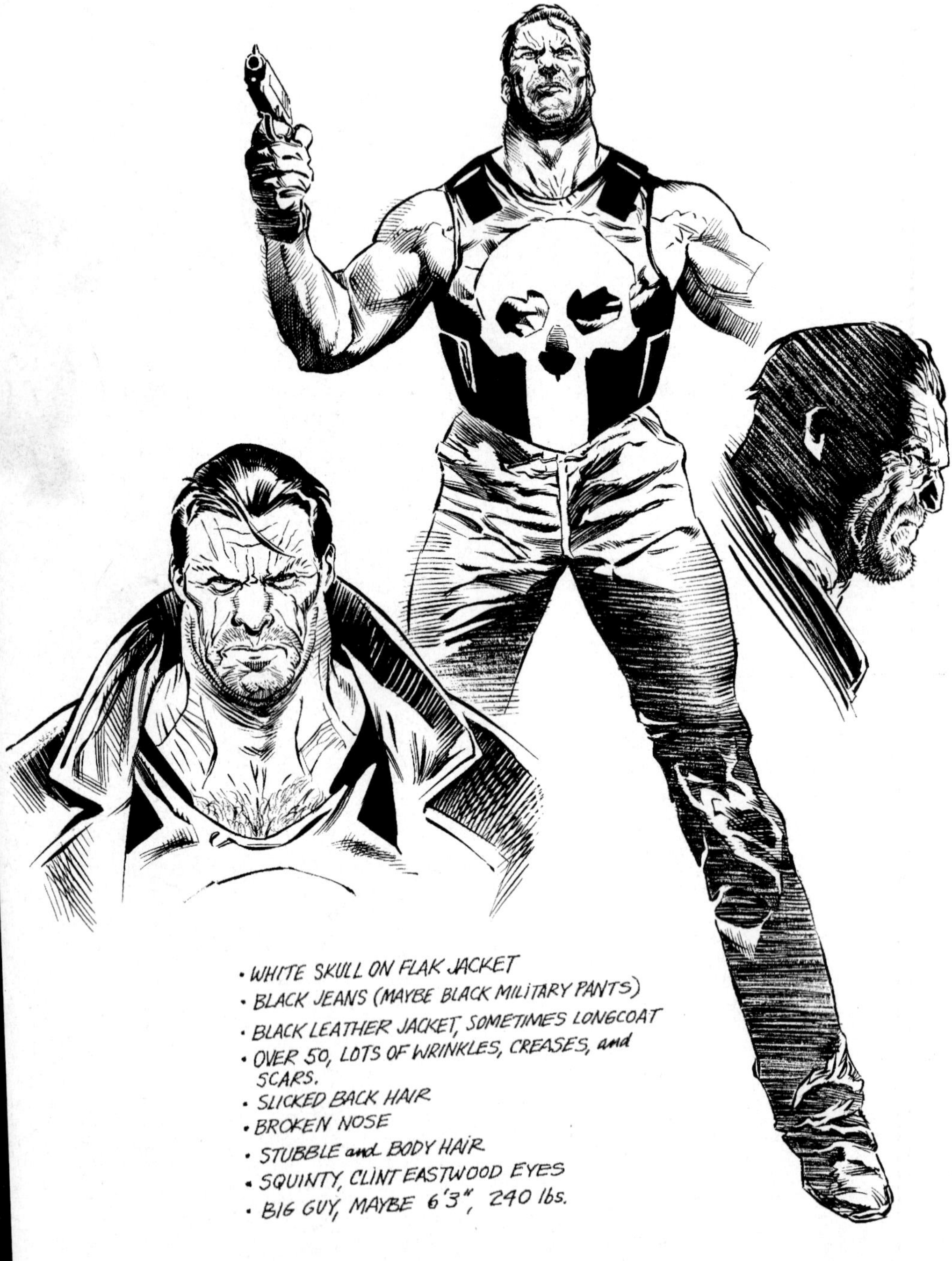

• WHITE SKULL ON FLAK JACKET
• BLACK JEANS (MAYBE BLACK MILITARY PANTS)
• BLACK LEATHER JACKET, SOMETIMES LONGCOAT
• OVER 50, LOTS OF WRINKLES, CREASES, and SCARS.
• SLICKED BACK HAIR
• BROKEN NOSE
• STUBBLE and BODY HAIR
• SQUINTY, CLINT EASTWOOD EYES
• BIG GUY, MAYBE 6'3", 240 lbs.